LIFE IS STRANGE

PARTNERS IN TIME

– TRACKS –

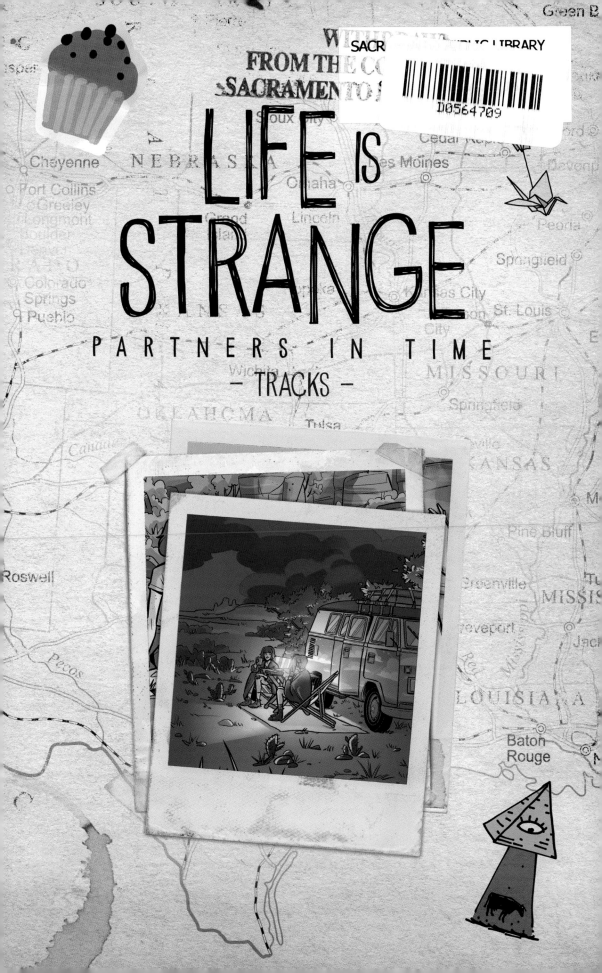

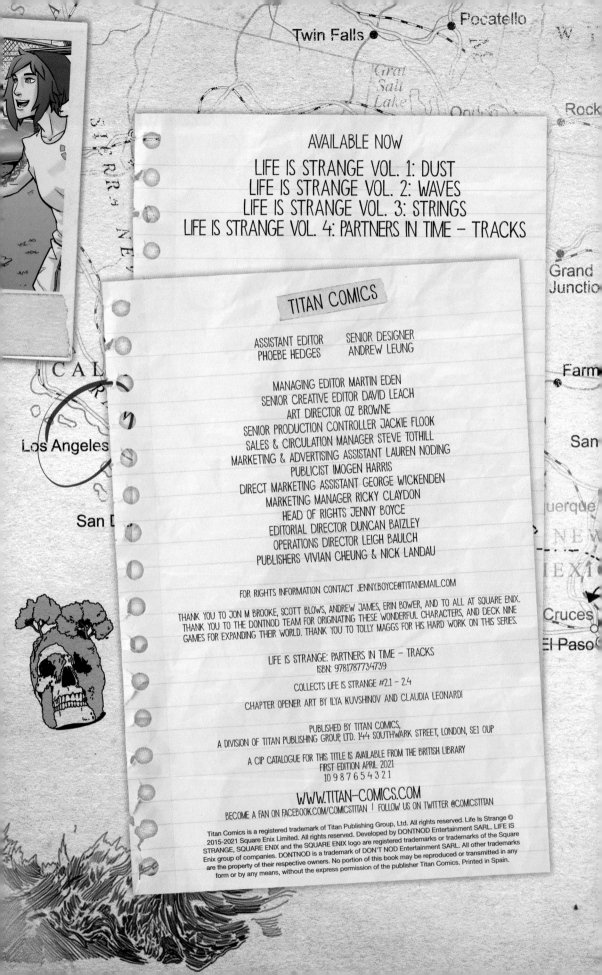

AVAILABLE NOW

LIFE IS STRANGE VOL. 1: DUST
LIFE IS STRANGE VOL. 2: WAVES
LIFE IS STRANGE VOL. 3: STRINGS
LIFE IS STRANGE VOL. 4: PARTNERS IN TIME – TRACKS

TITAN COMICS

ASSISTANT EDITOR   SENIOR DESIGNER
PHOEBE HEDGES   ANDREW LEUNG

MANAGING EDITOR MARTIN EDEN
SENIOR CREATIVE EDITOR DAVID LEACH
ART DIRECTOR OZ BROWNE
SENIOR PRODUCTION CONTROLLER JACKIE FLOOK
SALES & CIRCULATION MANAGER STEVE TOTHILL
MARKETING & ADVERTISING ASSISTANT LAUREN NODING
PUBLICIST IMOGEN HARRIS
DIRECT MARKETING ASSISTANT GEORGE WICKENDEN
MARKETING MANAGER RICKY CLAYDON
HEAD OF RIGHTS JENNY BOYCE
EDITORIAL DIRECTOR DUNCAN BAIZLEY
OPERATIONS DIRECTOR LEIGH BAULCH
PUBLISHERS VIVIAN CHEUNG & NICK LANDAU

FOR RIGHTS INFORMATION CONTACT JENNY.BOYCE@TITANEMAIL.COM

THANK YOU TO JON M BROOKE, SCOTT BLOWS, ANDREW JAMES, ERIN BOWER, AND TO ALL AT SQUARE ENIX.
THANK YOU TO THE DONTNOD TEAM FOR ORIGINATING THESE WONDERFUL CHARACTERS, AND DECK NINE
GAMES FOR EXPANDING THEIR WORLD. THANK YOU TO TOLLY MAGGS FOR HIS HARD WORK ON THIS SERIES.

LIFE IS STRANGE: PARTNERS IN TIME – TRACKS
ISBN: 9781787734739

COLLECTS LIFE IS STRANGE #2.1 – 2.4

CHAPTER OPENER ART BY ILYA KUVSHINOV AND CLAUDIA LEONARDI

PUBLISHED BY TITAN COMICS,
A DIVISION OF TITAN PUBLISHING GROUP, LTD. 144 SOUTHWARK STREET, LONDON, SE1 0UP

A CIP CATALOGUE FOR THIS TITLE IS AVAILABLE FROM THE BRITISH LIBRARY
FIRST EDITION APRIL 2021
10 9 8 7 6 5 4 3 2 1

WWW.TITAN-COMICS.COM
BECOME A FAN ON FACEBOOK.COM/COMICSTITAN | FOLLOW US ON TWITTER @COMICSTITAN

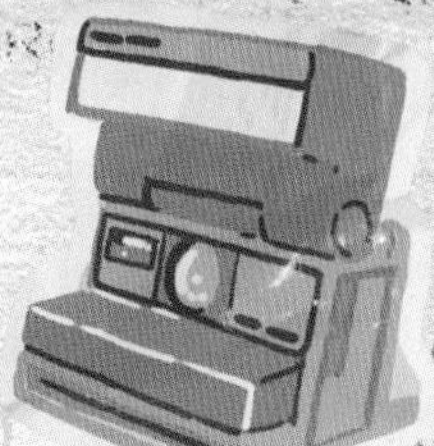

LIFE IS STRANGE

PARTNERS IN TIME

– TRACKS –

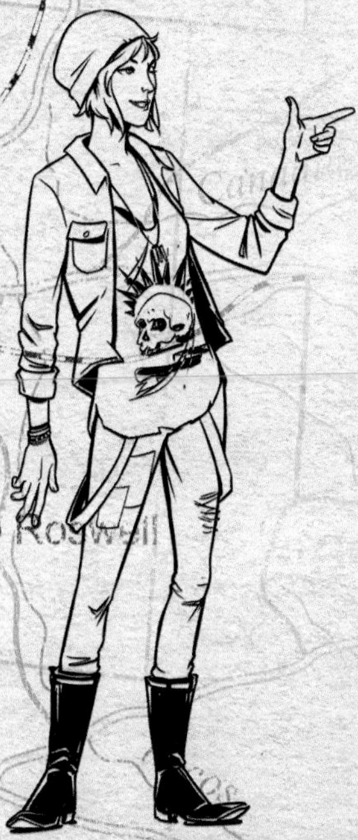

WRITTEN BY
EMMA VIECELI

ARTWORK BY
CLAUDIA LEONARDI

COLORS BY
ANDREA IZZO

LETTERS BY
RICHARD STARKINGS
& COMICRAFT'S
JIMMY BETANCOURT

ORIGINAL STORY AND CHARACTERS BY
RAOUL BARBET, JEAN-LUC CANO
AND MICHEL KOCH.

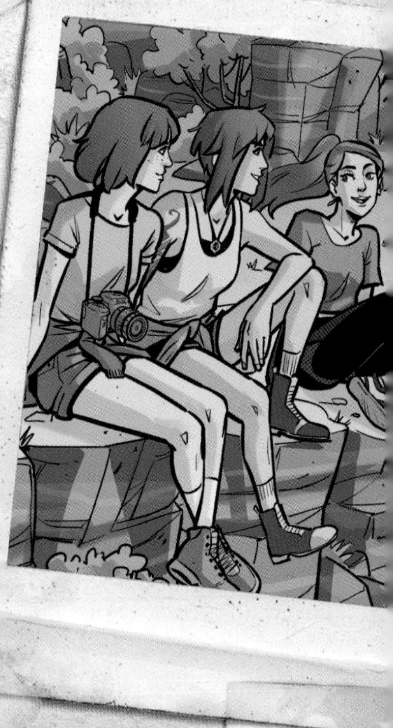

PREVIOUSLY...

Mysteriously gifted with the power to rewind time, photography student Max Caulfield became entangled in the dark secrets of Arcadia Bay. She used her strange new abilities to reconnect with her oldest friend, Chloe Price, and to bring to justice the men who had murdered Chloe's closest confidante, Rachel Amber. However, Max's abilities created a once-in-a-generation hurricane that threatened the town with total destruction, if Max didn't allow the original timeline – in which Chloe died – to play out. In one sequence of events, Max chose to save Chloe's life, sacrificing Arcadia Bay. Then, to escape the temporal forces that were tearing her apart, she leapt into a timeline where both Chloe and Rachel lived. Two years later, and with the help of Tristan, a young man who can phase out of reality, Max is trying to get back home. Caught between two timelines, traveling towards an uncertain destiny – can Chloe and Max find each other again?

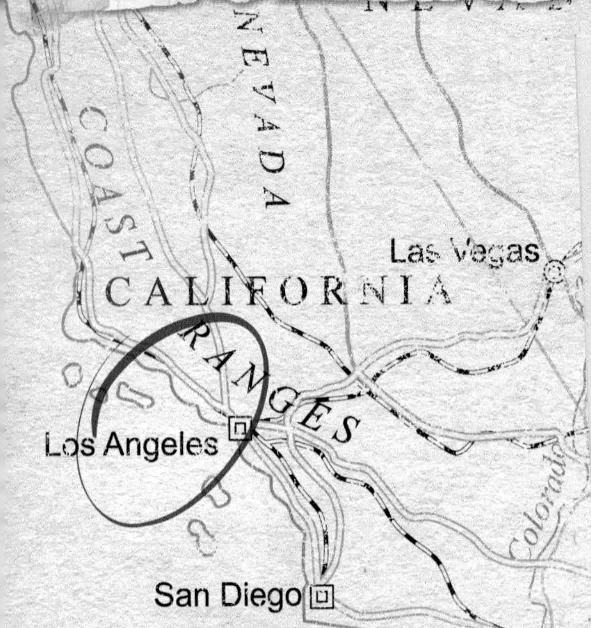
Twin Falls
Pocatello
NEVADA
COAST
CALIFORNIA
RANGES
Las Vegas
Los Angeles
San Diego
Colorado
Las Cruces
El Paso

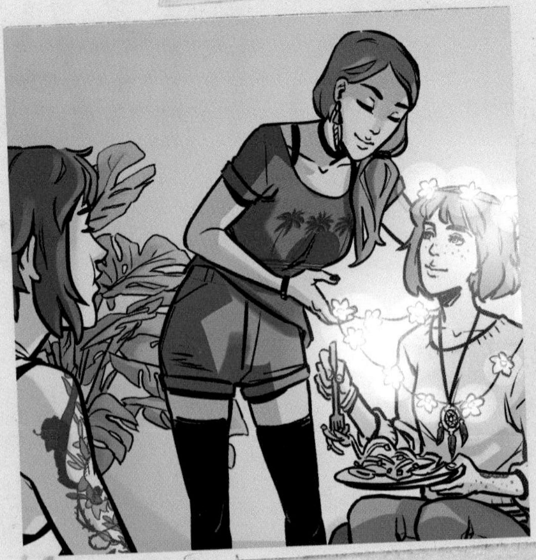

1. Max has lived in this new timeline for several years, becoming friends and housemates with Chloe and Rachel, and believing that there was no way home.

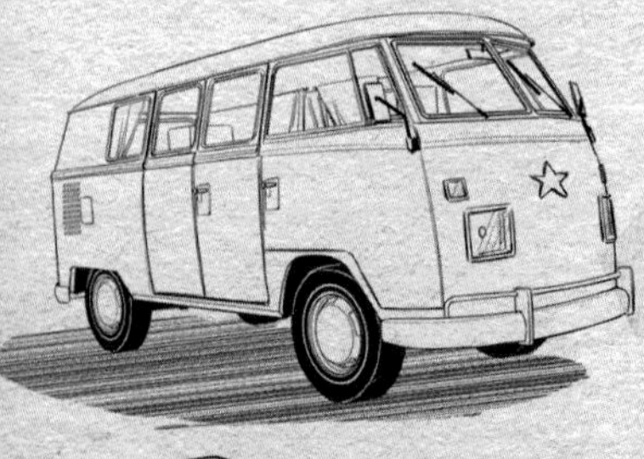

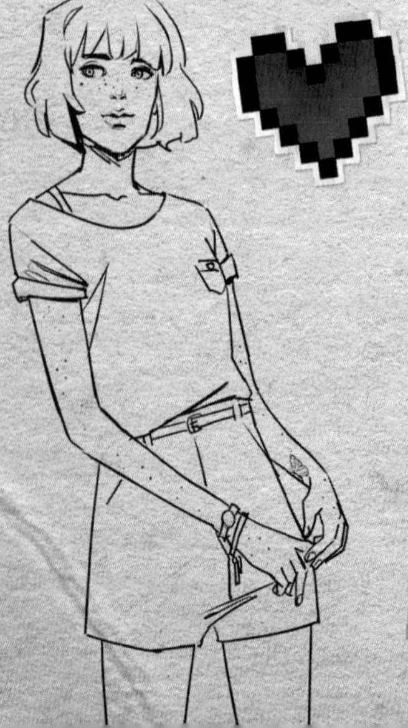

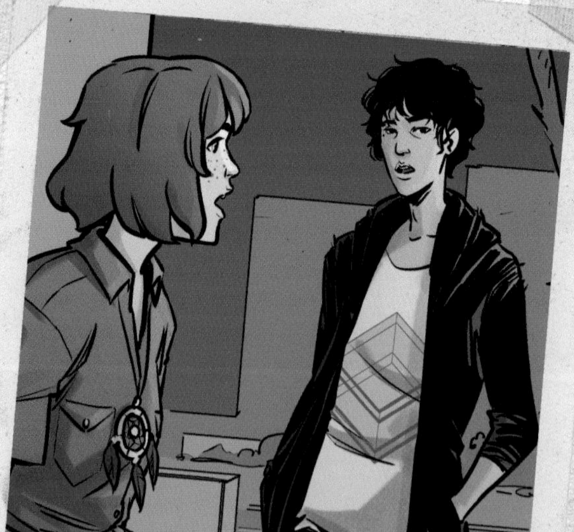

2. Then she met Tristan, a homeless drifter with the ability to 'phase' out of reality, becoming invisible and intangible. When Tristan confessed his power to Chloe and Rachel, Max also confesses her powers... and her true past in another universe.

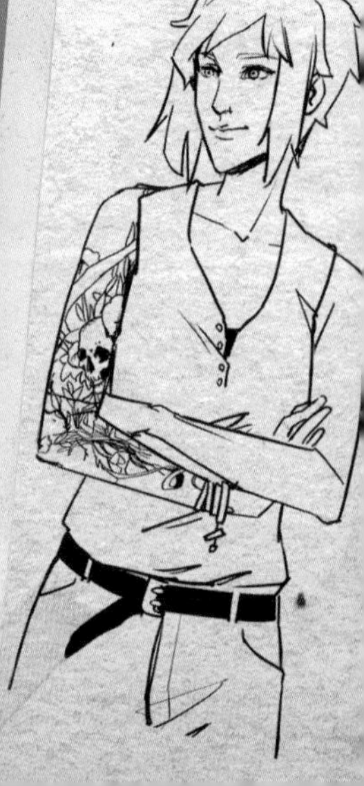

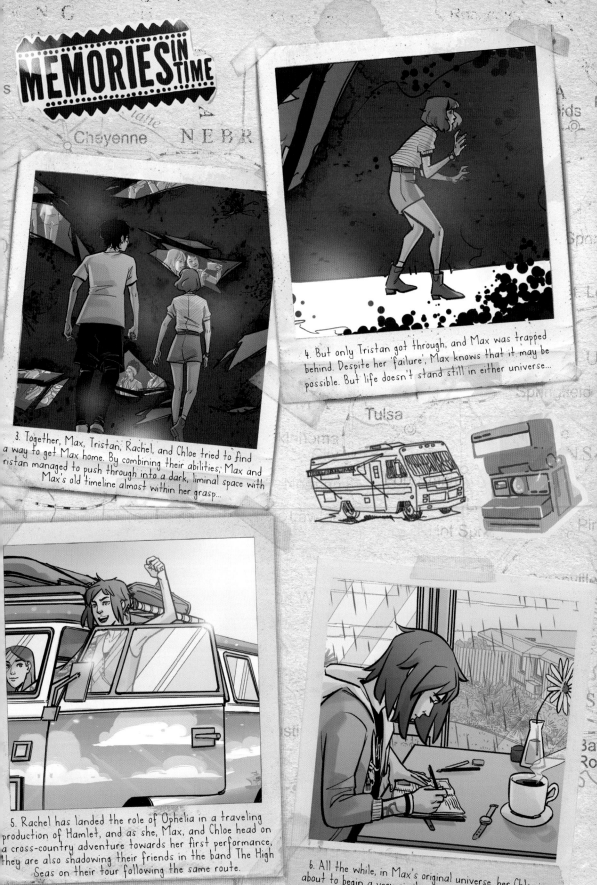

MEMORIES IN TIME

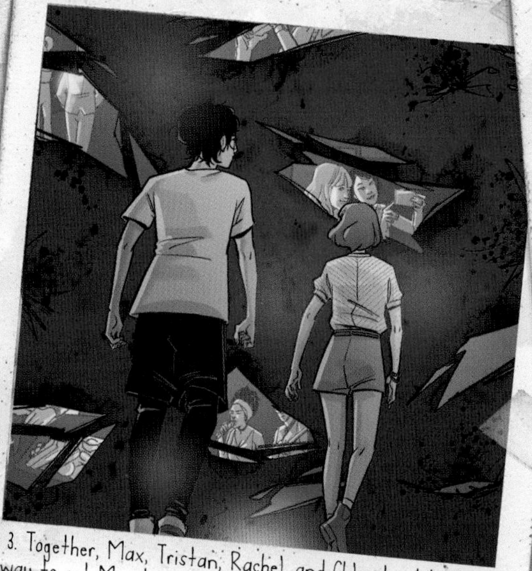

3. Together, Max, Tristan, Rachel, and Chloe tried to find a way to get Max home. By combining their abilities, Max and Tristan managed to push through into a dark, liminal space with Max's old timeline almost within her grasp...

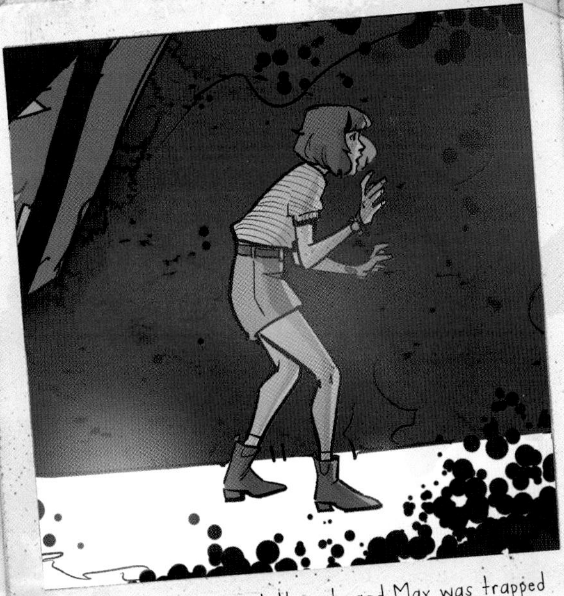

4. But only Tristan got through, and Max was trapped behind. Despite her 'failure', Max knows that it may be possible. But life doesn't stand still in either universe...

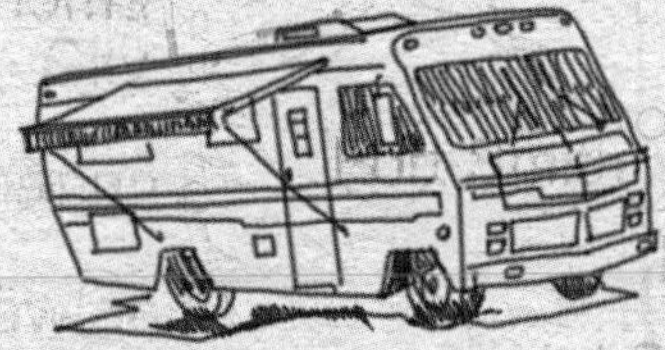

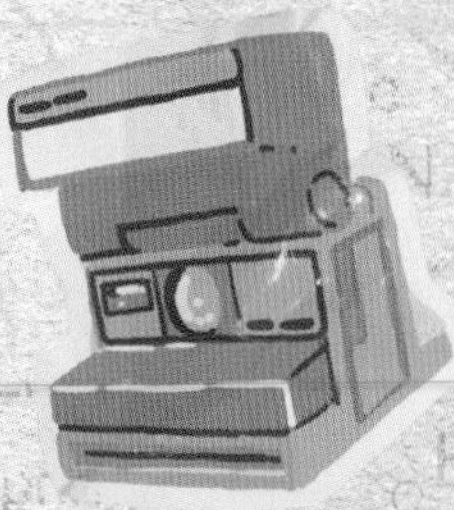

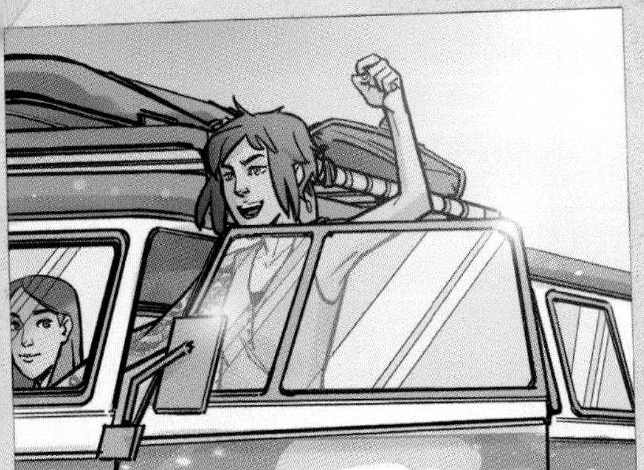

5. Rachel has landed the role of Ophelia in a traveling production of Hamlet, and as she, Max, and Chloe head on a cross-country adventure towards her first performance, they are also shadowing their friends in the band The High Seas on their tour following the same route.

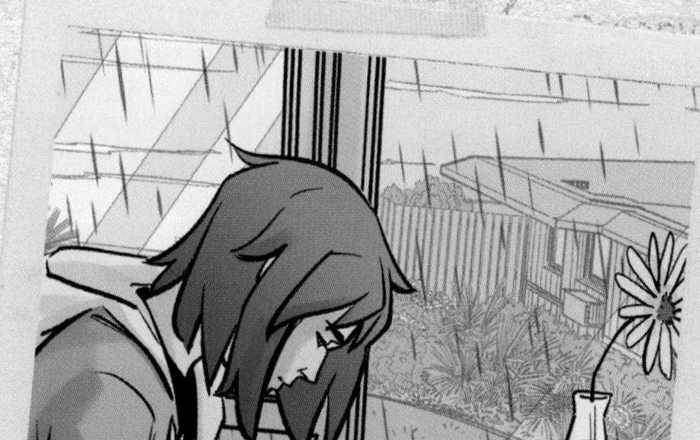

6. All the while, in Max's original universe, her Chloe is about to begin a very similar cross-country road trip, and she's going to be accompanied by a familiar face...

CAST OF CHARACTERS

CHLOE AND RACHEL'S UNIVERSE

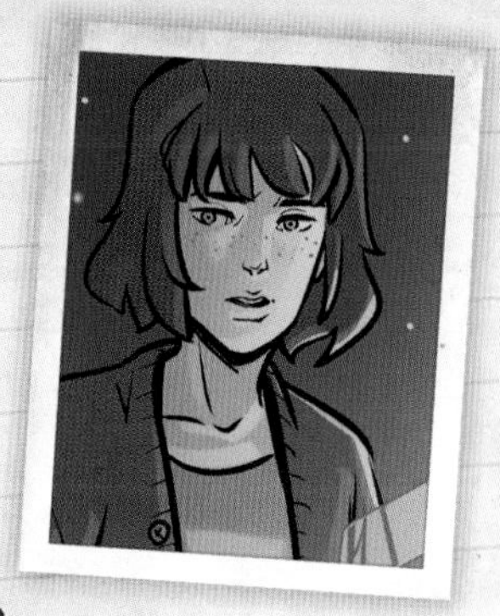

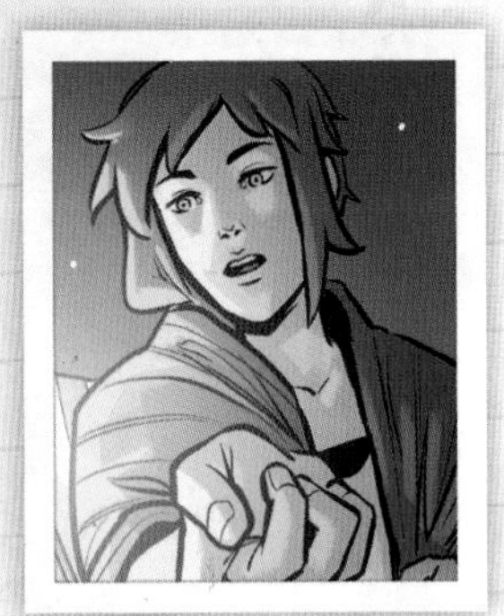

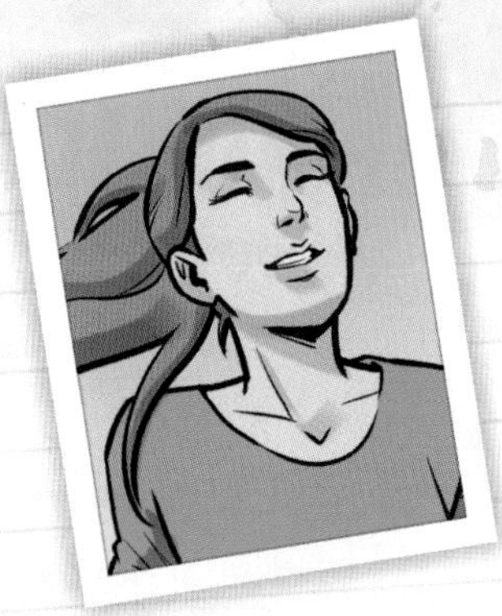

MAX

Time traveler. Photographer. Refugee from her original universe, now trying to get back to the Chloe she loves.

CHLOE

A different Chloe from the one Max fell in love with. Still a punky rebel mechanic with an artistic side. Only recently discovered Max's secret. Dating Rachel.

RACHEL

Influencer, actor, just heading out on her first theatrical tour with Hamlet. Dating Chloe. Murdered in Max's original timeline, but alive and kicking in this one.

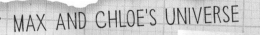

MAX AND CHLOE'S UNIVERSE

TRISTAN

Timeline castaway with the ability to phase out of reality. After befriending Max, he tried to use their combined powers to get home. It didn't work... but Tristan crossed into Max's original universe alone!

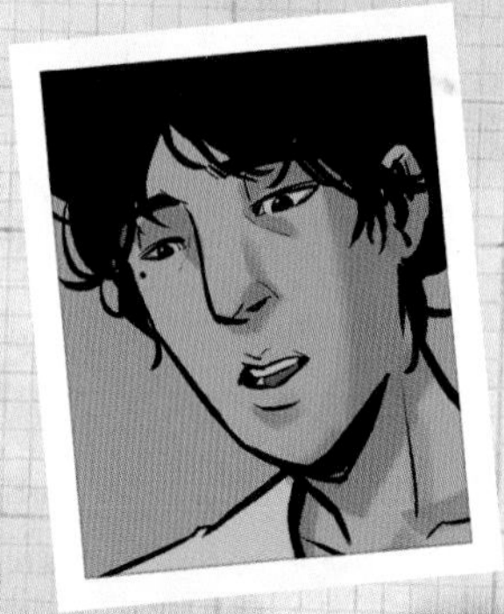

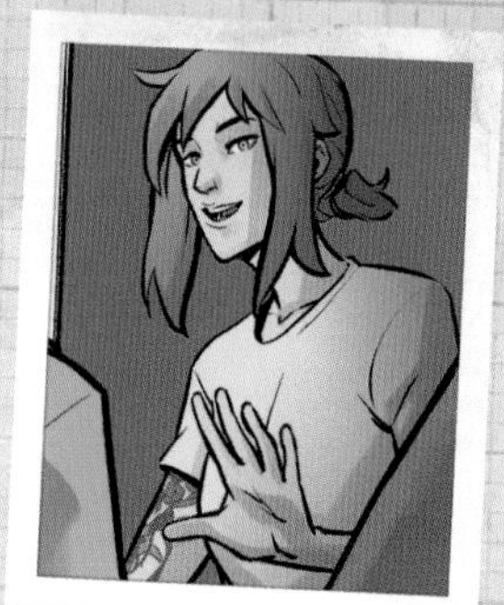

CHLOE

The Chloe Max had to leave behind. Now that both are aware that the other is still alive, Chloe is actively looking for a way to bring Max home.

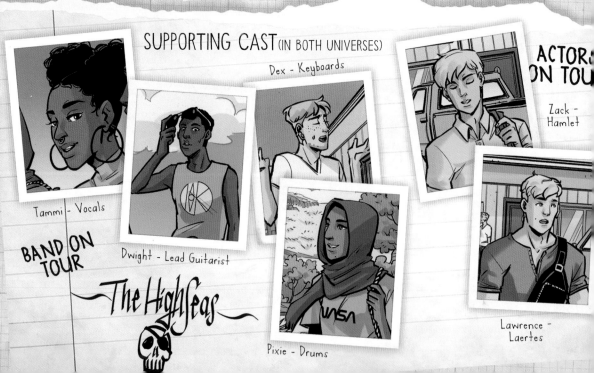

SUPPORTING CAST (IN BOTH UNIVERSES)

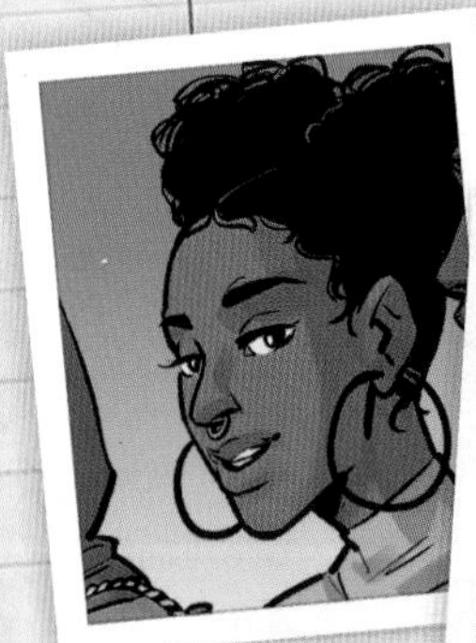

Tammi - Vocals

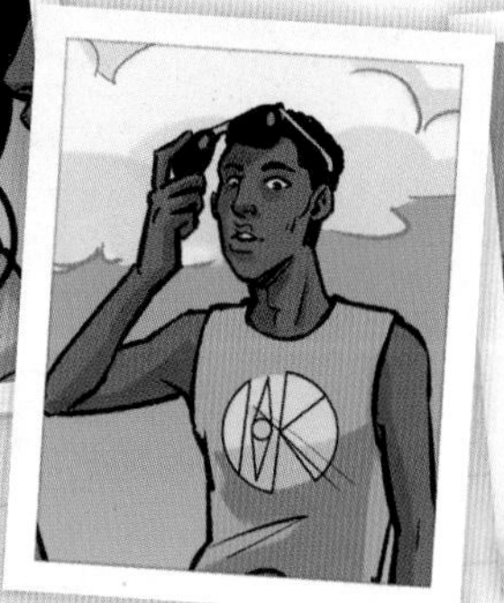

Dwight - Lead Guitarist

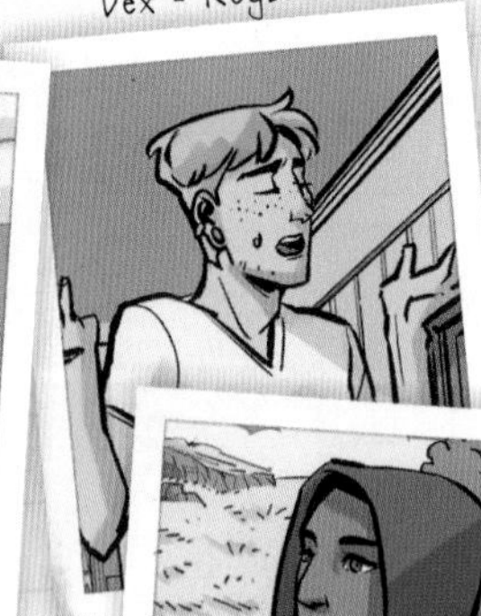

Dex - Keyboards

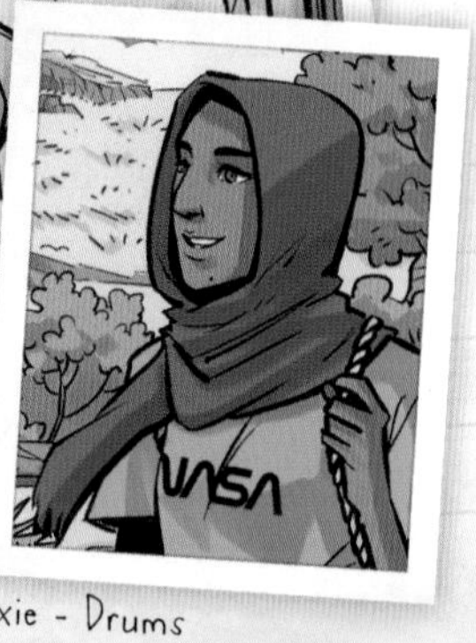

Pixie - Drums

BAND ON TOUR

The HighSeas

ACTORS ON TOUR

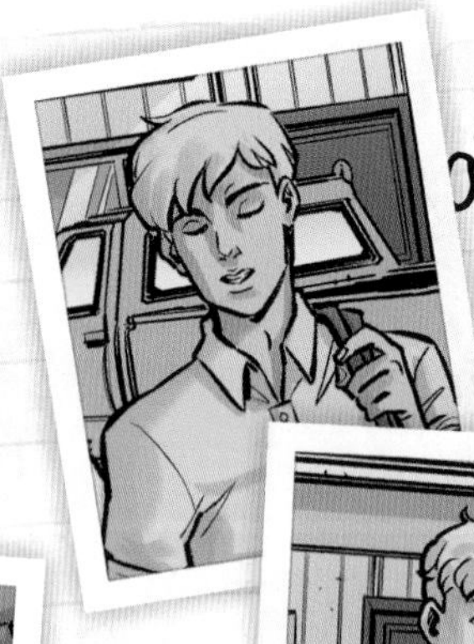

Zack - Hamlet

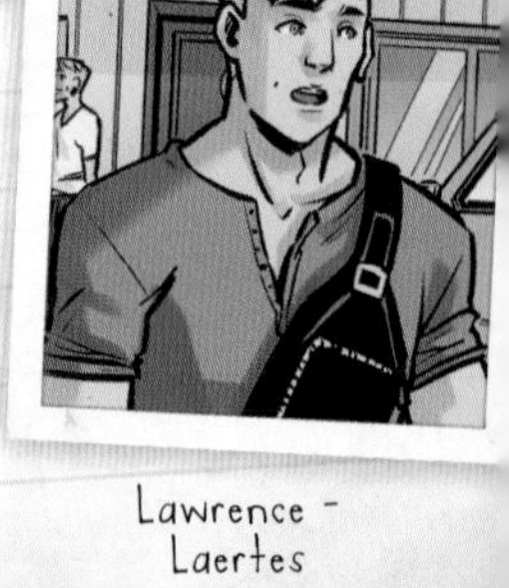

Lawrence - Laertes

CHAPTER 1

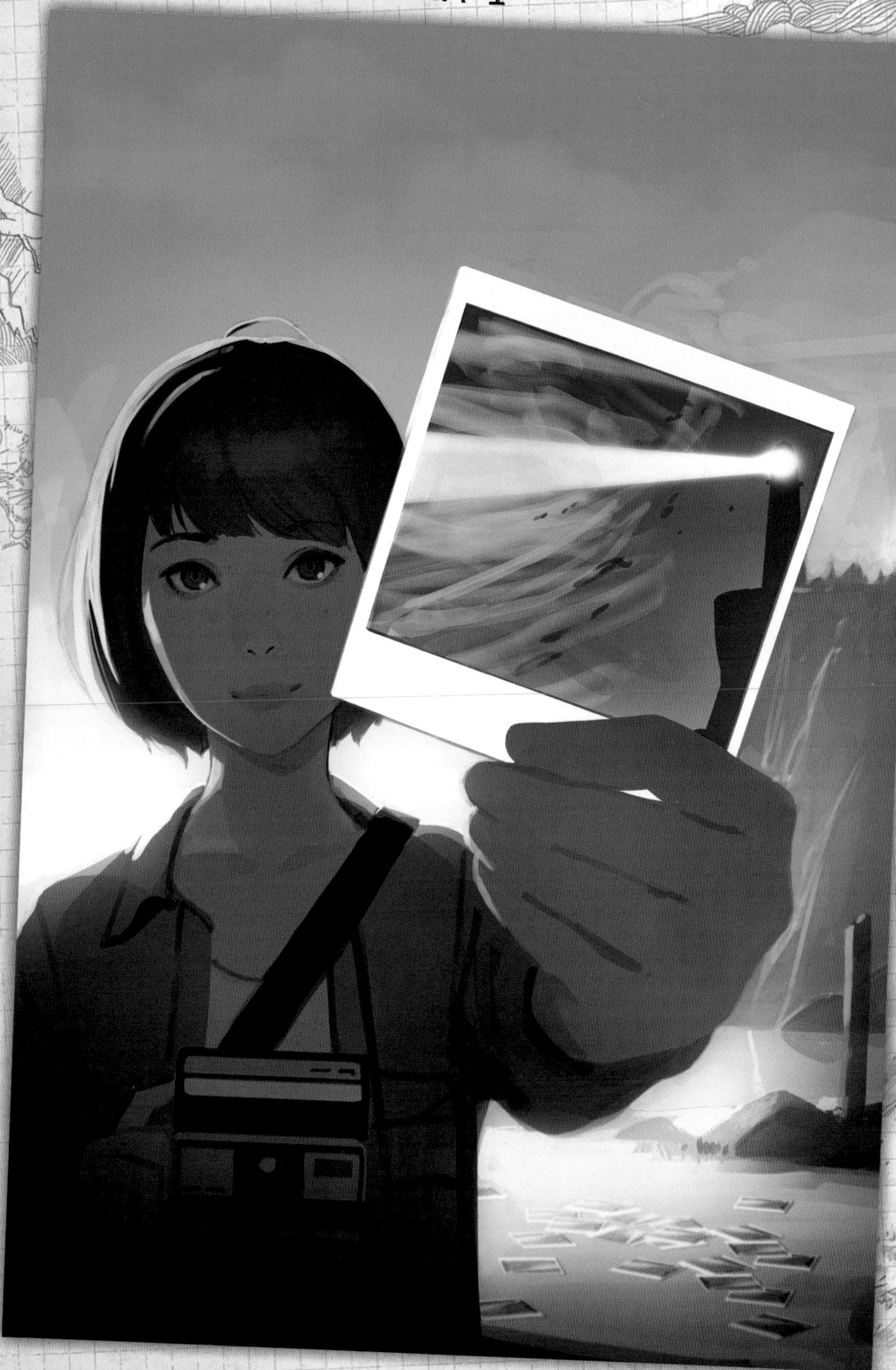

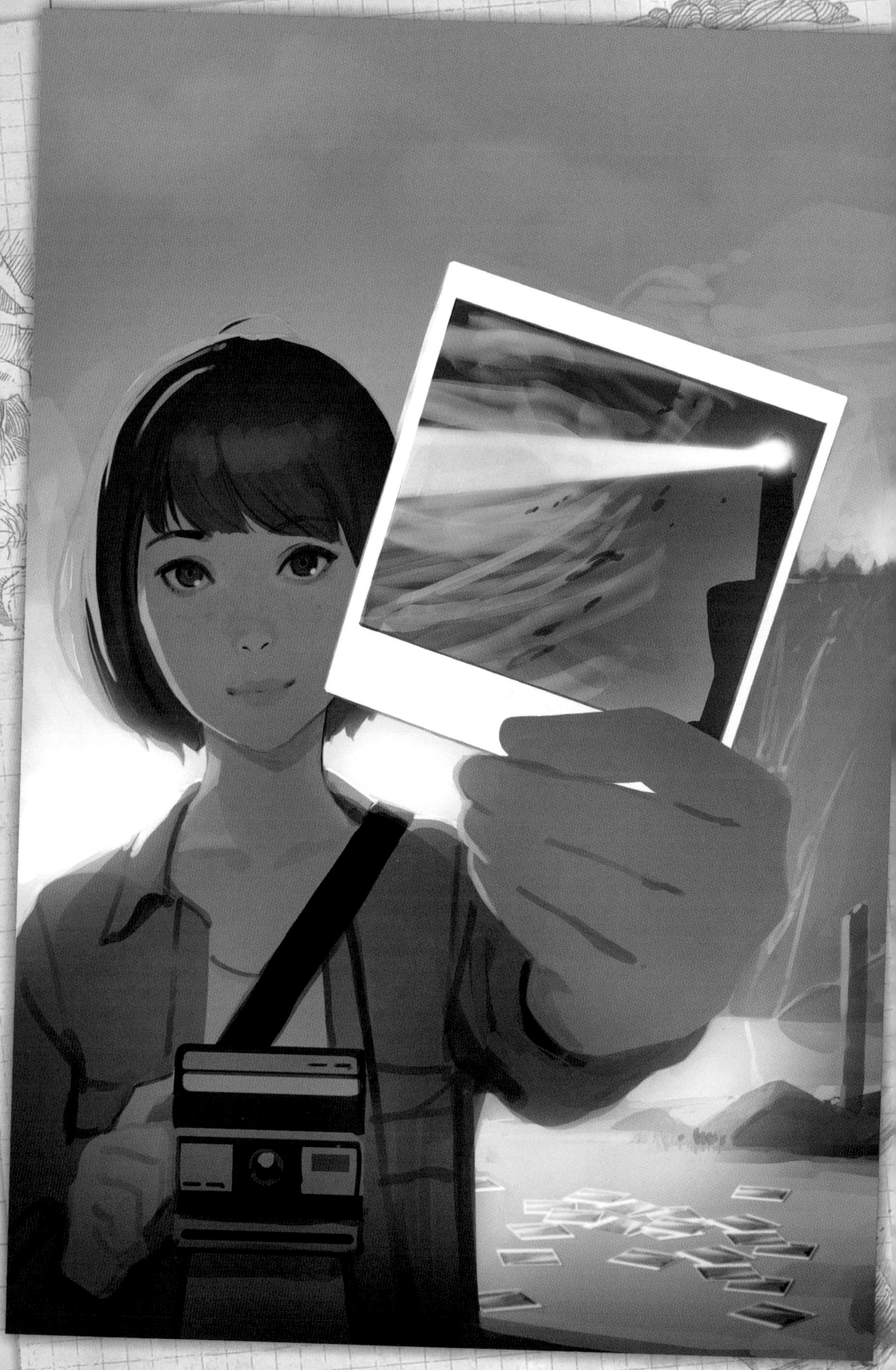

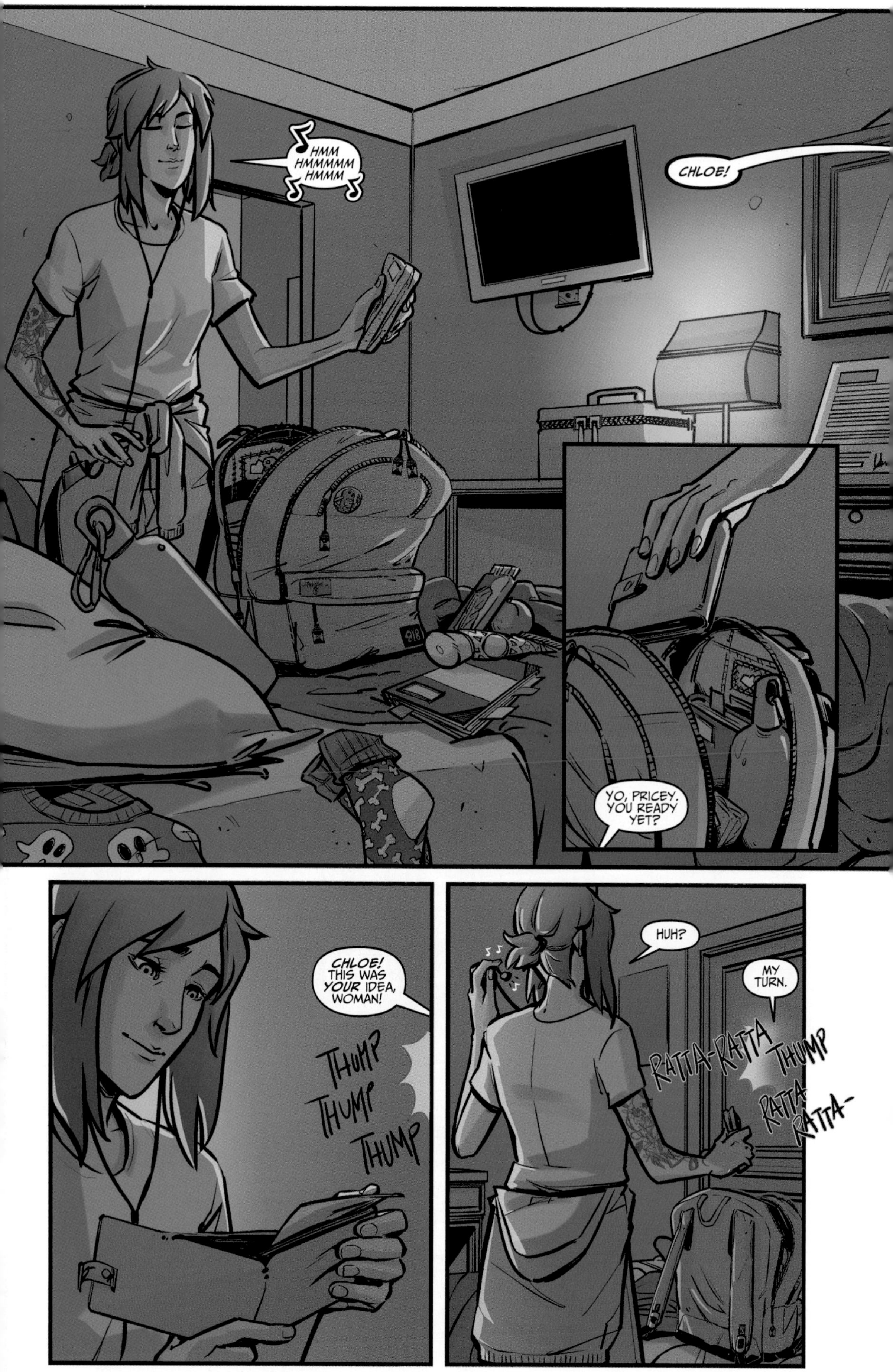
HMM HMMMMM HMMM
CHLOE!
YO, PRICEY. YOU READY YET?
CHLOE! THIS WAS YOUR IDEA, WOMAN!
THUMP THUMP THUMP
HUH?
MY TURN.
RATTA-RATTA THUMP
RATTA RATTA-

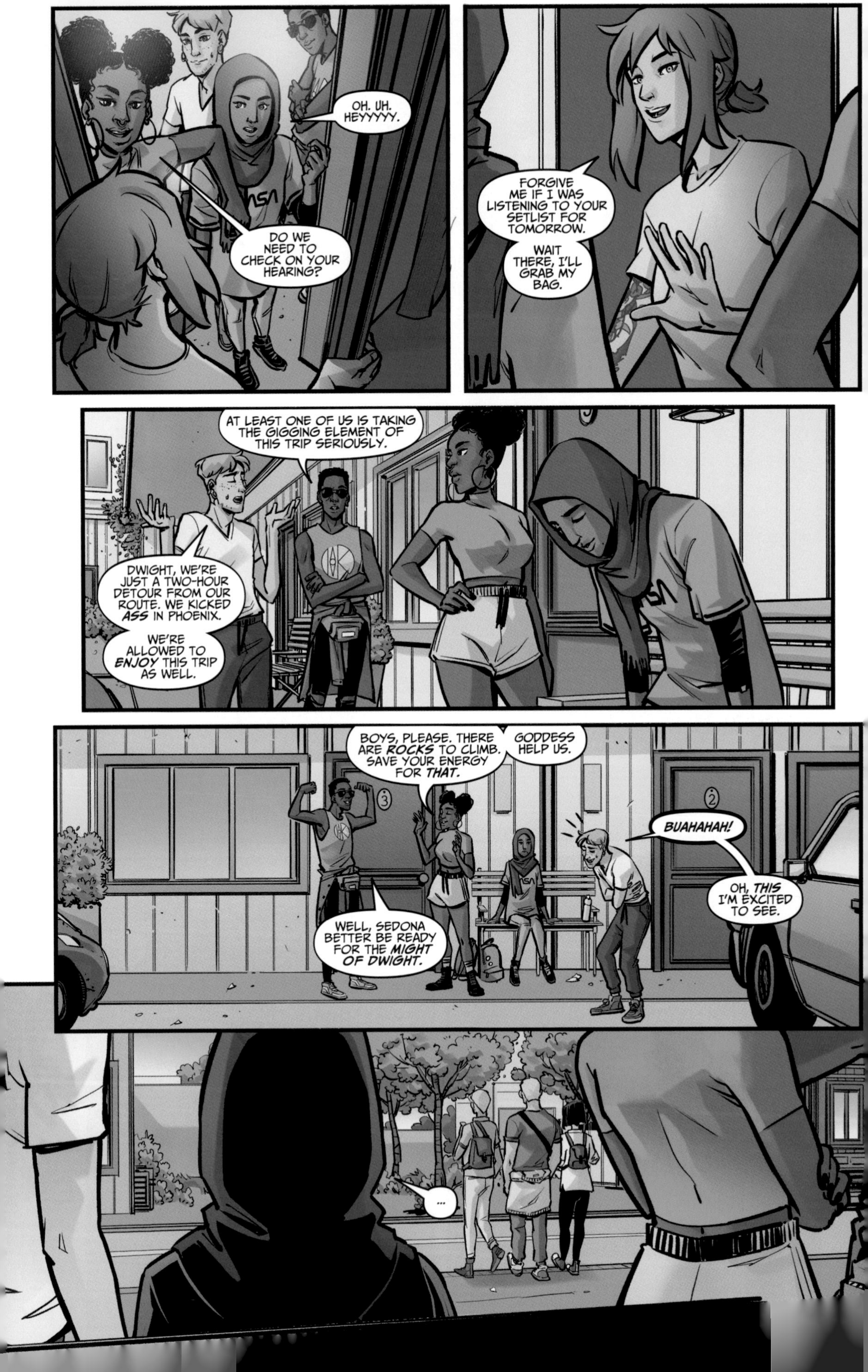
OH. UH. HEYYYYY.
DO WE NEED TO CHECK ON YOUR HEARING?
FORGIVE ME IF I WAS LISTENING TO YOUR SETLIST FOR TOMORROW.
WAIT THERE, I'LL GRAB MY BAG.
AT LEAST ONE OF US IS TAKING THE GIGGING ELEMENT OF THIS TRIP SERIOUSLY.
DWIGHT, WE'RE JUST A TWO-HOUR DETOUR FROM OUR ROUTE. WE KICKED ASS IN PHOENIX.
WE'RE ALLOWED TO ENJOY THIS TRIP AS WELL.
BOYS, PLEASE. THERE ARE ROCKS TO CLIMB. SAVE YOUR ENERGY FOR THAT.
GODDESS HELP US.
WELL, SEDONA BETTER BE READY FOR THE MIGHT OF DWIGHT.
BUAHAHAH!
OH, THIS I'M EXCITED TO SEE.
...

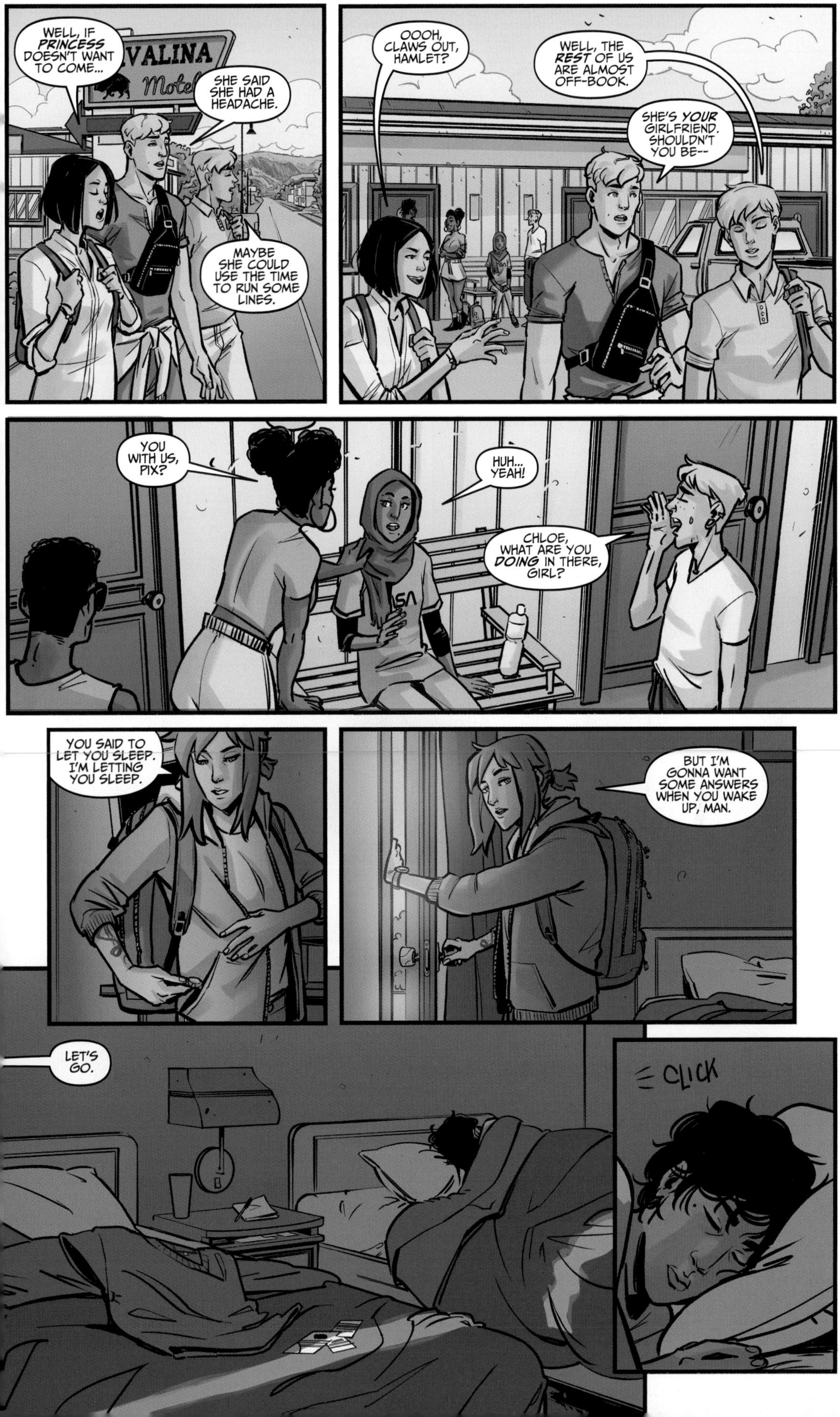
WELL, IF PRINCESS DOESN'T WANT TO COME...
VALINA Motel
SHE SAID SHE HAD A HEADACHE.
MAYBE SHE COULD USE THE TIME TO RUN SOME LINES.
OOOH, CLAWS OUT, HAMLET?
WELL, THE REST OF US ARE ALMOST OFF-BOOK.
SHE'S YOUR GIRLFRIEND. SHOULDN'T YOU BE--
YOU WITH US, PIX?
HUH... YEAH!
CHLOE, WHAT ARE YOU DOING IN THERE, GIRL?
YOU SAID TO LET YOU SLEEP. I'M LETTING YOU SLEEP.
BUT I'M GONNA WANT SOME ANSWERS WHEN YOU WAKE UP, MAN.
LET'S GO.
CLICK

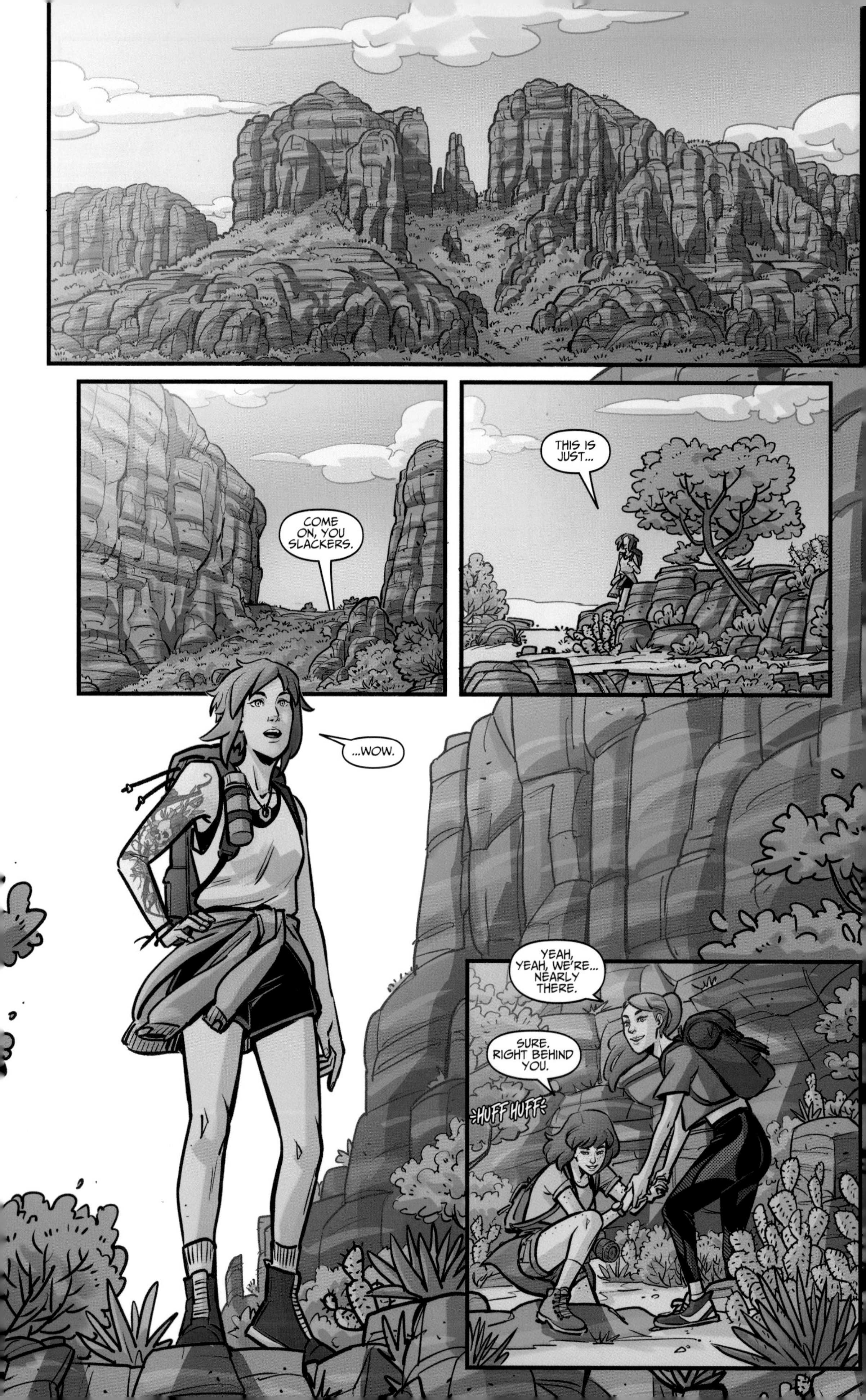
COME ON, YOU SLACKERS.
THIS IS JUST...
...WOW.
YEAH, YEAH, WE'RE... NEARLY THERE.
SURE. RIGHT BEHIND YOU.
HUFF HUFF

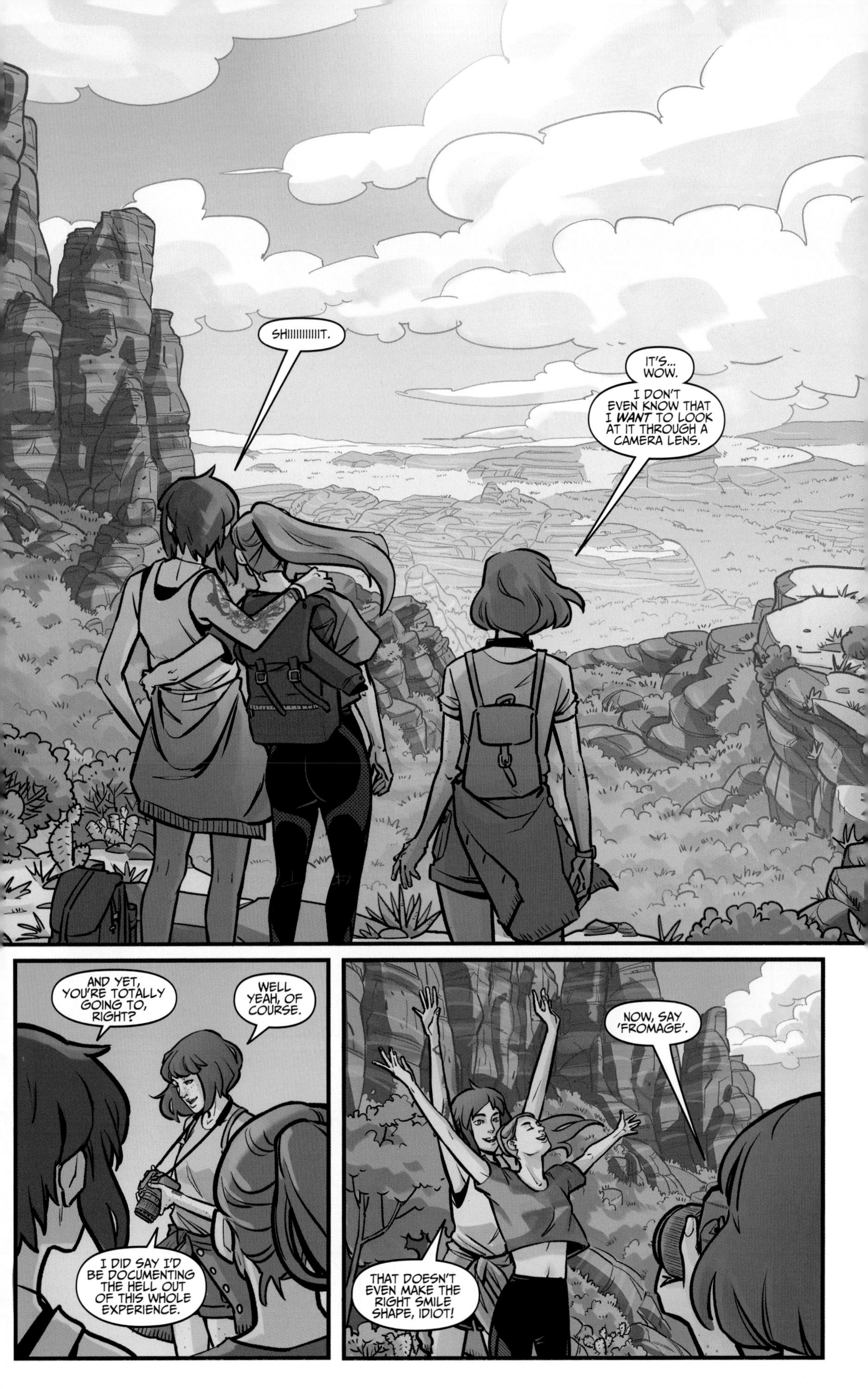
SHIIIIIIIIIIT.
IT'S... WOW.
I DON'T EVEN KNOW THAT I *WANT* TO LOOK AT IT THROUGH A CAMERA LENS.
AND YET, YOU'RE TOTALLY GOING TO, RIGHT?
WELL YEAH, OF COURSE.
I DID SAY I'D BE DOCUMENTING THE HELL OUT OF THIS WHOLE EXPERIENCE.
NOW, SAY 'FROMAGE'.
THAT DOESN'T EVEN MAKE THE RIGHT SMILE SHAPE, IDIOT!

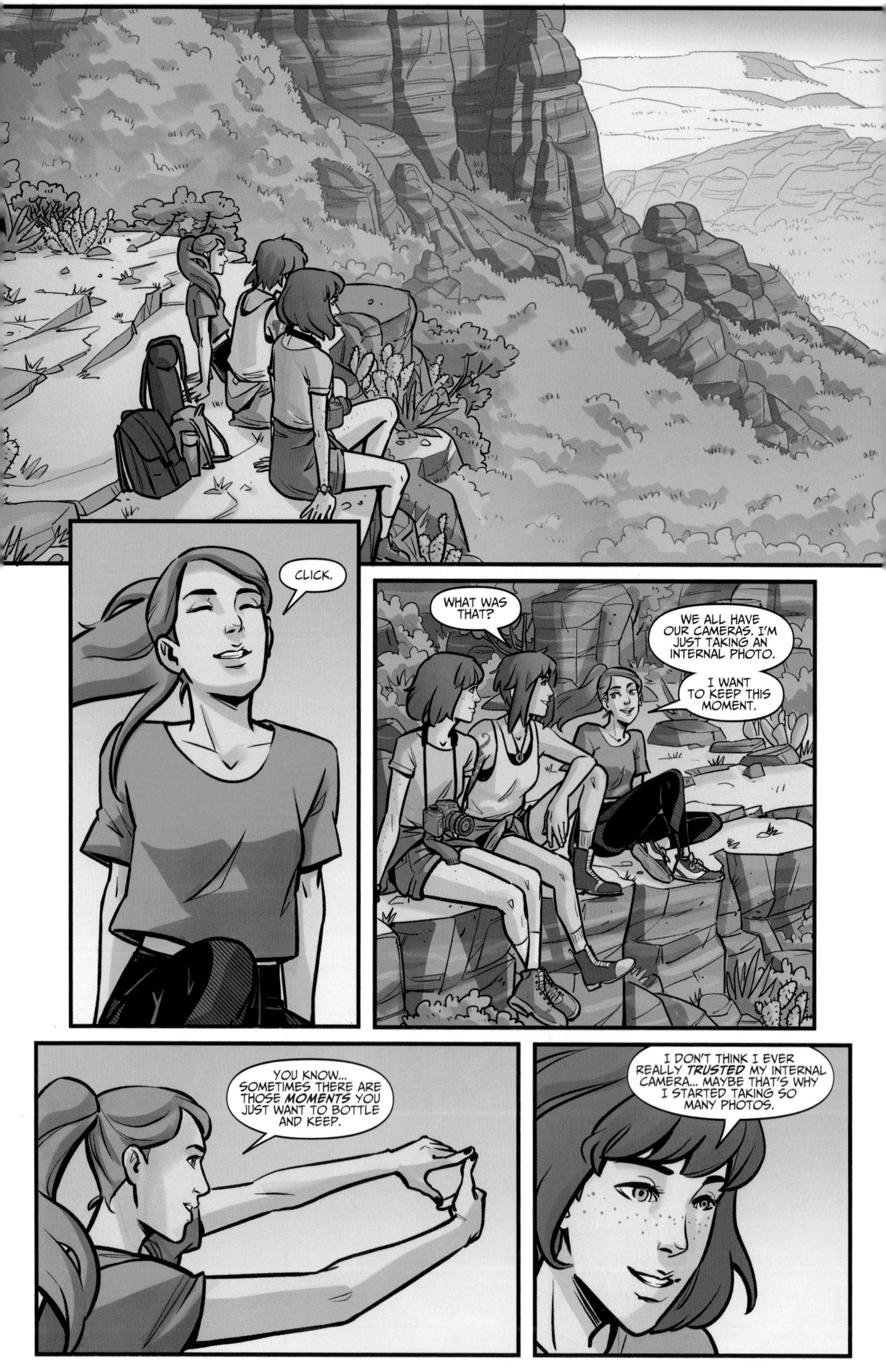
CLICK.
WHAT WAS THAT?
WE ALL HAVE OUR CAMERAS. I'M JUST TAKING AN INTERNAL PHOTO.
I WANT TO KEEP THIS MOMENT.
YOU KNOW... SOMETIMES THERE ARE THOSE MOMENTS YOU JUST WANT TO BOTTLE AND KEEP.
I DON'T THINK I EVER REALLY TRUSTED MY INTERNAL CAMERA... MAYBE THAT'S WHY I STARTED TAKING SO MANY PHOTOS.

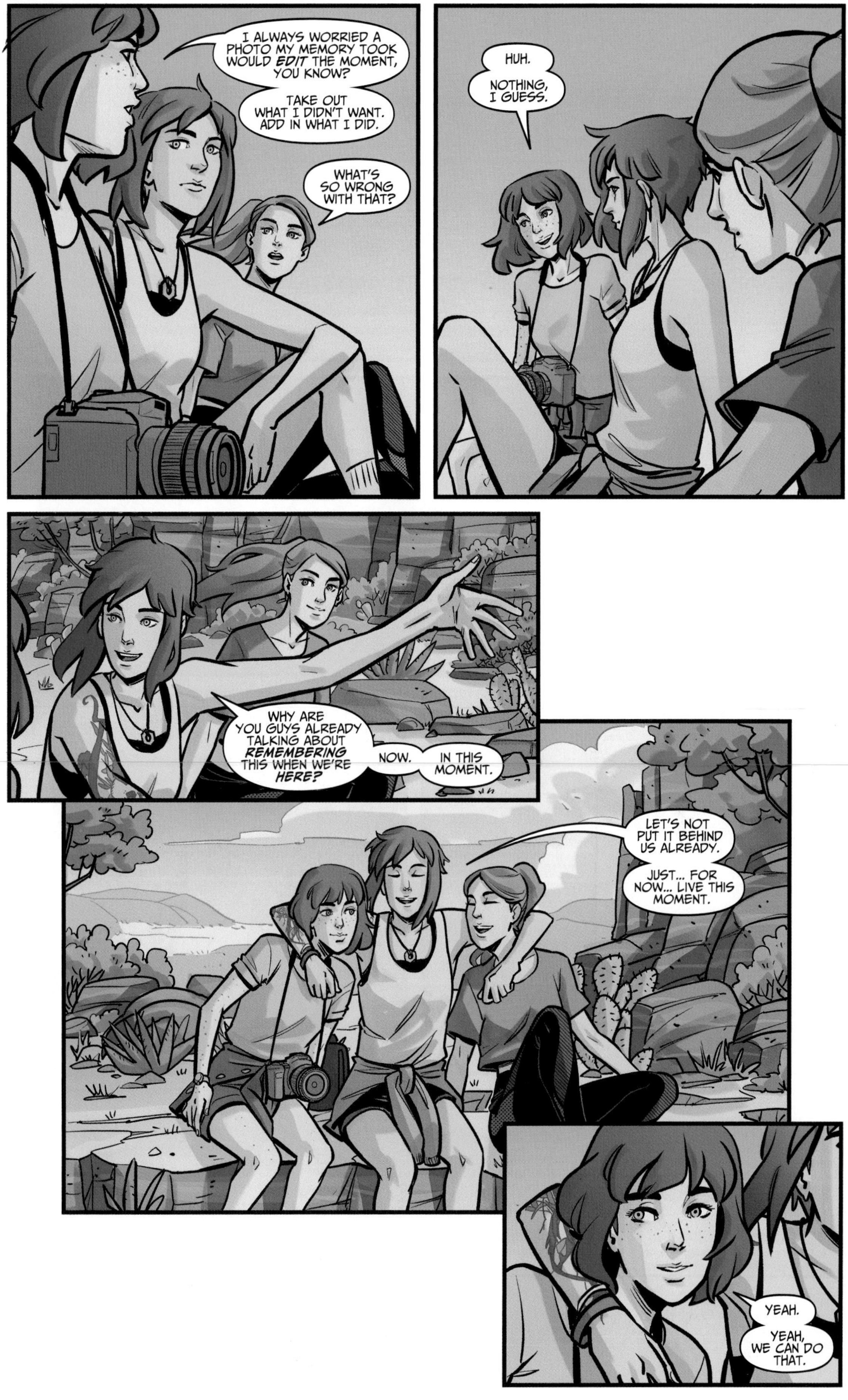
I ALWAYS WORRIED A PHOTO MY MEMORY TOOK WOULD EDIT THE MOMENT, YOU KNOW?
TAKE OUT WHAT I DIDN'T WANT. ADD IN WHAT I DID.
WHAT'S SO WRONG WITH THAT?
HUH.
NOTHING, I GUESS.
WHY ARE YOU GUYS ALREADY TALKING ABOUT REMEMBERING THIS WHEN WE'RE HERE?
NOW.
IN THIS MOMENT.
LET'S NOT PUT IT BEHIND US ALREADY.
JUST... FOR NOW... LIVE THIS MOMENT.
YEAH.
YEAH, WE CAN DO THAT.

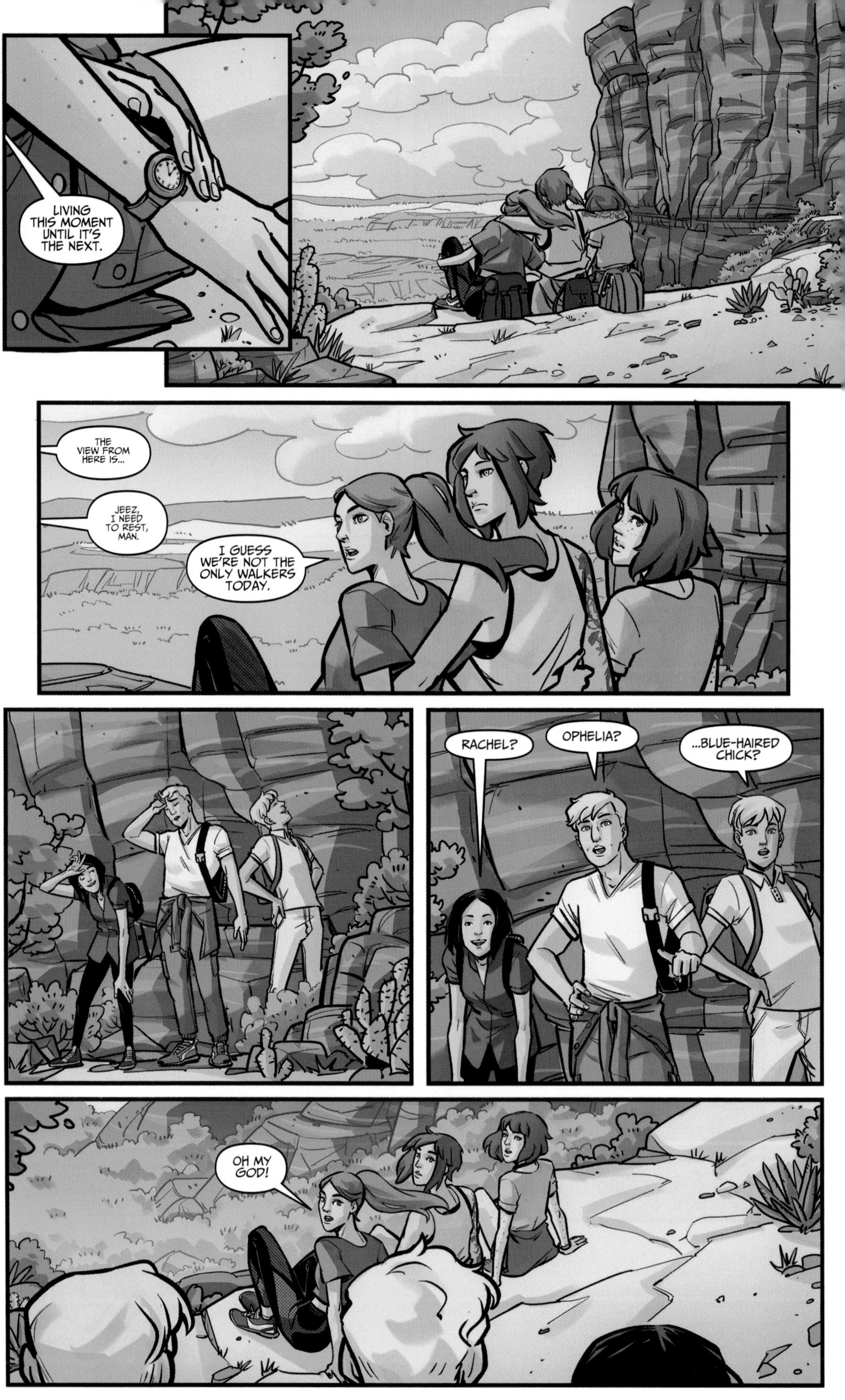
LIVING THIS MOMENT UNTIL IT'S THE NEXT.
THE VIEW FROM HERE IS...
JEEZ, I NEED TO REST, MAN.
I GUESS WE'RE NOT THE ONLY WALKERS TODAY.
RACHEL?
OPHELIA?
...BLUE-HAIRED CHICK?
OH MY GOD!

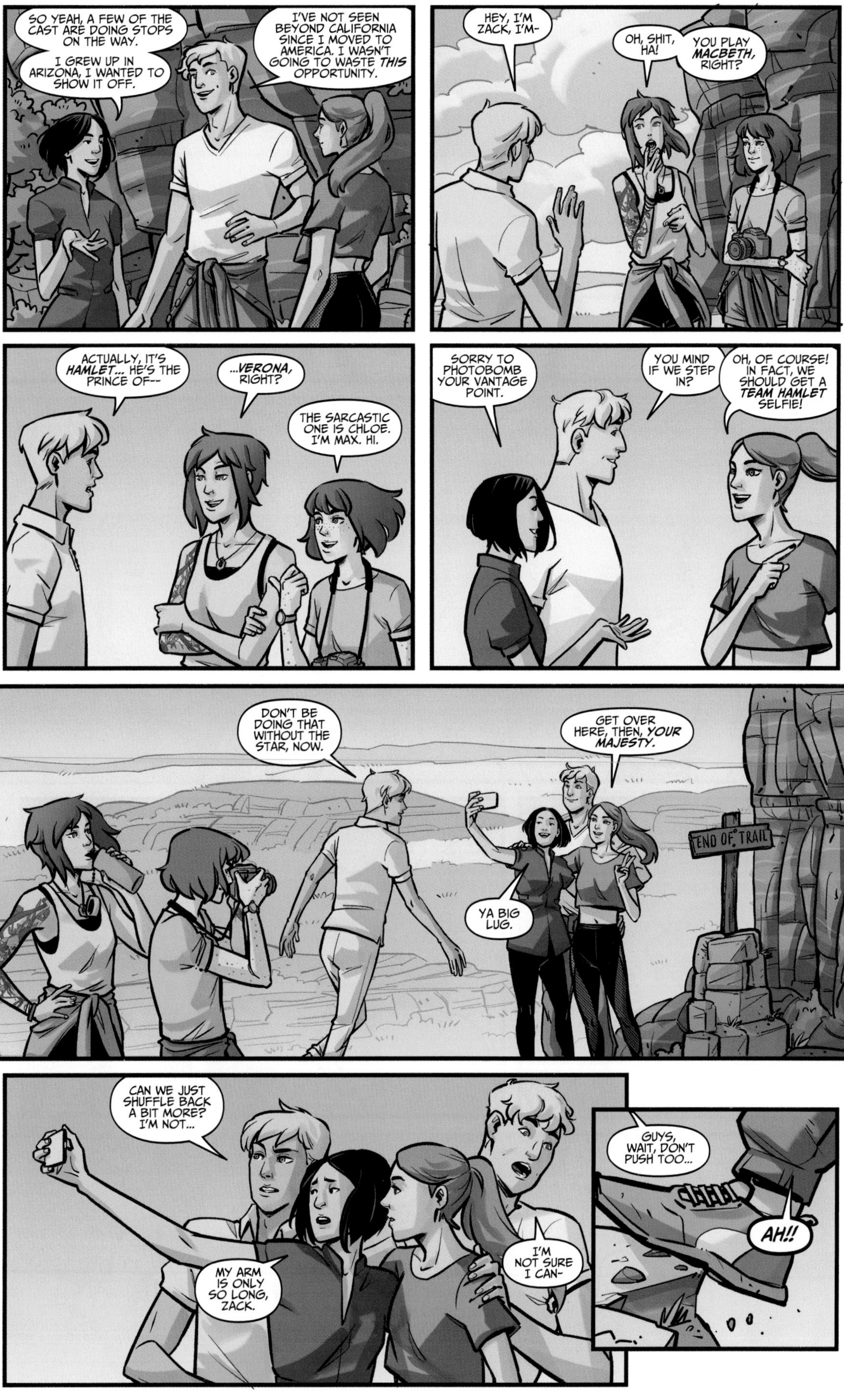
SO YEAH, A FEW OF THE CAST ARE DOING STOPS ON THE WAY.
I GREW UP IN ARIZONA, I WANTED TO SHOW IT OFF.
I'VE NOT SEEN BEYOND CALIFORNIA SINCE I MOVED TO AMERICA. I WASN'T GOING TO WASTE THIS OPPORTUNITY.
HEY, I'M ZACK, I'M-
OH, SHIT, HA!
YOU PLAY MACBETH, RIGHT?
ACTUALLY, IT'S HAMLET... HE'S THE PRINCE OF--
...VERONA, RIGHT?
THE SARCASTIC ONE IS CHLOE. I'M MAX. HI.
SORRY TO PHOTOBOMB YOUR VANTAGE POINT.
YOU MIND IF WE STEP IN?
OH, OF COURSE! IN FACT, WE SHOULD GET A TEAM HAMLET SELFIE!
DON'T BE DOING THAT WITHOUT THE STAR, NOW.
GET OVER HERE, THEN, YOUR MAJESTY.
END OF TRAIL
YA BIG LUG.
CAN WE JUST SHUFFLE BACK A BIT MORE? I'M NOT...
MY ARM IS ONLY SO LONG, ZACK.
I'M NOT SURE I CAN-
GUYS, WAIT, DON'T PUSH TOO...
AH!!

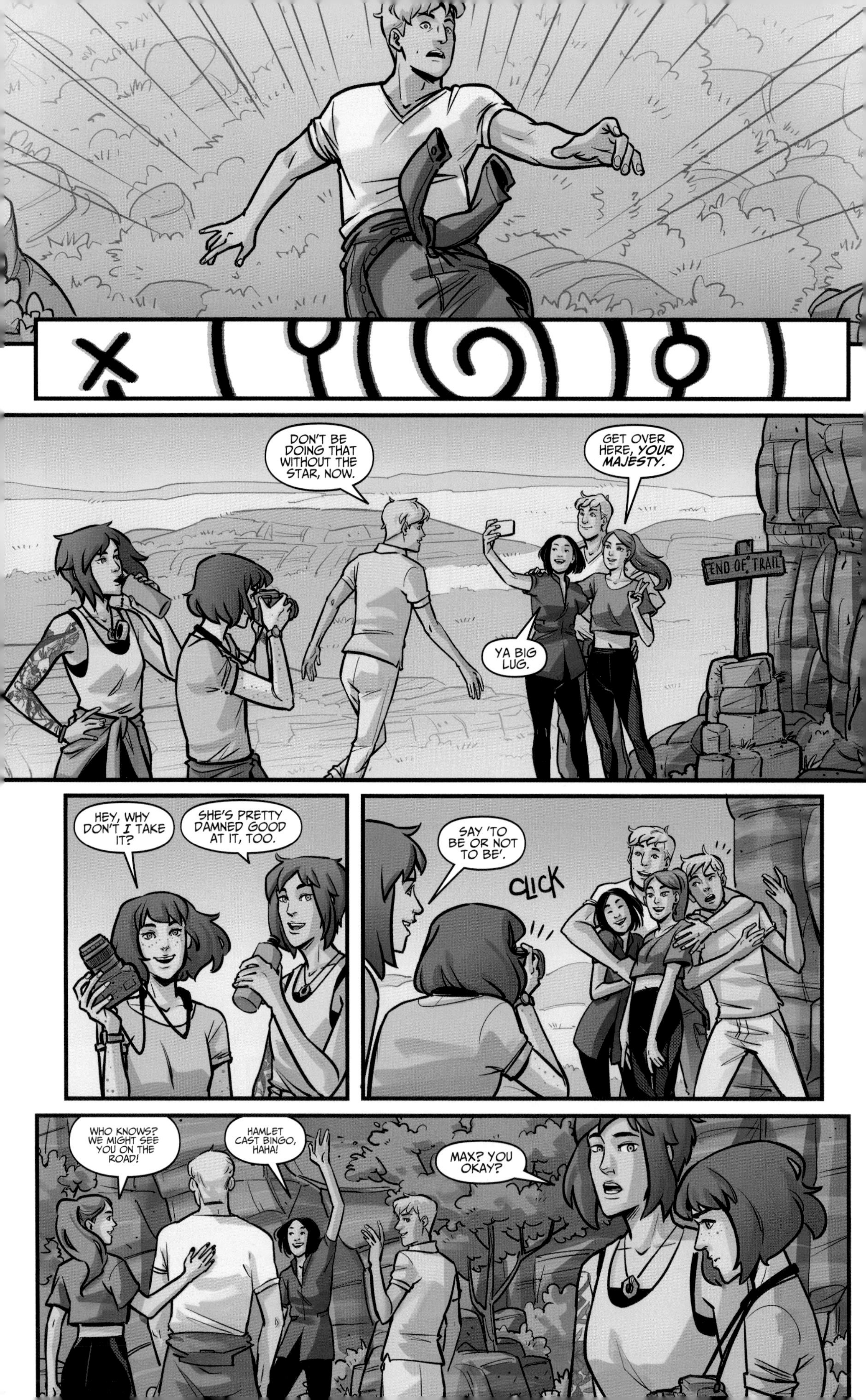

DON'T BE DOING THAT WITHOUT THE STAR, NOW.
GET OVER HERE, YOUR MAJESTY.
END OF TRAIL
YA BIG LUG.
HEY, WHY DON'T I TAKE IT?
SHE'S PRETTY DAMNED GOOD AT IT, TOO.
SAY 'TO BE OR NOT TO BE'.
CLICK
WHO KNOWS? WE MIGHT SEE YOU ON THE ROAD!
HAMLET CAST BINGO, HAHA!
MAX? YOU OKAY?

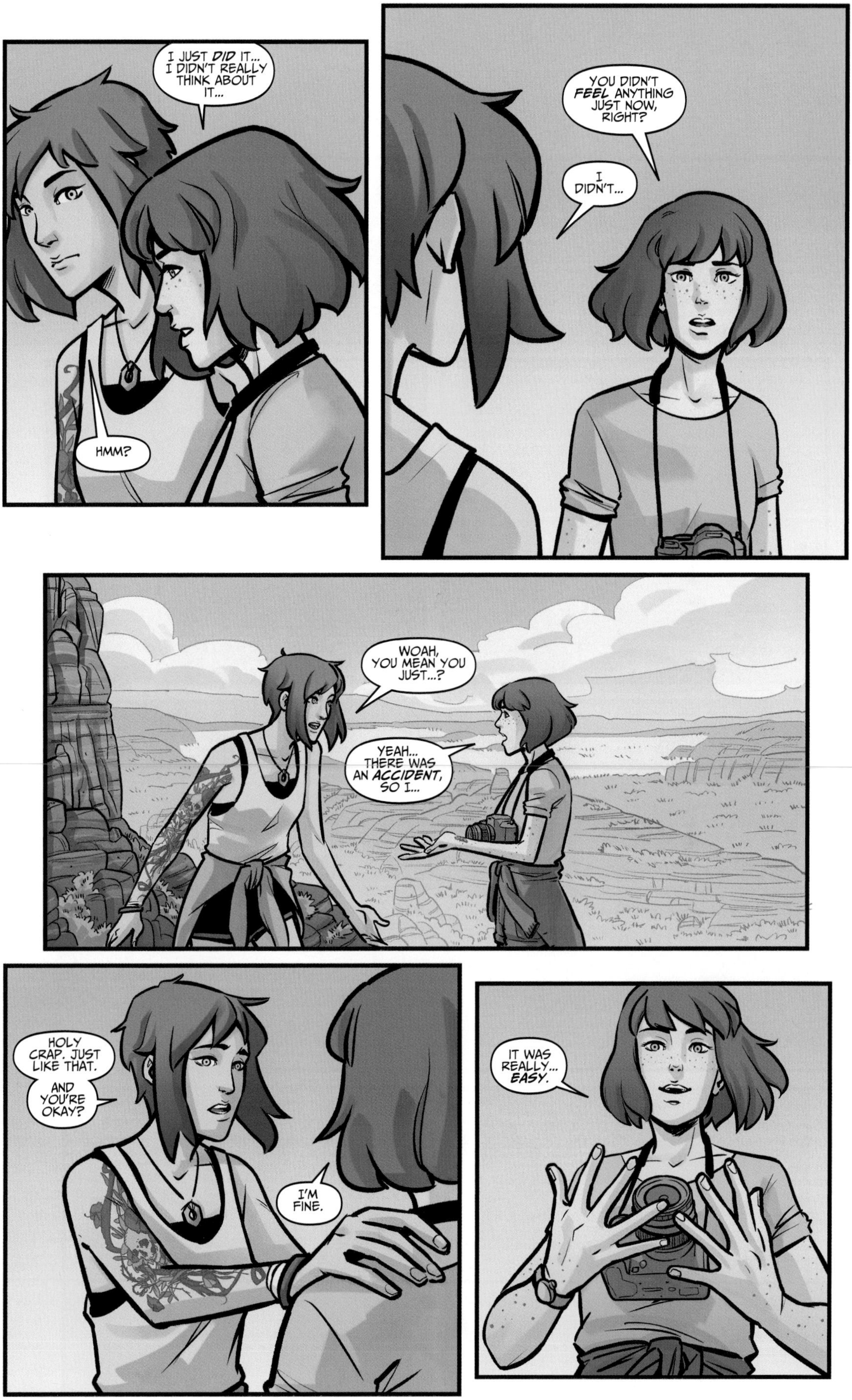
I JUST *DID* IT... I DIDN'T REALLY THINK ABOUT IT...
HMM?
YOU DIDN'T *FEEL* ANYTHING JUST NOW, RIGHT?
I DIDN'T...
WOAH, YOU MEAN YOU JUST...?
YEAH... THERE WAS AN *ACCIDENT*, SO I...
HOLY CRAP. JUST LIKE THAT.
AND YOU'RE OKAY?
I'M FINE.
IT WAS REALLY... *EASY*.

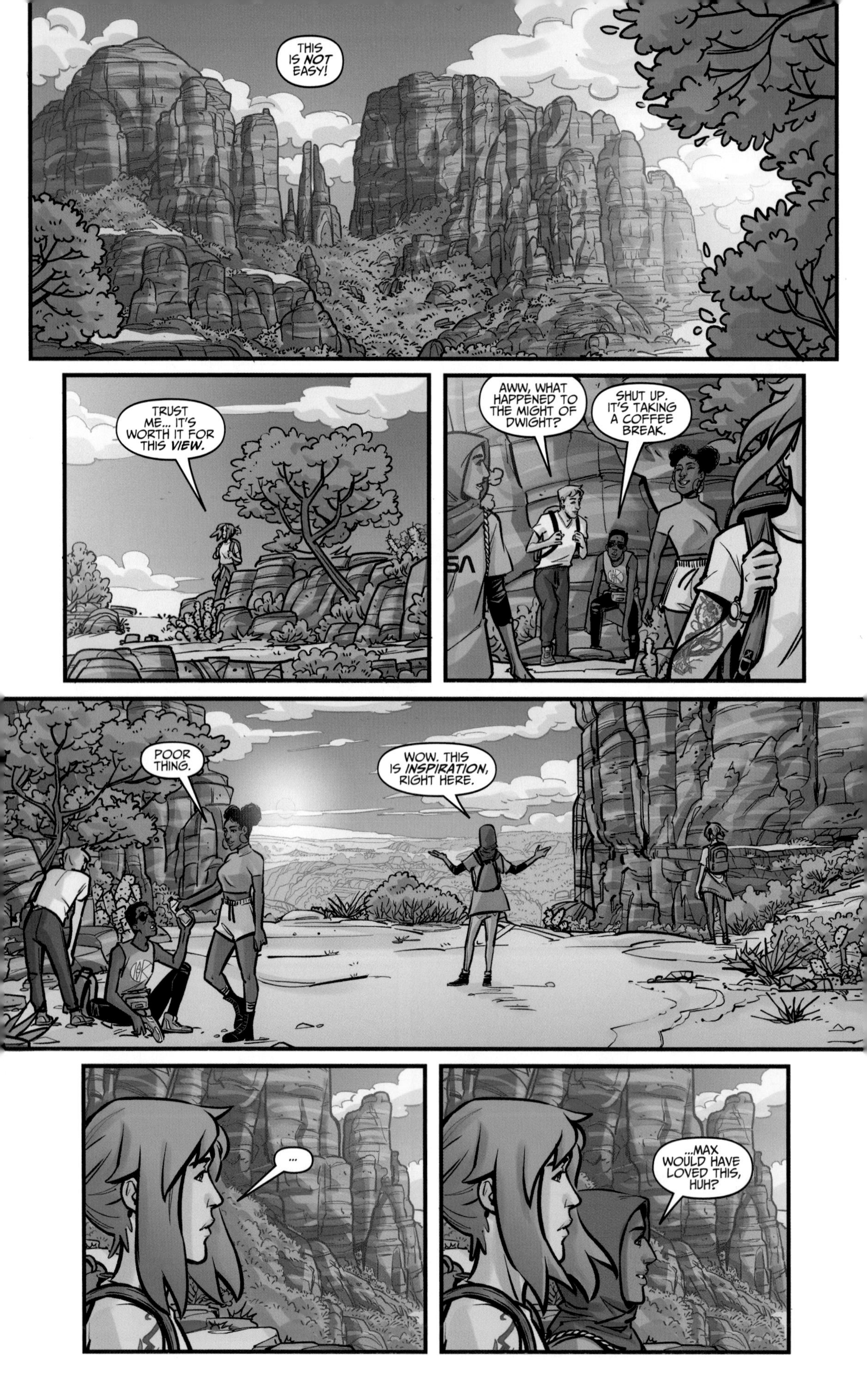
THIS IS NOT EASY!
TRUST ME... IT'S WORTH IT FOR THIS VIEW.
AWW, WHAT HAPPENED TO THE MIGHT OF DWIGHT?
SHUT UP. IT'S TAKING A COFFEE BREAK.
POOR THING.
WOW. THIS IS INSPIRATION, RIGHT HERE.
...
...MAX WOULD HAVE LOVED THIS, HUH?

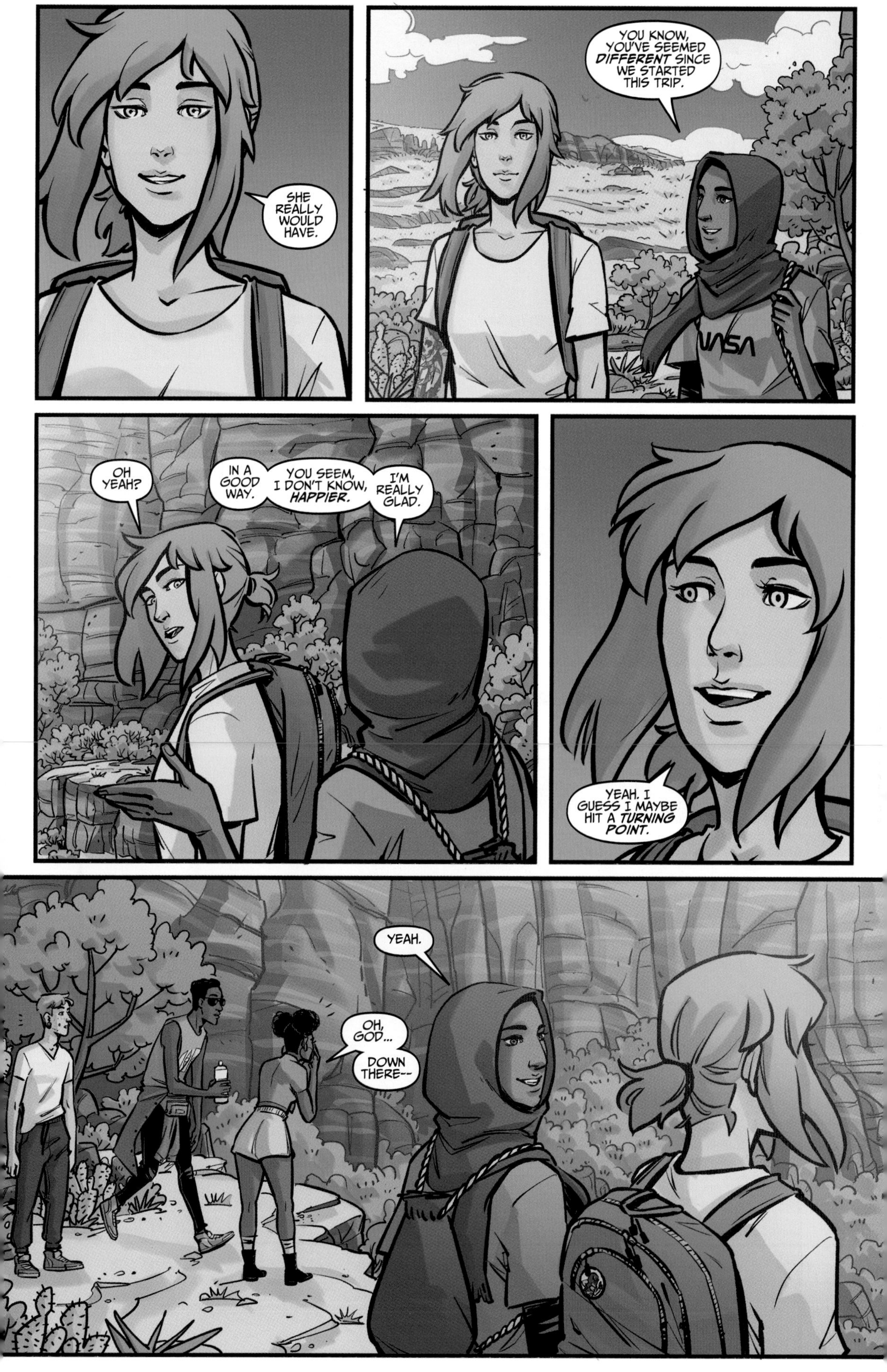
SHE REALLY WOULD HAVE.
YOU KNOW, YOU'VE SEEMED *DIFFERENT* SINCE WE STARTED THIS TRIP.
NASA
OH YEAH?
IN A GOOD WAY.
YOU SEEM, I DON'T KNOW, *HAPPIER.*
I'M REALLY GLAD.
YEAH. I GUESS I MAYBE HIT A *TURNING POINT*.
YEAH.
OH, GOD...
DOWN THERE--

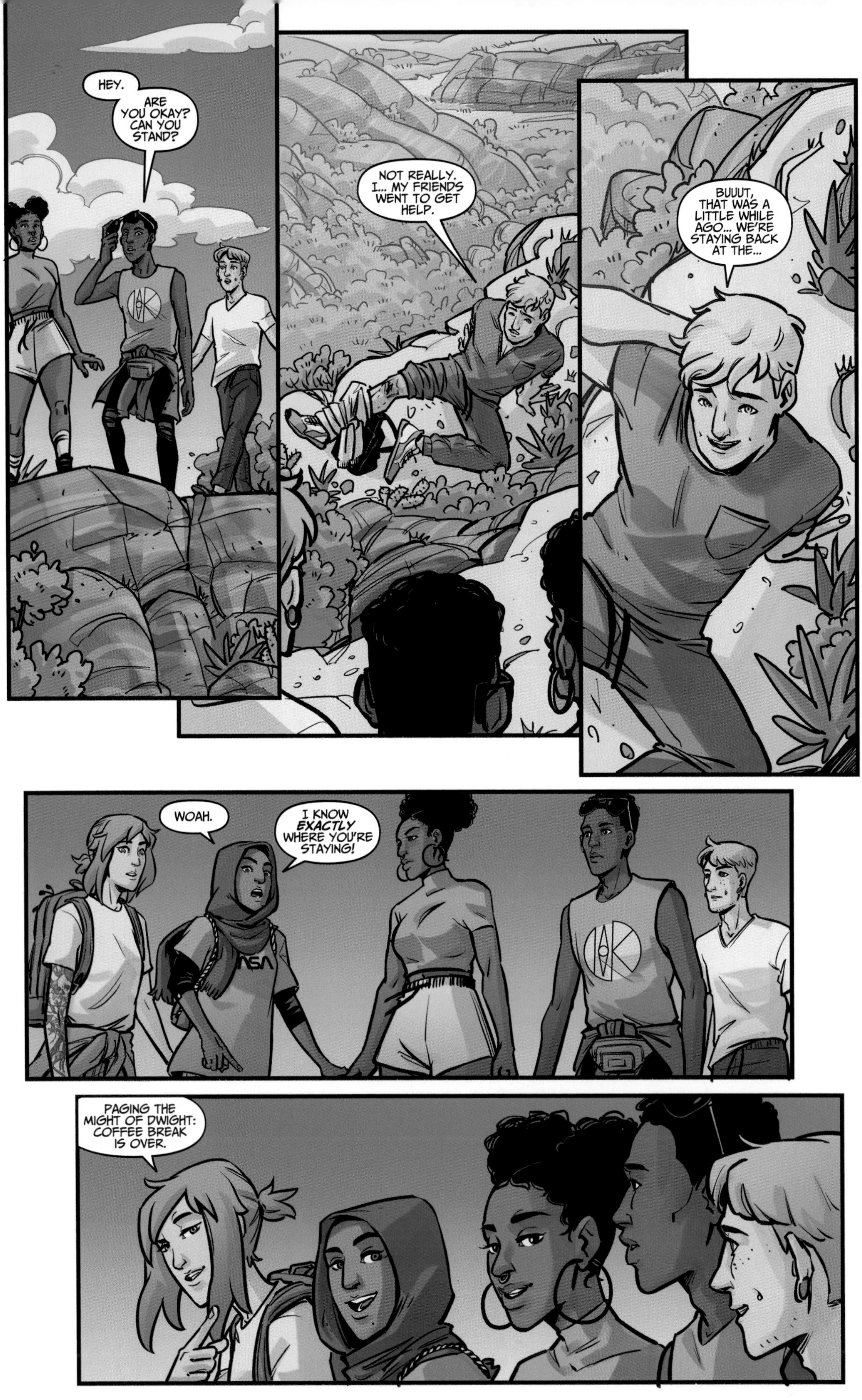
HEY.
ARE YOU OKAY? CAN YOU STAND?
NOT REALLY. I... MY FRIENDS WENT TO GET HELP.
BUUUT, THAT WAS A LITTLE WHILE AGO... WE'RE STAYING BACK AT THE...
WOAH.
I KNOW *EXACTLY* WHERE YOU'RE STAYING!
PAGING THE MIGHT OF DWIGHT: COFFEE BREAK IS OVER.

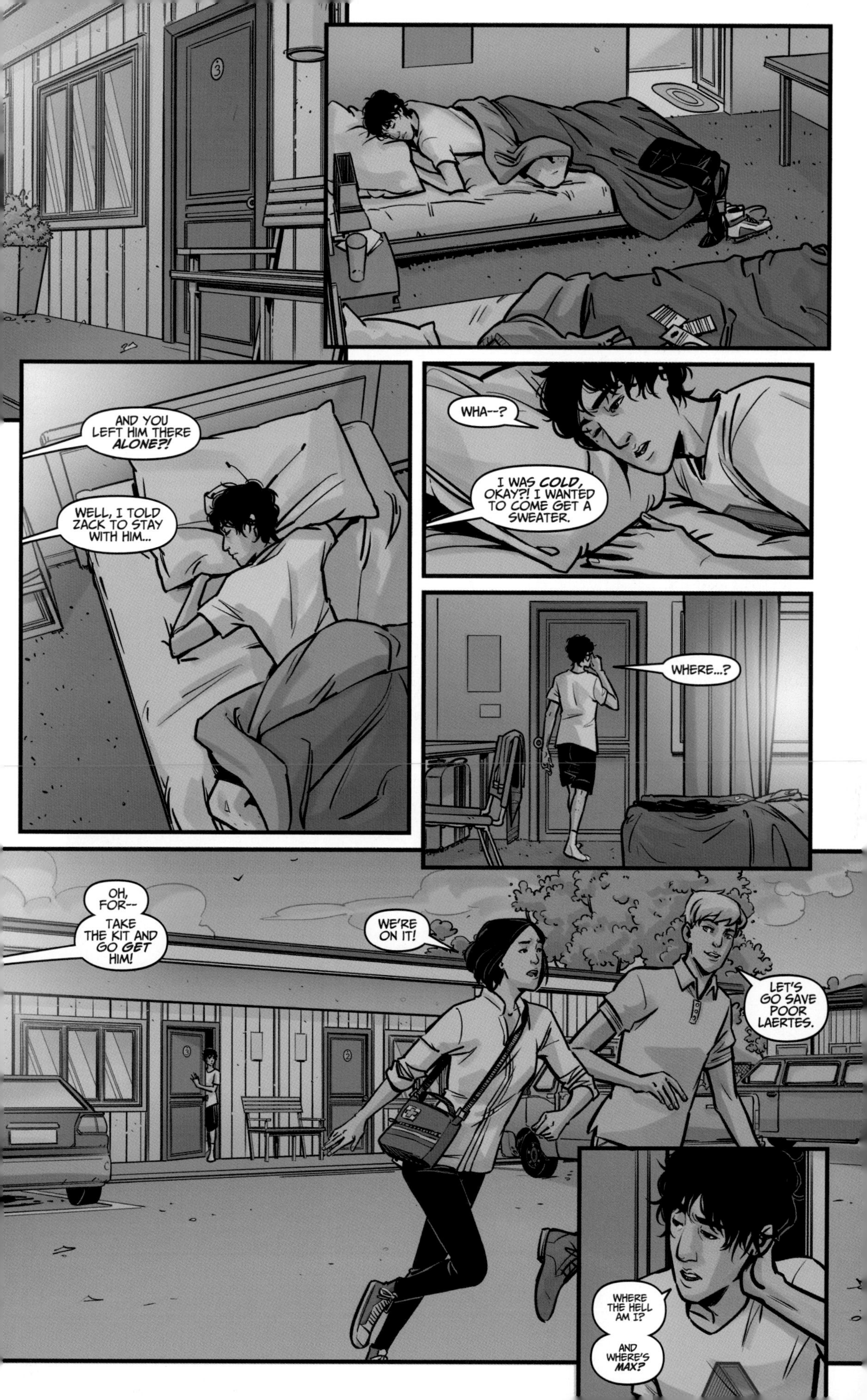
AND YOU LEFT HIM THERE ALONE?!
WELL, I TOLD ZACK TO STAY WITH HIM...
WHA--?
I WAS COLD, OKAY?! I WANTED TO COME GET A SWEATER.
WHERE...?
OH, FOR--
TAKE THE KIT AND GO GET HIM!
WE'RE ON IT!
LET'S GO SAVE POOR LAERTES.
WHERE THE HELL AM I?
AND WHERE'S MAX?

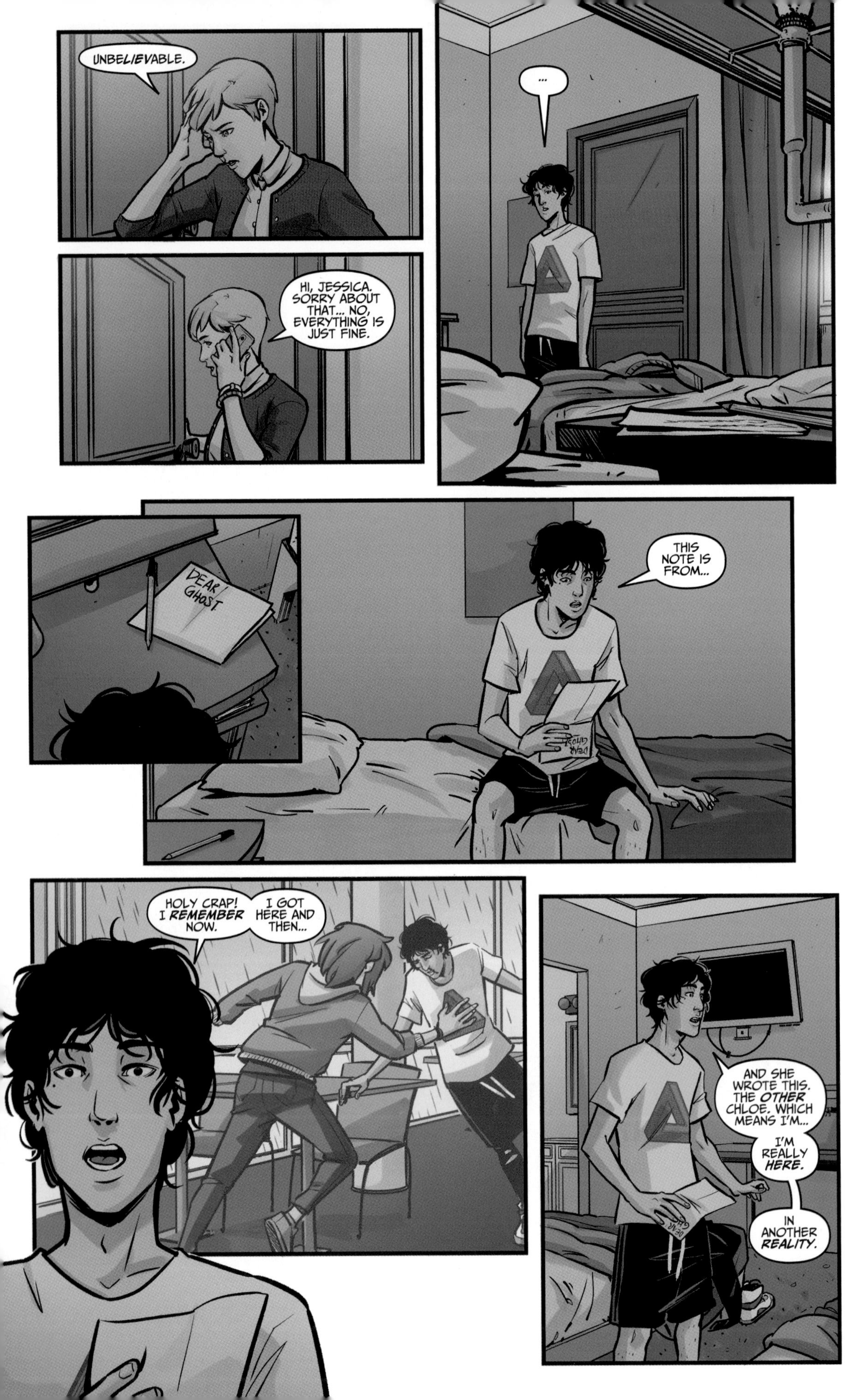
UNBELIEVABLE.
...
HI, JESSICA. SORRY ABOUT THAT... NO, EVERYTHING IS JUST FINE.
DEAR GHOST.
THIS NOTE IS FROM...
HOLY CRAP! I REMEMBER NOW.
I GOT HERE AND THEN...
AND SHE WROTE THIS. THE OTHER CHLOE. WHICH MEANS I'M...
I'M REALLY HERE.
IN ANOTHER REALITY.

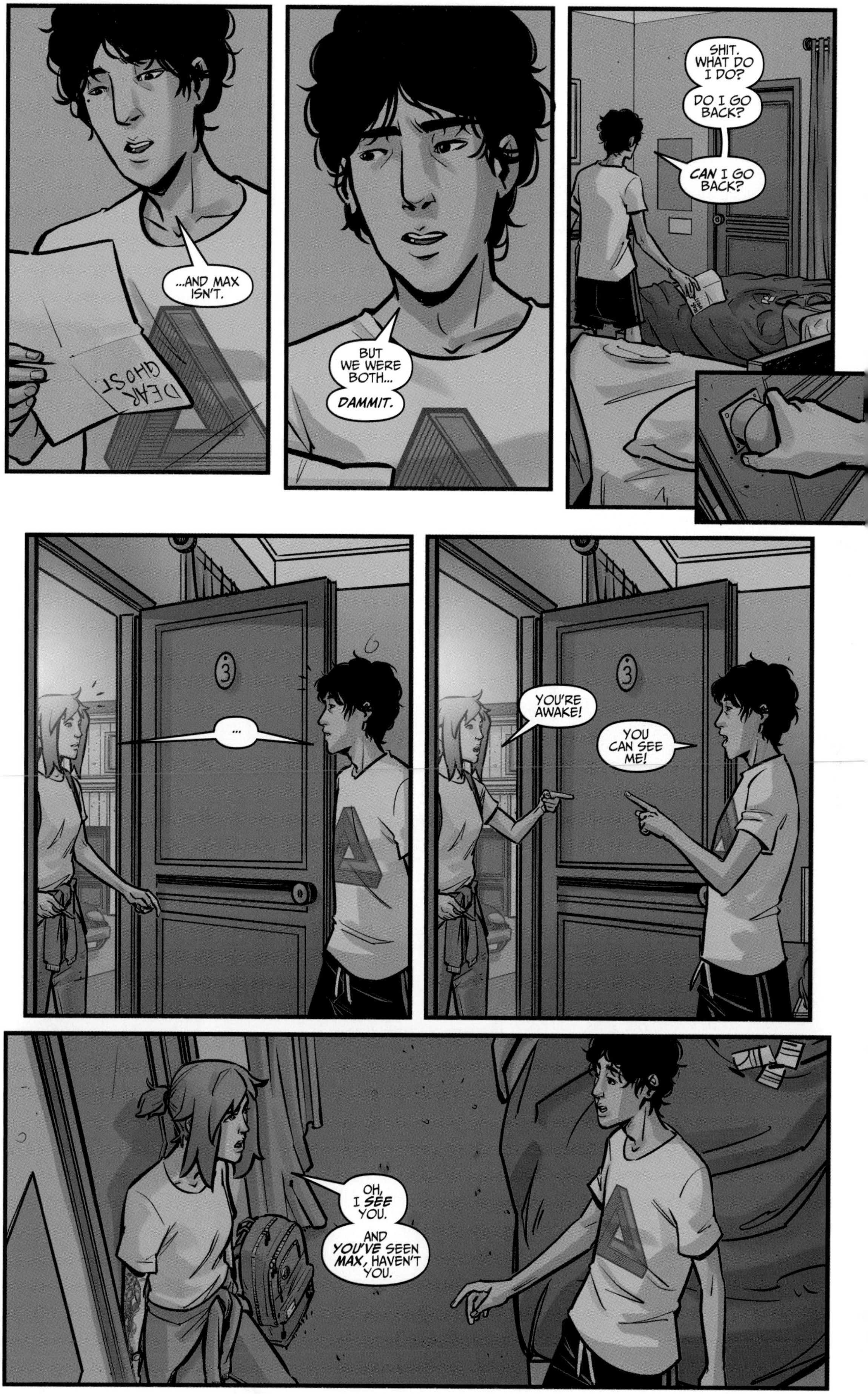
...AND MAX ISN'T.
DEAR GHOST.
BUT WE WERE BOTH...
DAMMIT.
SHIT. WHAT DO I DO?
DO I GO BACK?
CAN I GO BACK?
...
YOU'RE AWAKE!
YOU CAN SEE ME!
OH, I SEE YOU.
AND YOU'VE SEEN MAX, HAVEN'T YOU.

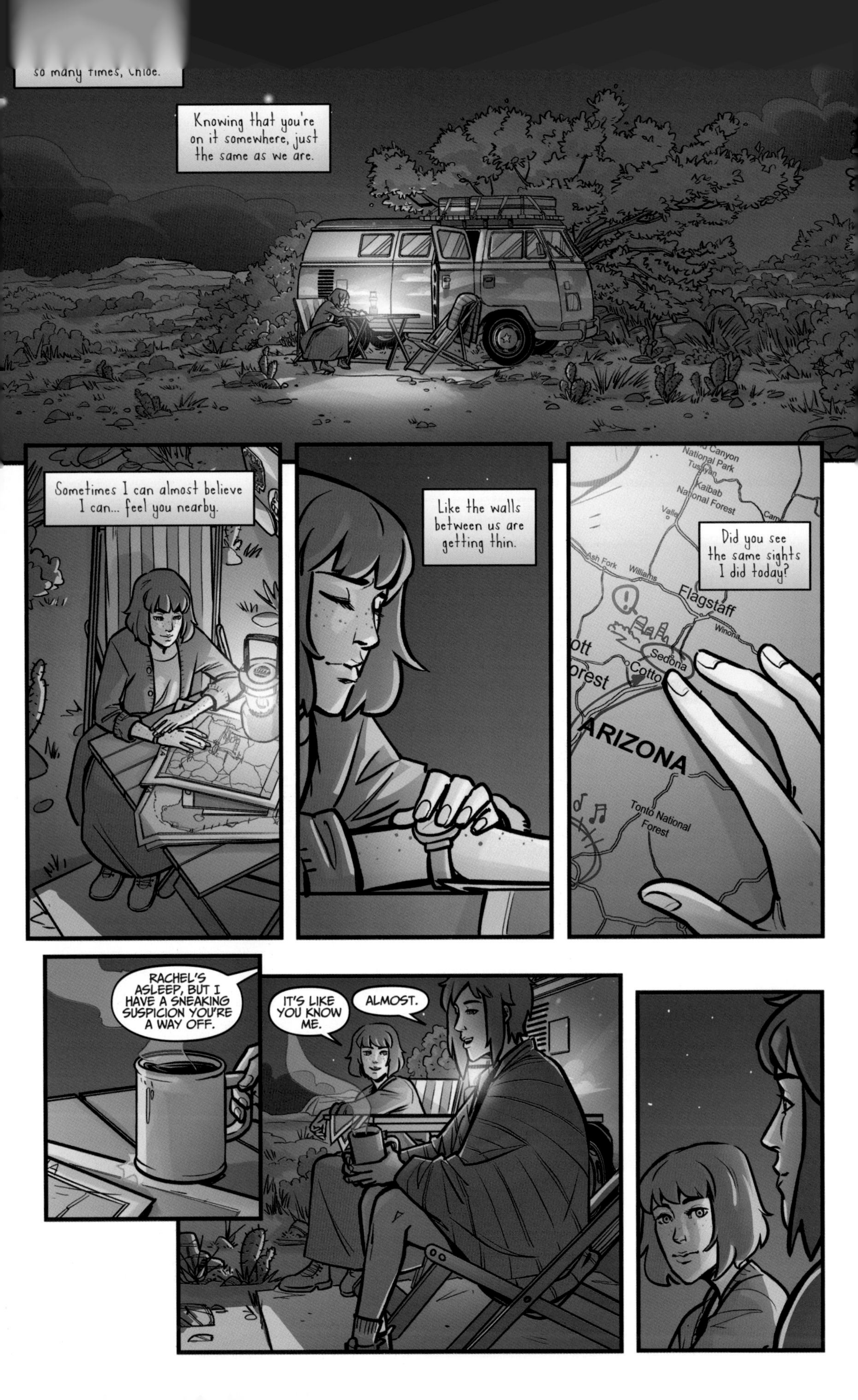

so many times, Chloe.
Knowing that you're on it somewhere, just the same as we are.
Sometimes I can almost believe I can... feel you nearby.
Like the walls between us are getting thin.
National Park
Tusayan
Kaibab National Forest
Valle
Ash Fork
Williams
Flagstaff
Winona
Sedona
ARIZONA
Tonto National Forest
Did you see the same sights I did today?
RACHEL'S ASLEEP, BUT I HAVE A SNEAKING SUSPICION YOU'RE A WAY OFF.
IT'S LIKE YOU KNOW ME.
ALMOST.

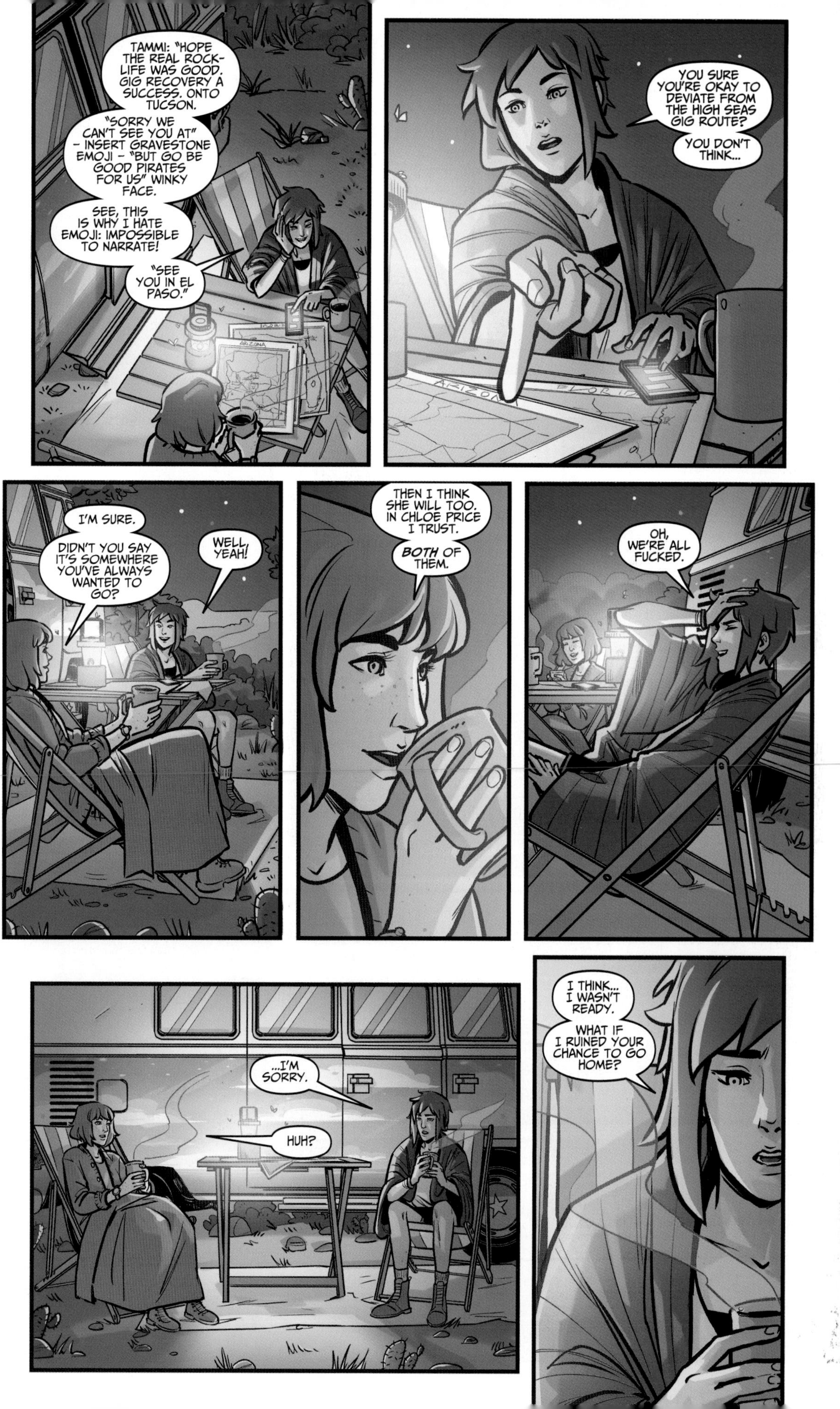
TAMMI: "HOPE THE REAL ROCK-LIFE WAS GOOD. GIG RECOVERY A SUCCESS. ONTO TUCSON.
"SORRY WE CAN'T SEE YOU AT" – INSERT GRAVESTONE EMOJI – "BUT GO BE GOOD PIRATES FOR US" WINKY FACE.
SEE, THIS IS WHY I HATE EMOJI: IMPOSSIBLE TO NARRATE!
"SEE YOU IN EL PASO."
ARIZONA
YOU SURE YOU'RE OKAY TO DEVIATE FROM THE HIGH SEAS GIG ROUTE?
YOU DON'T THINK...
I'M SURE.
DIDN'T YOU SAY IT'S SOMEWHERE YOU'VE ALWAYS WANTED TO GO?
WELL, YEAH!
THEN I THINK SHE WILL TOO. IN CHLOE PRICE I TRUST.
BOTH OF THEM.
OH, WE'RE ALL FUCKED.
...I'M SORRY.
HUH?
I THINK... I WASN'T READY.
WHAT IF I RUINED YOUR CHANCE TO GO HOME?

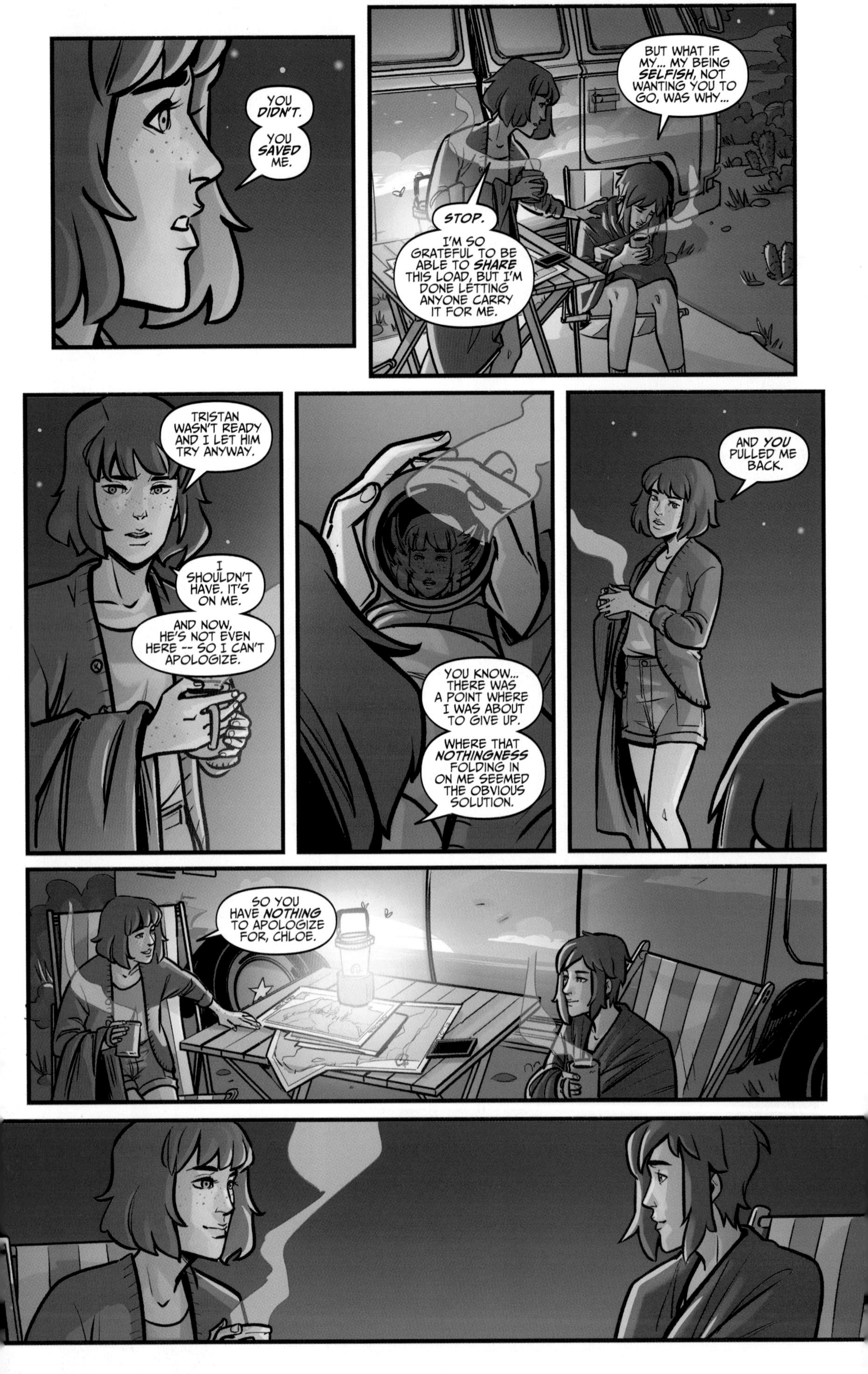
YOU DIDN'T.
YOU SAVED ME.
BUT WHAT IF MY... MY BEING SELFISH, NOT WANTING YOU TO GO, WAS WHY...
STOP.
I'M SO GRATEFUL TO BE ABLE TO SHARE THIS LOAD, BUT I'M DONE LETTING ANYONE CARRY IT FOR ME.
TRISTAN WASN'T READY AND I LET HIM TRY ANYWAY.
I SHOULDN'T HAVE. IT'S ON ME.
AND NOW, HE'S NOT EVEN HERE -- SO I CAN'T APOLOGIZE.
YOU KNOW... THERE WAS A POINT WHERE I WAS ABOUT TO GIVE UP.
WHERE THAT NOTHINGNESS FOLDING IN ON ME SEEMED THE OBVIOUS SOLUTION.
AND YOU PULLED ME BACK.
SO YOU HAVE NOTHING TO APOLOGIZE FOR, CHLOE.

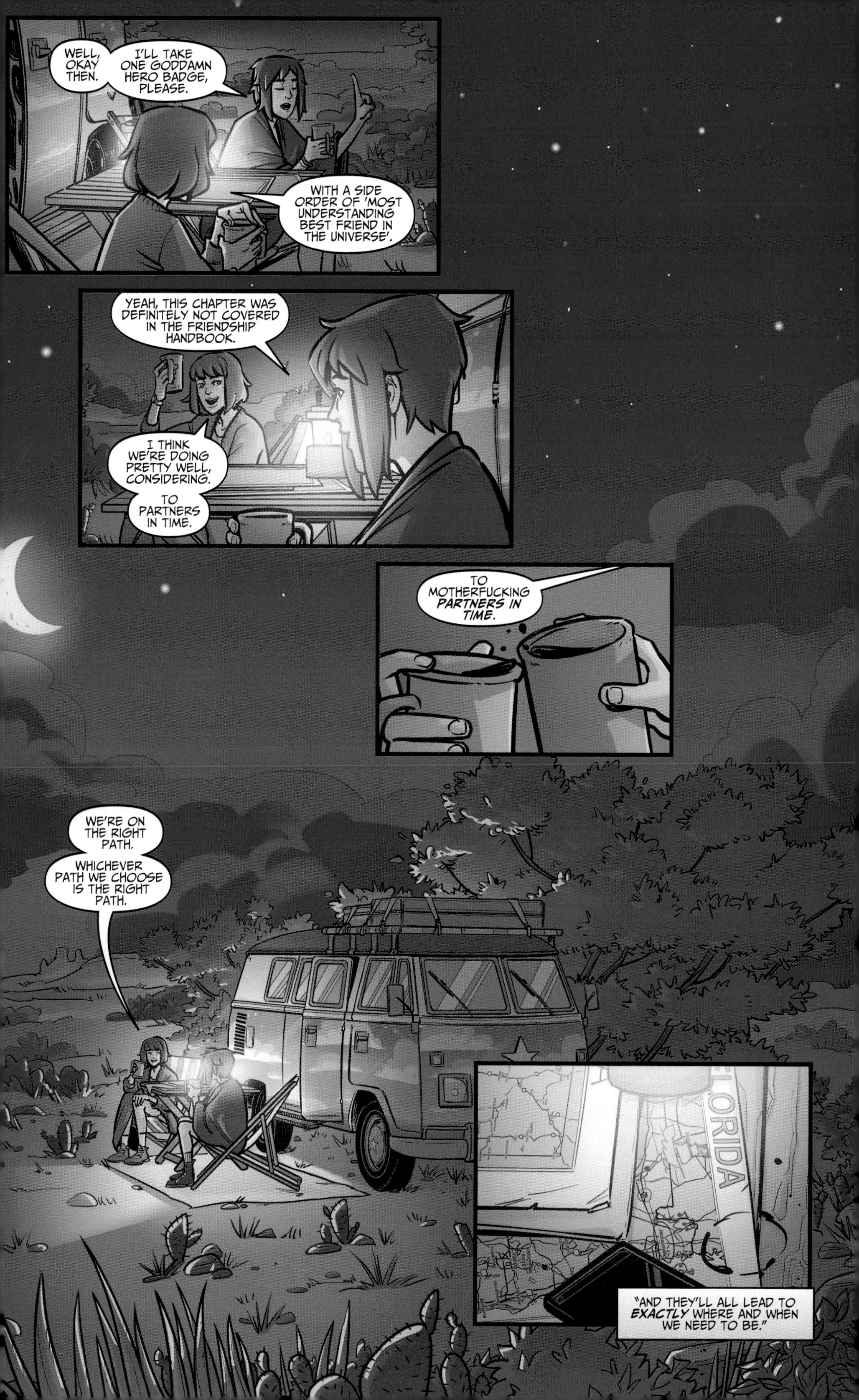
WELL, OKAY THEN.
I'LL TAKE ONE GODDAMN HERO BADGE, PLEASE.
WITH A SIDE ORDER OF 'MOST UNDERSTANDING BEST FRIEND IN THE UNIVERSE'.
YEAH, THIS CHAPTER WAS DEFINITELY NOT COVERED IN THE FRIENDSHIP HANDBOOK.
I THINK WE'RE DOING PRETTY WELL, CONSIDERING.
TO PARTNERS IN TIME.
TO MOTHERFUCKING *PARTNERS IN TIME.*
WE'RE ON THE RIGHT PATH.
WHICHEVER PATH WE CHOOSE IS THE RIGHT PATH.
FLORIDA
"AND THEY'LL ALL LEAD TO *EXACTLY* WHERE AND WHEN WE NEED TO BE."

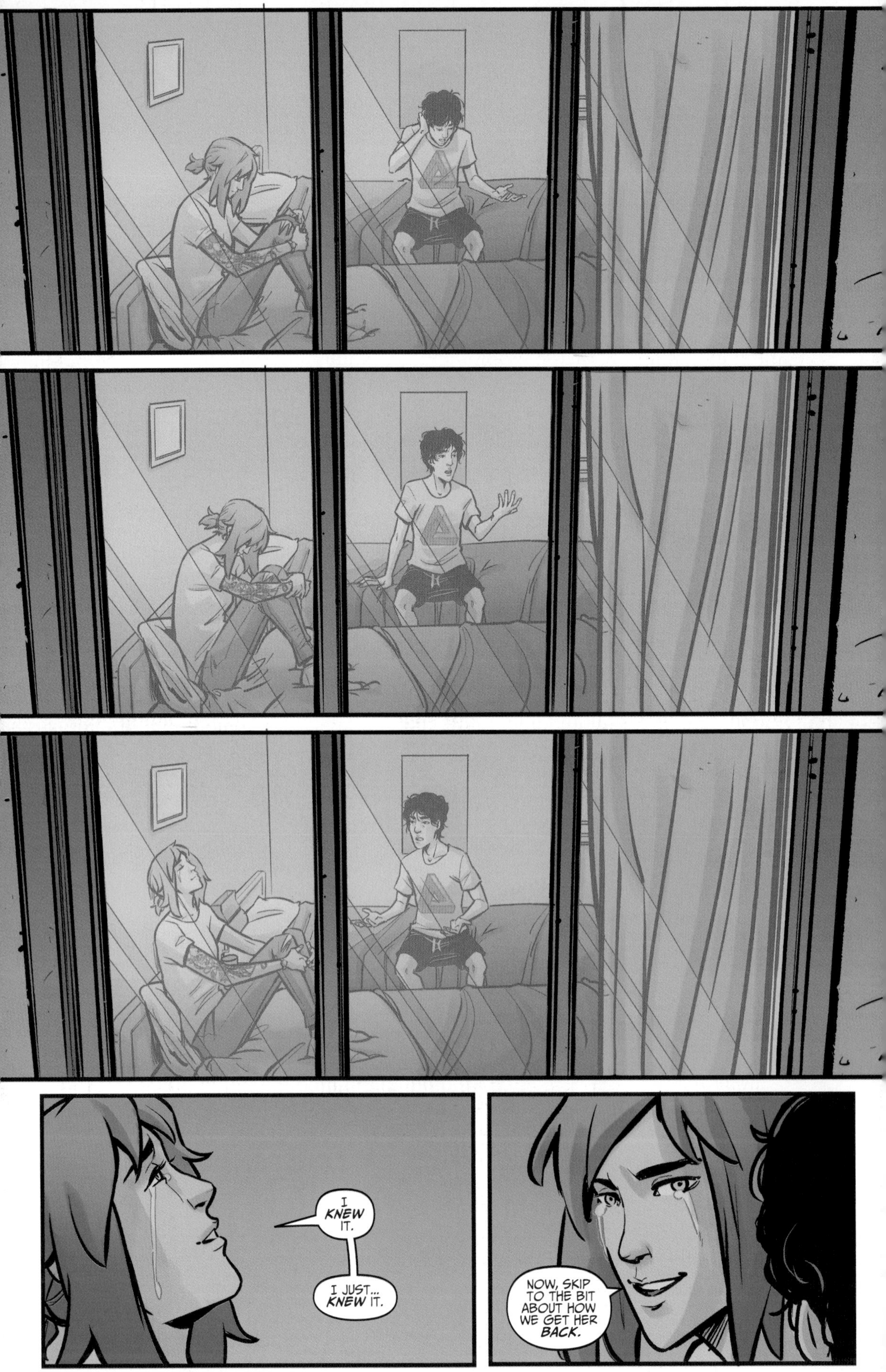
I KNEW IT.
I JUST... KNEW IT.
NOW, SKIP TO THE BIT ABOUT HOW WE GET HER BACK.

firewalk

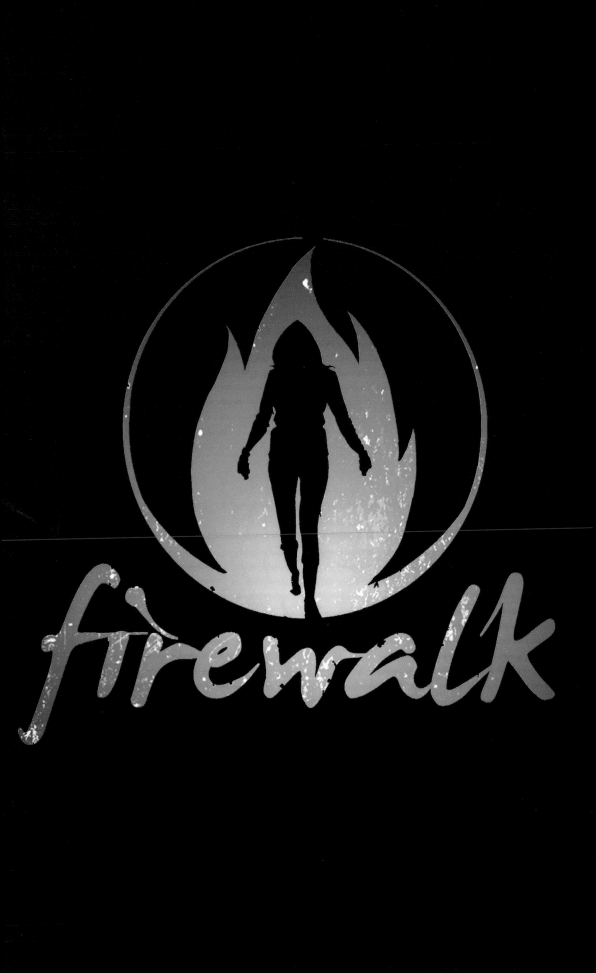

CHAPTER 2

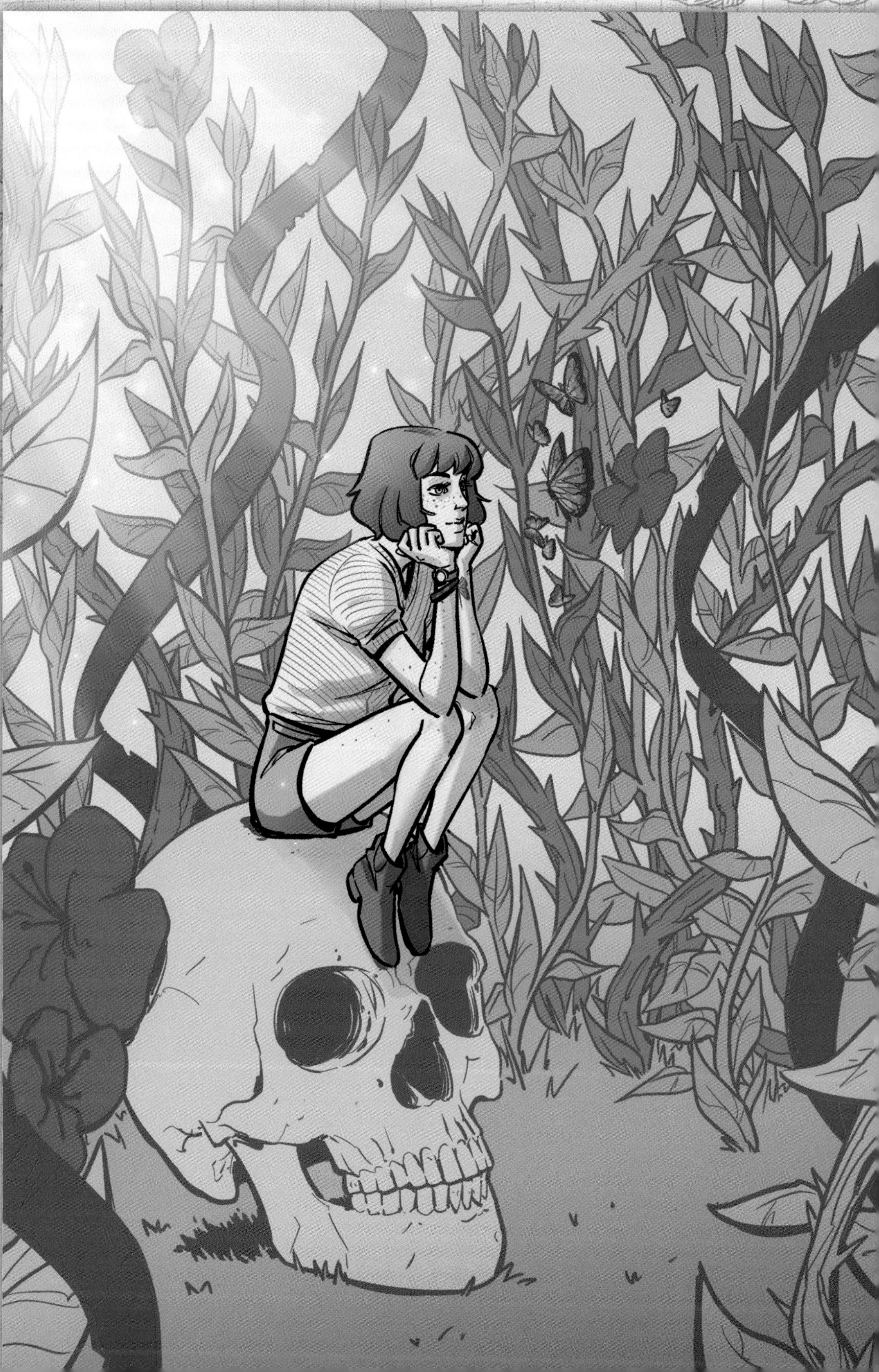

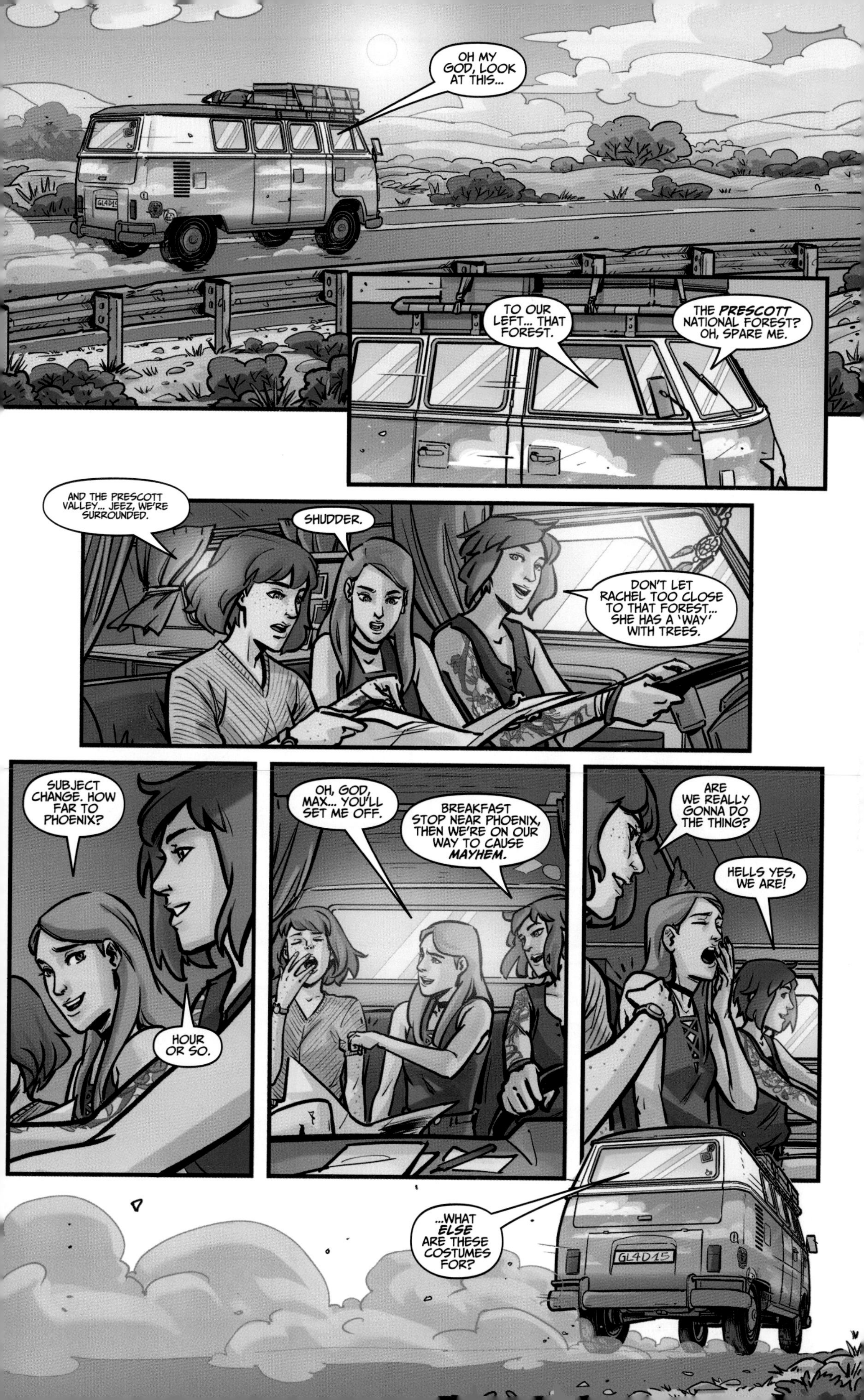
OH MY GOD, LOOK AT THIS...
TO OUR LEFT... THAT FOREST.
THE PRESCOTT NATIONAL FOREST? OH, SPARE ME.
AND THE PRESCOTT VALLEY... JEEZ, WE'RE SURROUNDED.
SHUDDER.
DON'T LET RACHEL TOO CLOSE TO THAT FOREST... SHE HAS A 'WAY' WITH TREES.
SUBJECT CHANGE. HOW FAR TO PHOENIX?
HOUR OR SO.
OH, GOD, MAX... YOU'LL SET ME OFF.
BREAKFAST STOP NEAR PHOENIX, THEN WE'RE ON OUR WAY TO CAUSE MAYHEM.
ARE WE REALLY GONNA DO THE THING?
HELLS YES, WE ARE!
...WHAT ELSE ARE THESE COSTUMES FOR?
GL4D15

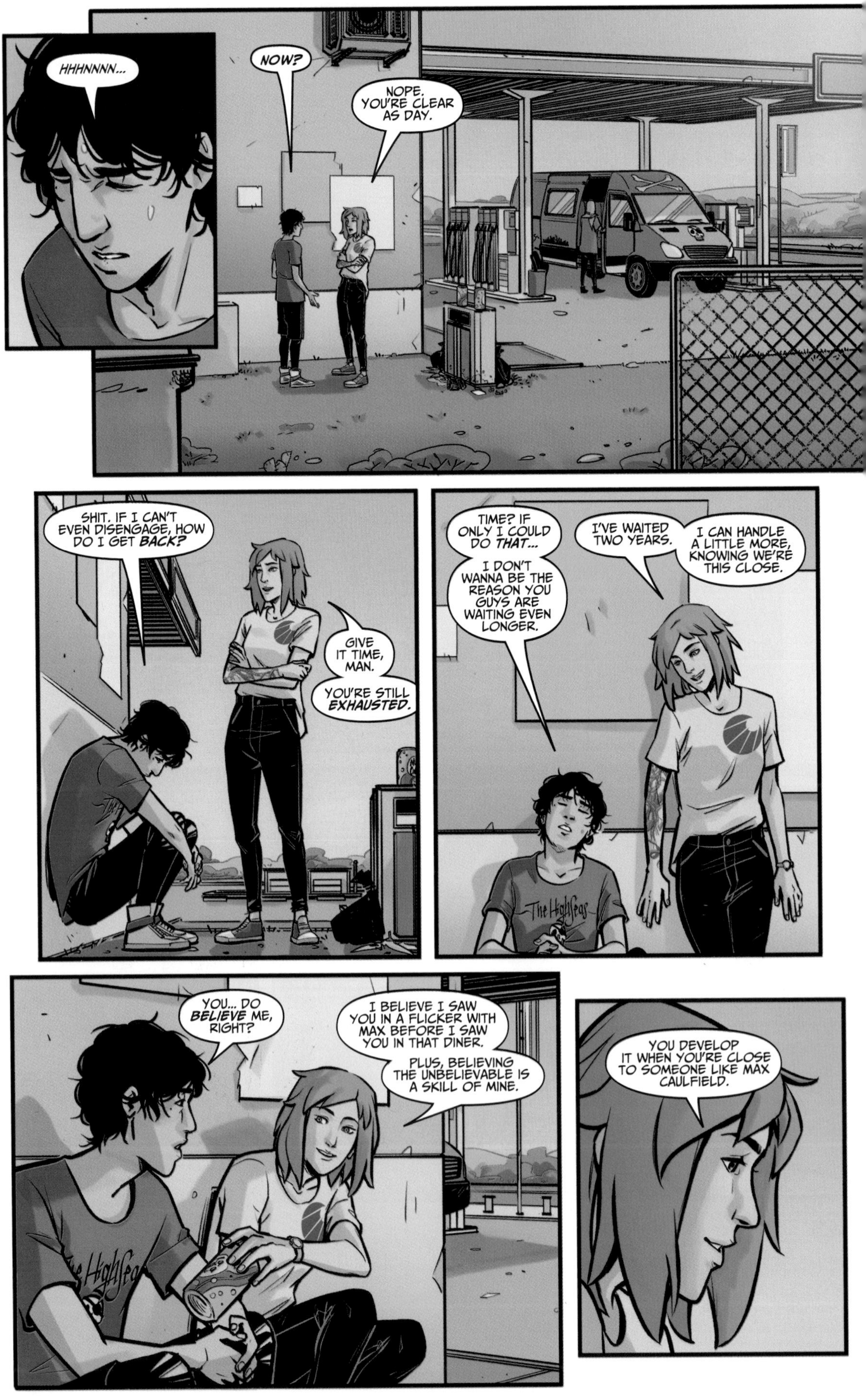
HHHNNNN...
NOW?
NOPE. YOU'RE CLEAR AS DAY.
SHIT. IF I CAN'T EVEN DISENGAGE, HOW DO I GET BACK?
GIVE IT TIME, MAN.
YOU'RE STILL EXHAUSTED.
TIME? IF ONLY I COULD DO THAT...
I DON'T WANNA BE THE REASON YOU GUYS ARE WAITING EVEN LONGER.
I'VE WAITED TWO YEARS.
I CAN HANDLE A LITTLE MORE, KNOWING WE'RE THIS CLOSE.
The HighSeas
YOU... DO BELIEVE ME, RIGHT?
I BELIEVE I SAW YOU IN A FLICKER WITH MAX BEFORE I SAW YOU IN THAT DINER.
PLUS, BELIEVING THE UNBELIEVABLE IS A SKILL OF MINE.
YOU DEVELOP IT WHEN YOU'RE CLOSE TO SOMEONE LIKE MAX CAULFIELD.

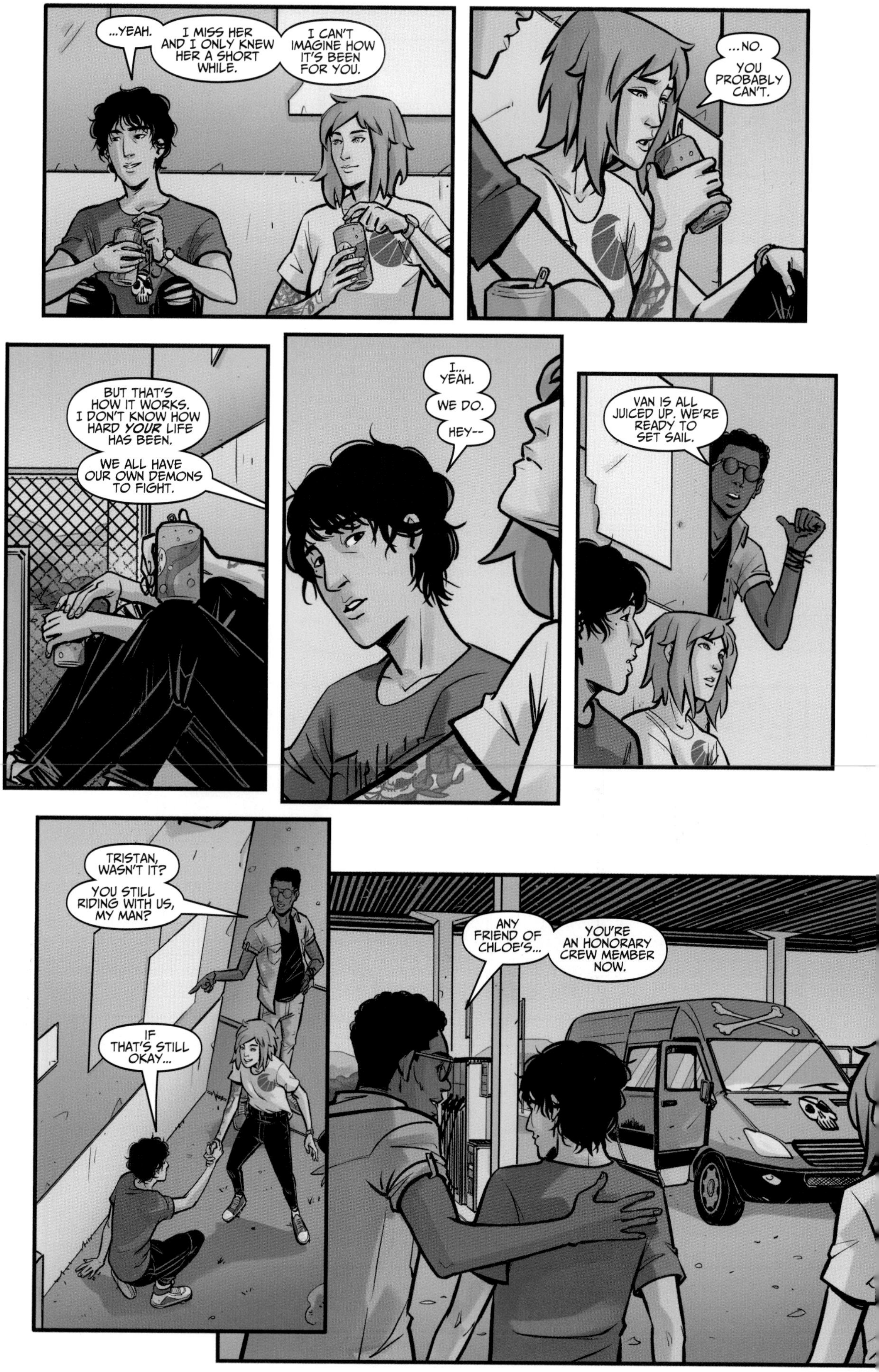
...YEAH.
I MISS HER AND I ONLY KNEW HER A SHORT WHILE.
I CAN'T IMAGINE HOW IT'S BEEN FOR YOU.
...NO.
YOU PROBABLY CAN'T.
BUT THAT'S HOW IT WORKS. I DON'T KNOW HOW HARD YOUR LIFE HAS BEEN.
WE ALL HAVE OUR OWN DEMONS TO FIGHT.
I... YEAH.
WE DO.
HEY--
VAN IS ALL JUICED UP. WE'RE READY TO SET SAIL.
TRISTAN, WASN'T IT?
YOU STILL RIDING WITH US, MY MAN?
IF THAT'S STILL OKAY...
ANY FRIEND OF CHLOE'S...
YOU'RE AN HONORARY CREW MEMBER NOW.

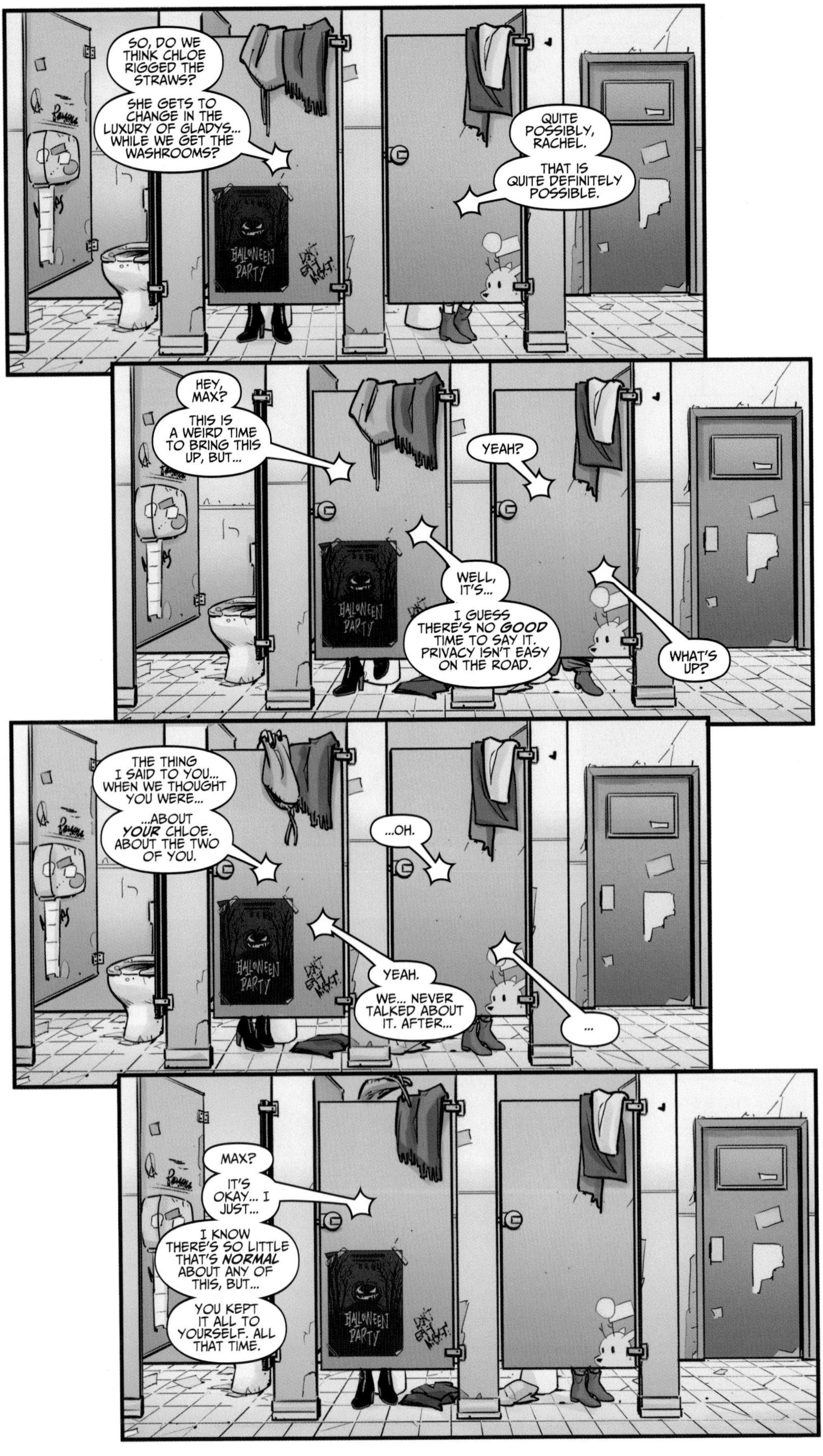
SO, DO WE THINK CHLOE RIGGED THE STRAWS?
SHE GETS TO CHANGE IN THE LUXURY OF GLADYS... WHILE WE GET THE WASHROOMS?
QUITE POSSIBLY, RACHEL.
THAT IS QUITE DEFINITELY POSSIBLE.
HALLOWEEN PARTY
HEY, MAX?
THIS IS A WEIRD TIME TO BRING THIS UP, BUT...
YEAH?
WELL, IT'S...
I GUESS THERE'S NO GOOD TIME TO SAY IT. PRIVACY ISN'T EASY ON THE ROAD.
WHAT'S UP?
THE THING I SAID TO YOU... WHEN WE THOUGHT YOU WERE...
...ABOUT YOUR CHLOE. ABOUT THE TWO OF YOU.
...OH.
YEAH.
WE... NEVER TALKED ABOUT IT. AFTER...
...
MAX?
IT'S OKAY... I JUST...
I KNOW THERE'S SO LITTLE THAT'S NORMAL ABOUT ANY OF THIS, BUT...
YOU KEPT IT ALL TO YOURSELF. ALL THAT TIME.

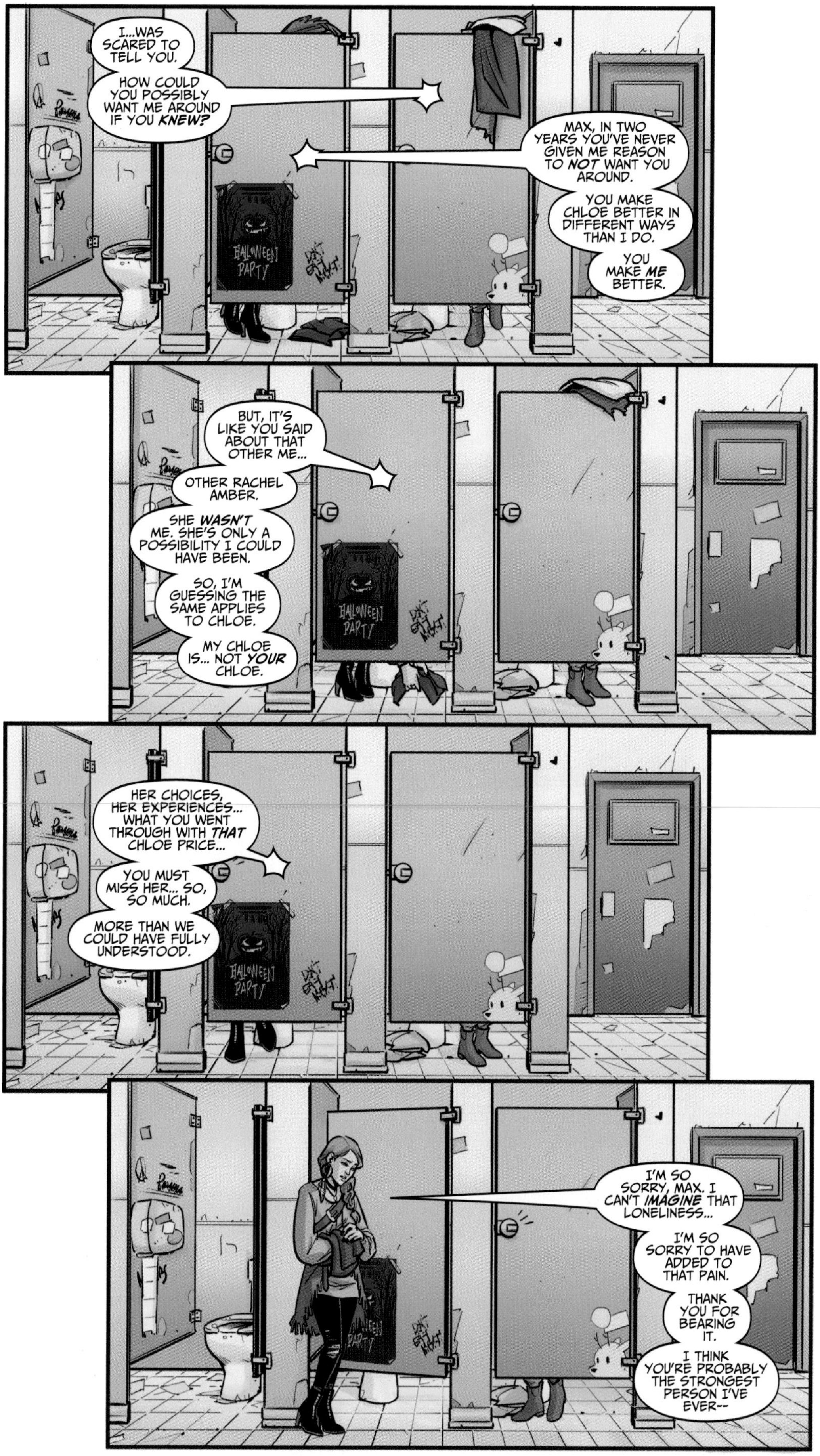
I...WAS SCARED TO TELL YOU.
HOW COULD YOU POSSIBLY WANT ME AROUND IF YOU *KNEW?*
MAX, IN TWO YEARS YOU'VE NEVER GIVEN ME REASON TO *NOT* WANT YOU AROUND.
YOU MAKE CHLOE BETTER IN DIFFERENT WAYS THAN I DO.
YOU MAKE *ME* BETTER.
BUT, IT'S LIKE YOU SAID ABOUT THAT OTHER ME...
OTHER RACHEL AMBER.
SHE *WASN'T* ME. SHE'S ONLY A POSSIBILITY I COULD HAVE BEEN.
SO, I'M GUESSING THE SAME APPLIES TO CHLOE.
MY CHLOE IS... NOT *YOUR* CHLOE.
HER CHOICES, HER EXPERIENCES... WHAT YOU WENT THROUGH WITH *THAT* CHLOE PRICE...
YOU MUST MISS HER... SO, SO MUCH.
MORE THAN WE COULD HAVE FULLY UNDERSTOOD.
I'M SO SORRY, MAX. I CAN'T *IMAGINE* THAT LONELINESS...
I'M SO SORRY TO HAVE ADDED TO THAT PAIN.
THANK YOU FOR BEARING IT.
I THINK YOU'RE PROBABLY THE STRONGEST PERSON I'VE EVER--

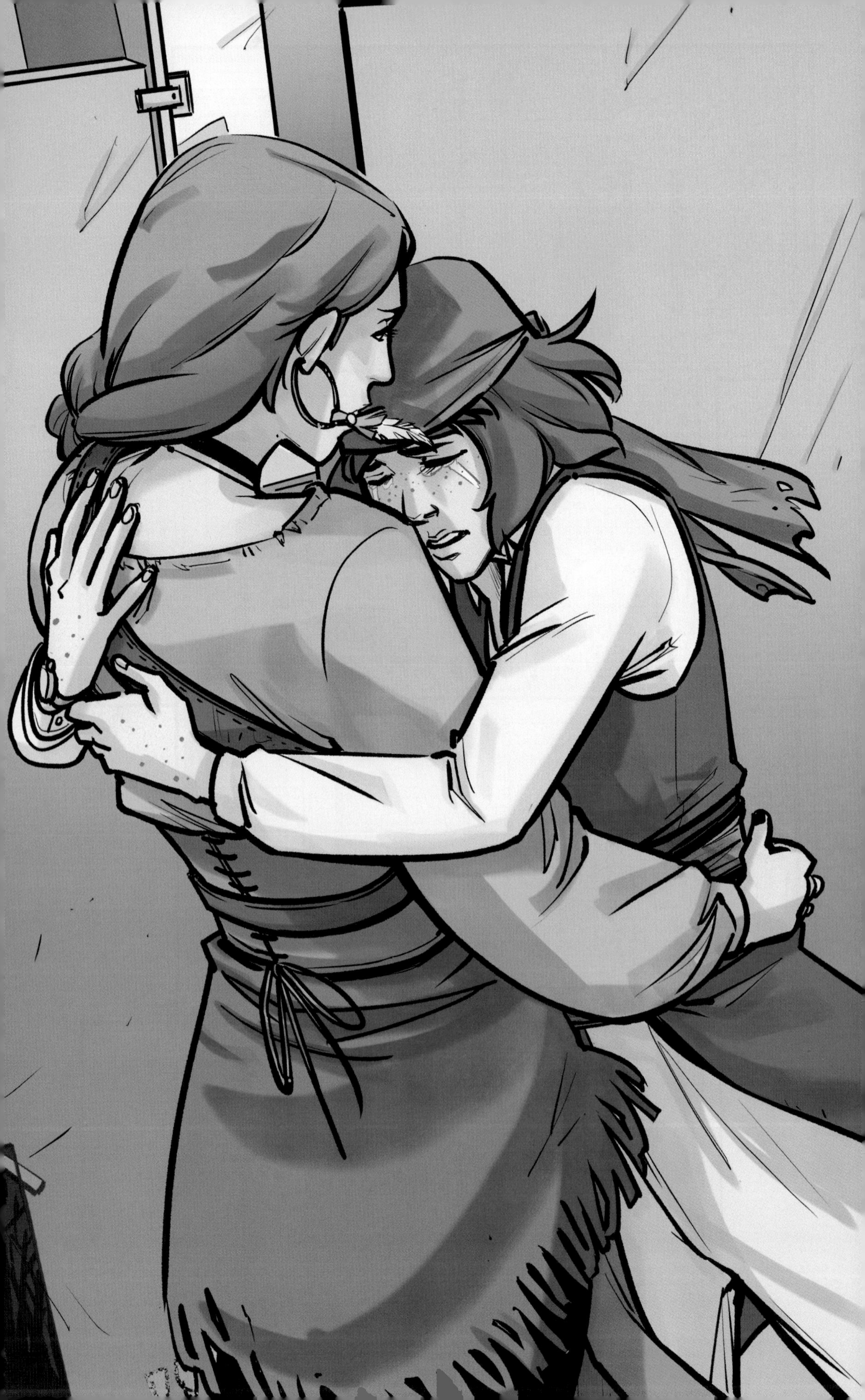

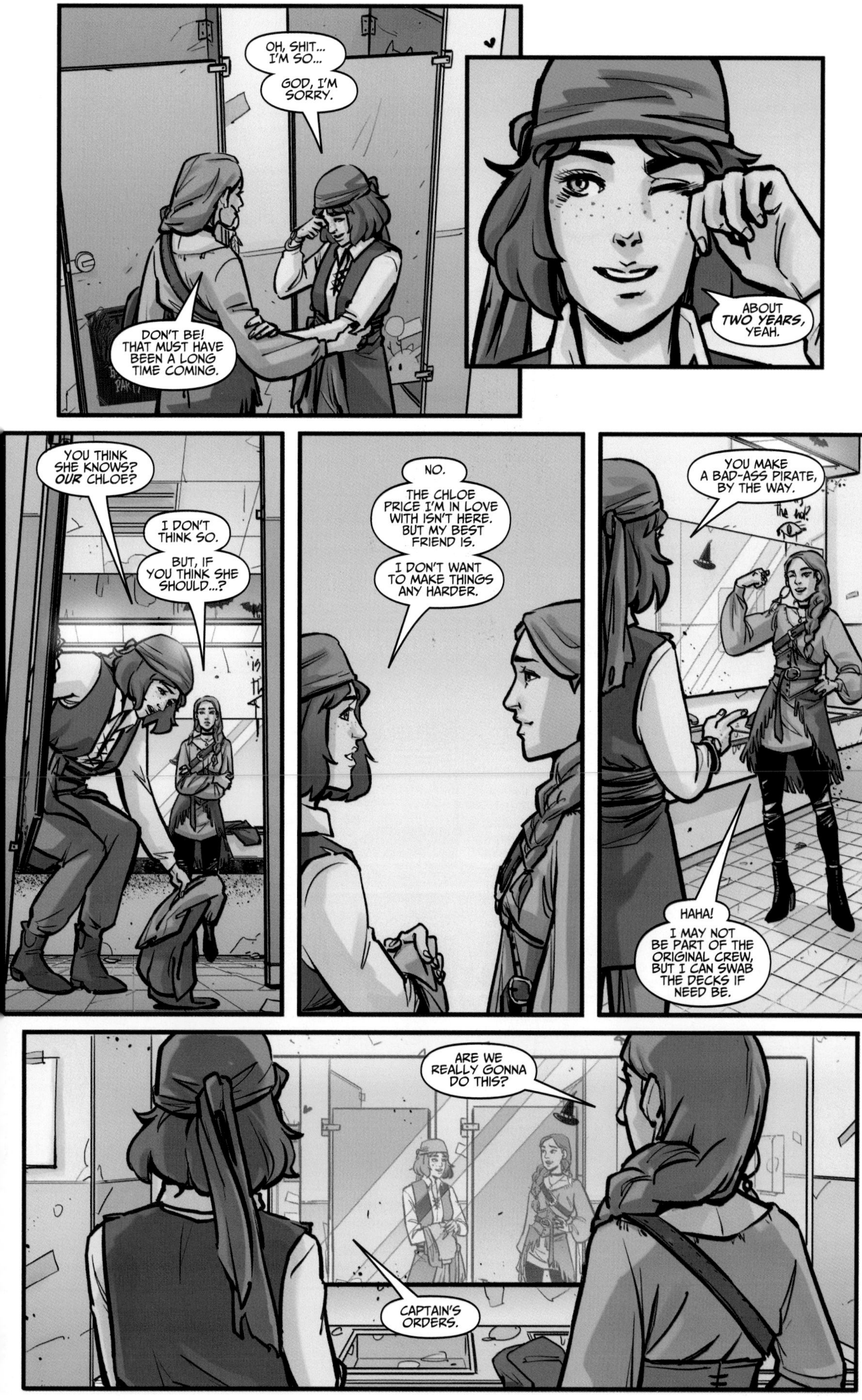
OH, SHIT... I'M SO...
GOD, I'M SORRY.
DON'T BE! THAT MUST HAVE BEEN A LONG TIME COMING.
ABOUT TWO YEARS, YEAH.
YOU THINK SHE KNOWS? OUR CHLOE?
I DON'T THINK SO.
BUT, IF YOU THINK SHE SHOULD...?
NO.
THE CHLOE PRICE I'M IN LOVE WITH ISN'T HERE. BUT MY BEST FRIEND IS.
I DON'T WANT TO MAKE THINGS ANY HARDER.
YOU MAKE A BAD-ASS PIRATE, BY THE WAY.
HAHA!
I MAY NOT BE PART OF THE ORIGINAL CREW, BUT I CAN SWAB THE DECKS IF NEED BE.
ARE WE REALLY GONNA DO THIS?
CAPTAIN'S ORDERS.

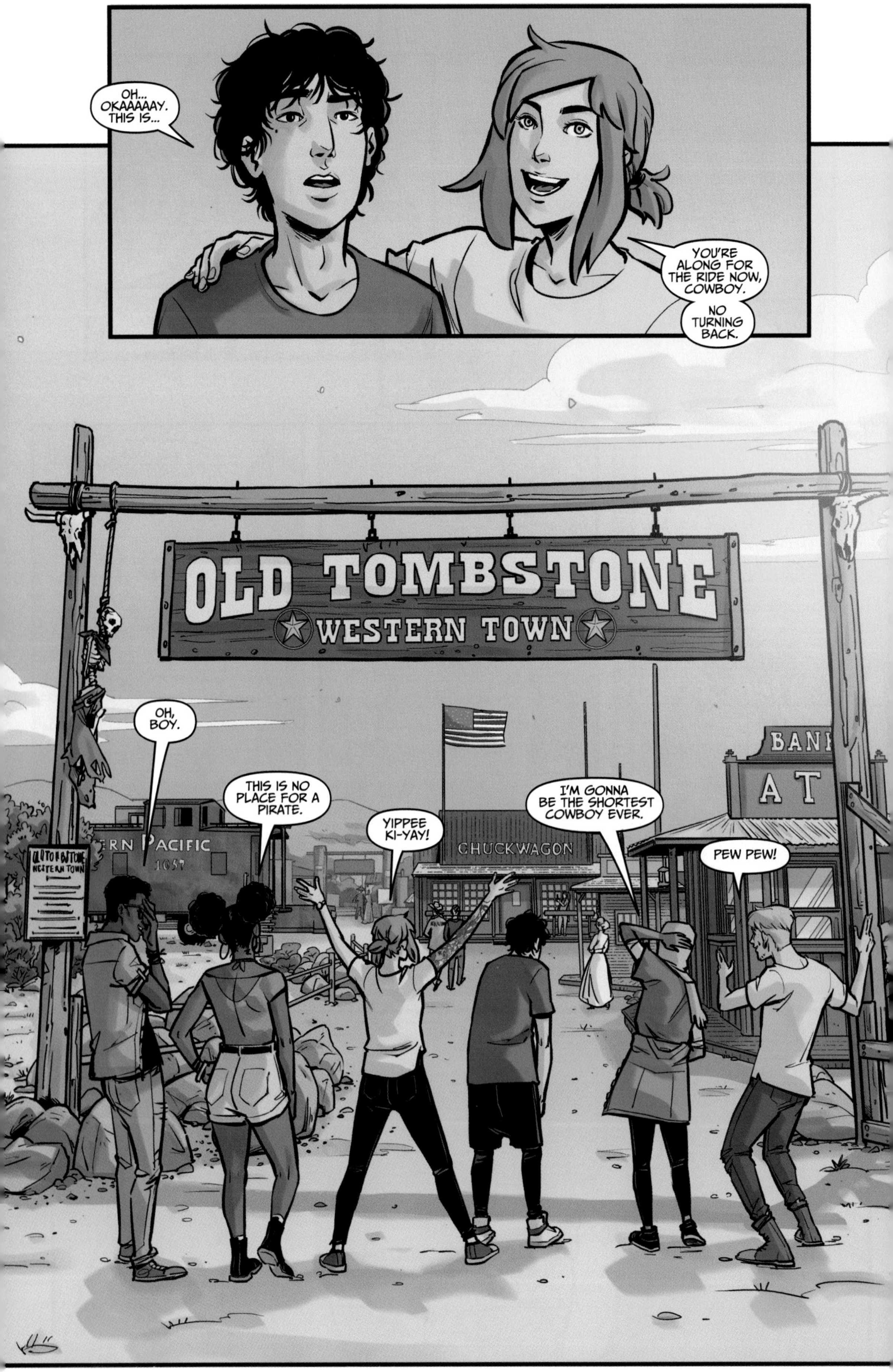
OH... OKAAAAAY. THIS IS...
YOU'RE ALONG FOR THE RIDE NOW, COWBOY.
NO TURNING BACK.
OLD TOMBSTONE
WESTERN TOWN
OH, BOY.
THIS IS NO PLACE FOR A PIRATE.
YIPPEE KI-YAY!
CHUCKWAGON
I'M GONNA BE THE SHORTEST COWBOY EVER.
PEW PEW!

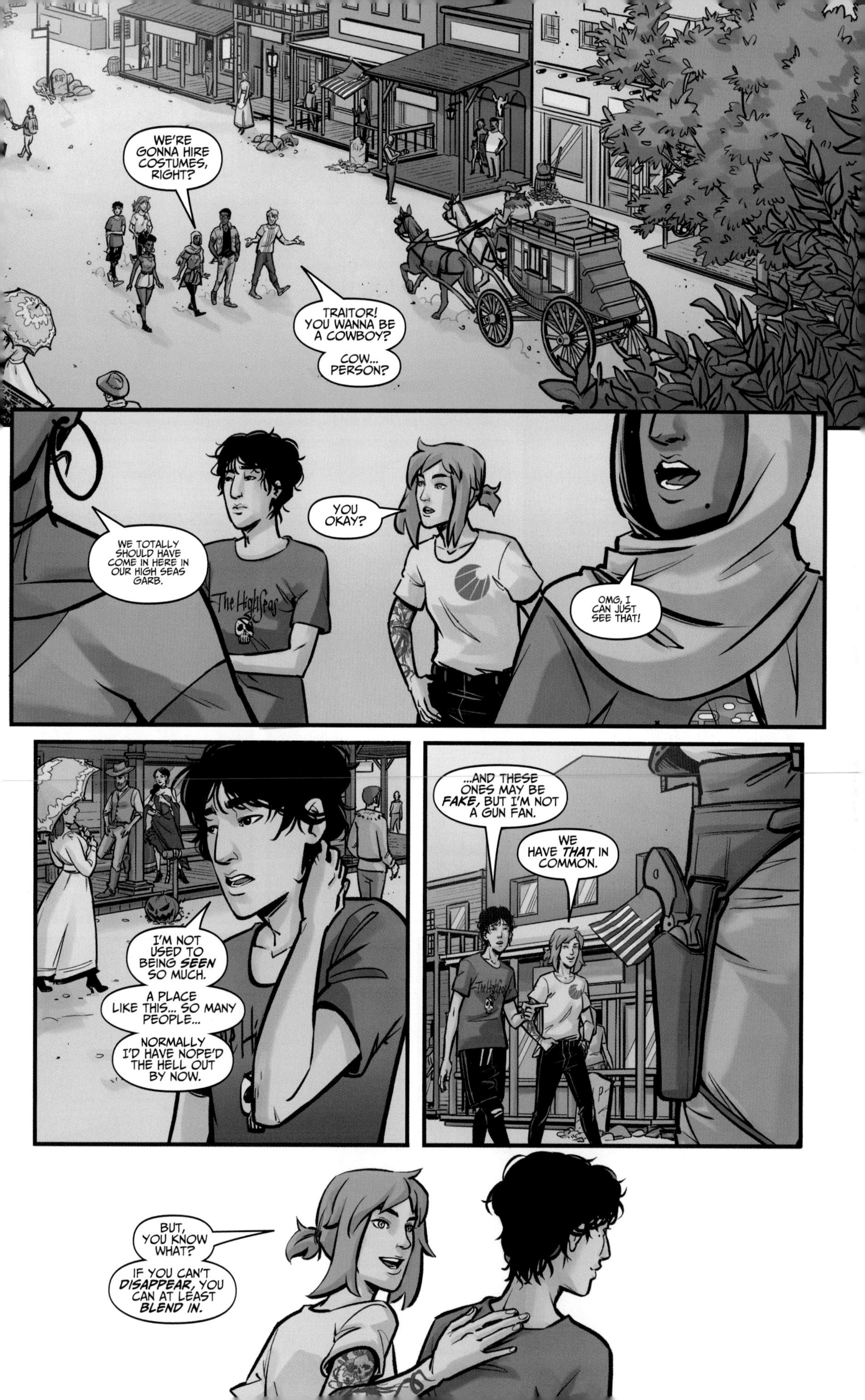
WE'RE GONNA HIRE COSTUMES, RIGHT?
TRAITOR! YOU WANNA BE A COWBOY?
COW... PERSON?
WE TOTALLY SHOULD HAVE COME IN HERE IN OUR HIGH SEAS GARB.
YOU OKAY?
OMG, I CAN JUST SEE THAT!
The HighSeas
I'M NOT USED TO BEING SEEN SO MUCH.
A PLACE LIKE THIS... SO MANY PEOPLE...
NORMALLY I'D HAVE NOPE'D THE HELL OUT BY NOW.
...AND THESE ONES MAY BE FAKE, BUT I'M NOT A GUN FAN.
WE HAVE THAT IN COMMON.
BUT, YOU KNOW WHAT?
IF YOU CAN'T DISAPPEAR, YOU CAN AT LEAST BLEND IN.

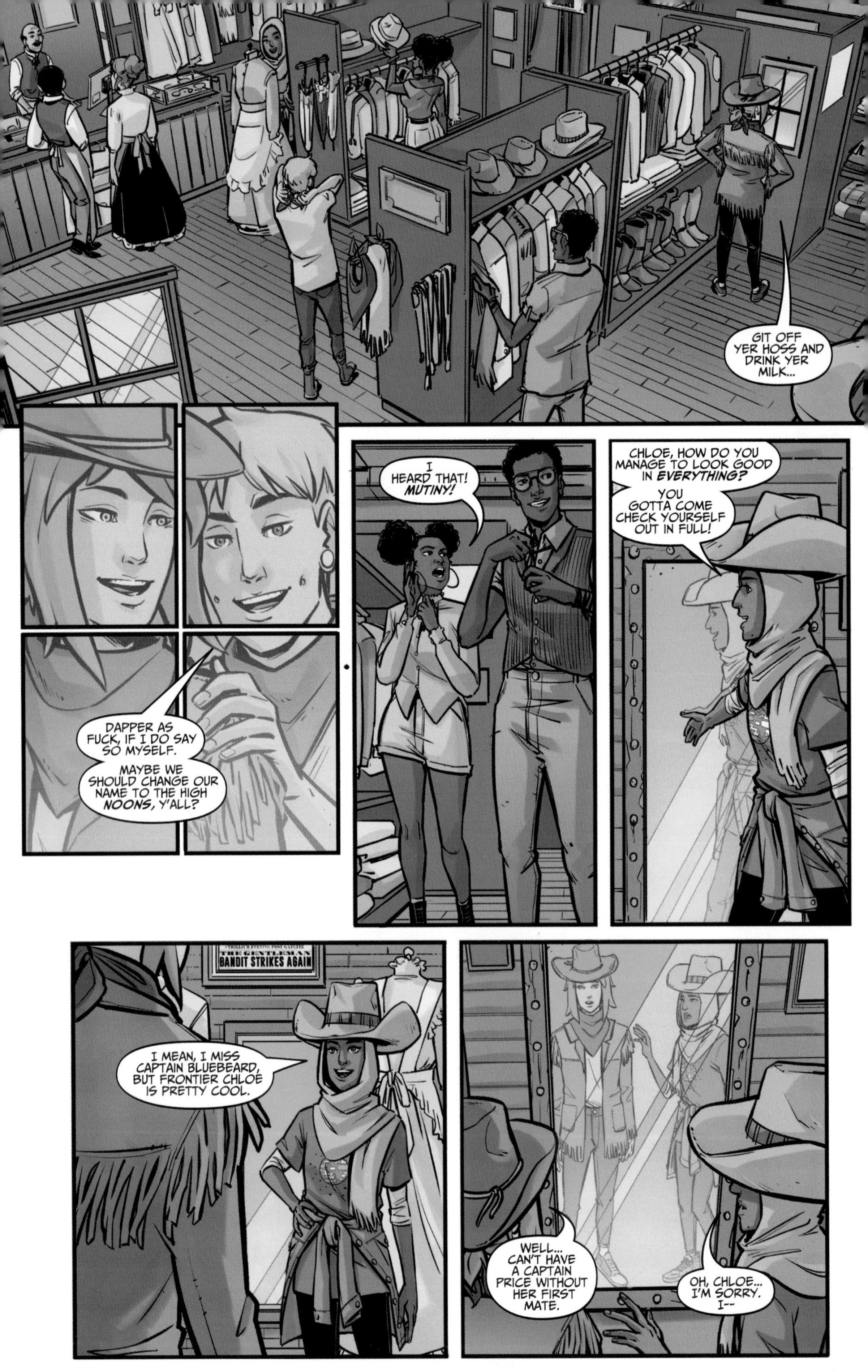
GIT OFF YER HOSS AND DRINK YER MILK...
DAPPER AS FUCK, IF I DO SAY SO MYSELF.
MAYBE WE SHOULD CHANGE OUR NAME TO THE HIGH *NOONS*, Y'ALL?
I HEARD THAT! *MUTINY!*
CHLOE, HOW DO YOU MANAGE TO LOOK GOOD IN *EVERYTHING?*
YOU GOTTA COME CHECK YOURSELF OUT IN FULL!
THE GENTLEMAN
BANDIT STRIKES AGAIN
I MEAN, I MISS CAPTAIN BLUEBEARD, BUT FRONTIER CHLOE IS PRETTY COOL.
WELL... CAN'T HAVE A CAPTAIN PRICE WITHOUT HER FIRST MATE.
OH, CHLOE... I'M SORRY. I--

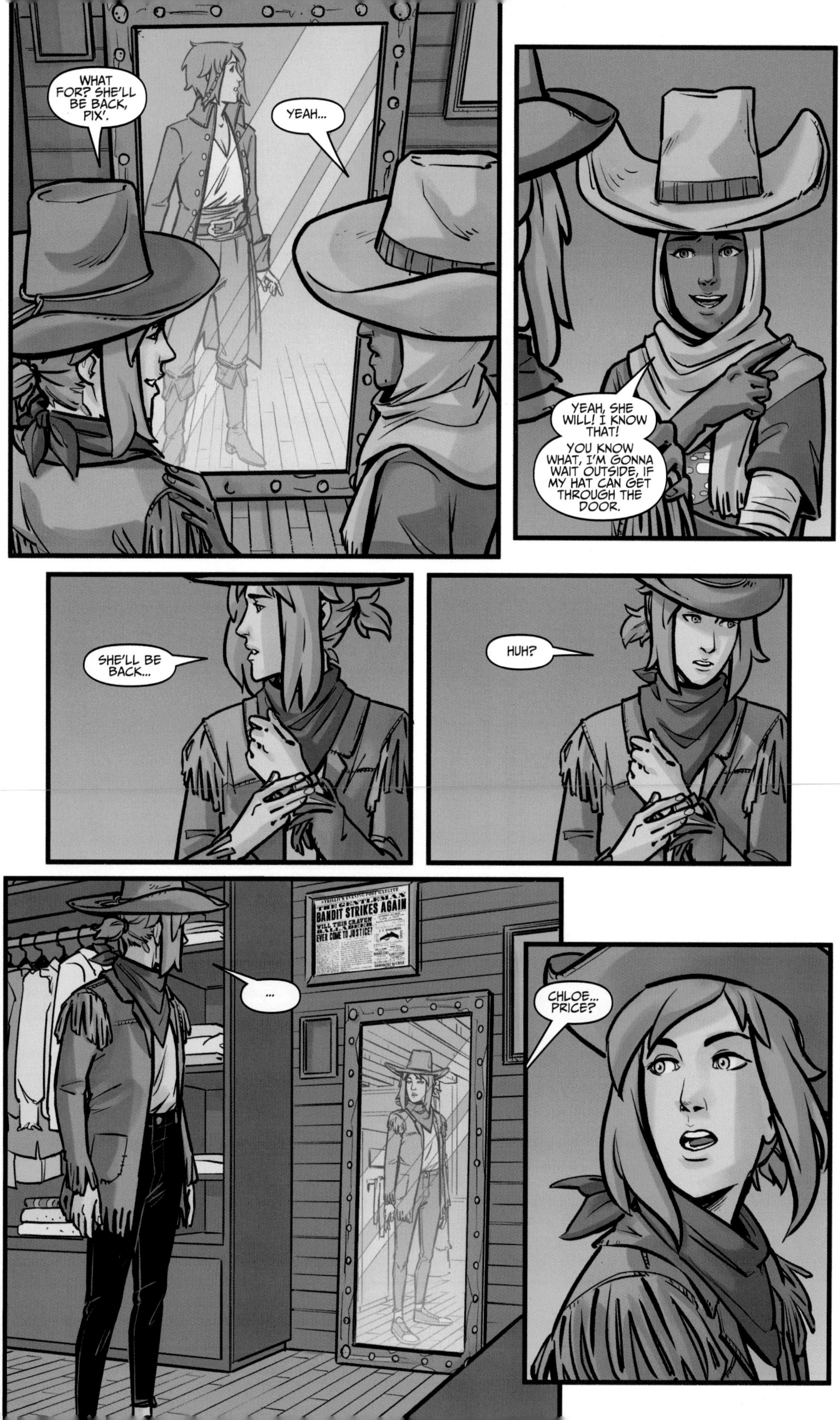
WHAT FOR? SHE'LL BE BACK, PIX'.
YEAH...
YEAH, SHE WILL! I KNOW THAT!
YOU KNOW WHAT, I'M GONNA WAIT OUTSIDE, IF MY HAT CAN GET THROUGH THE DOOR.
SHE'LL BE BACK...
HUH?
BANDIT STRIKES AGAIN
WILL THIS CRAVEN
EVER COME TO JUSTICE?
...
CHLOE... PRICE?

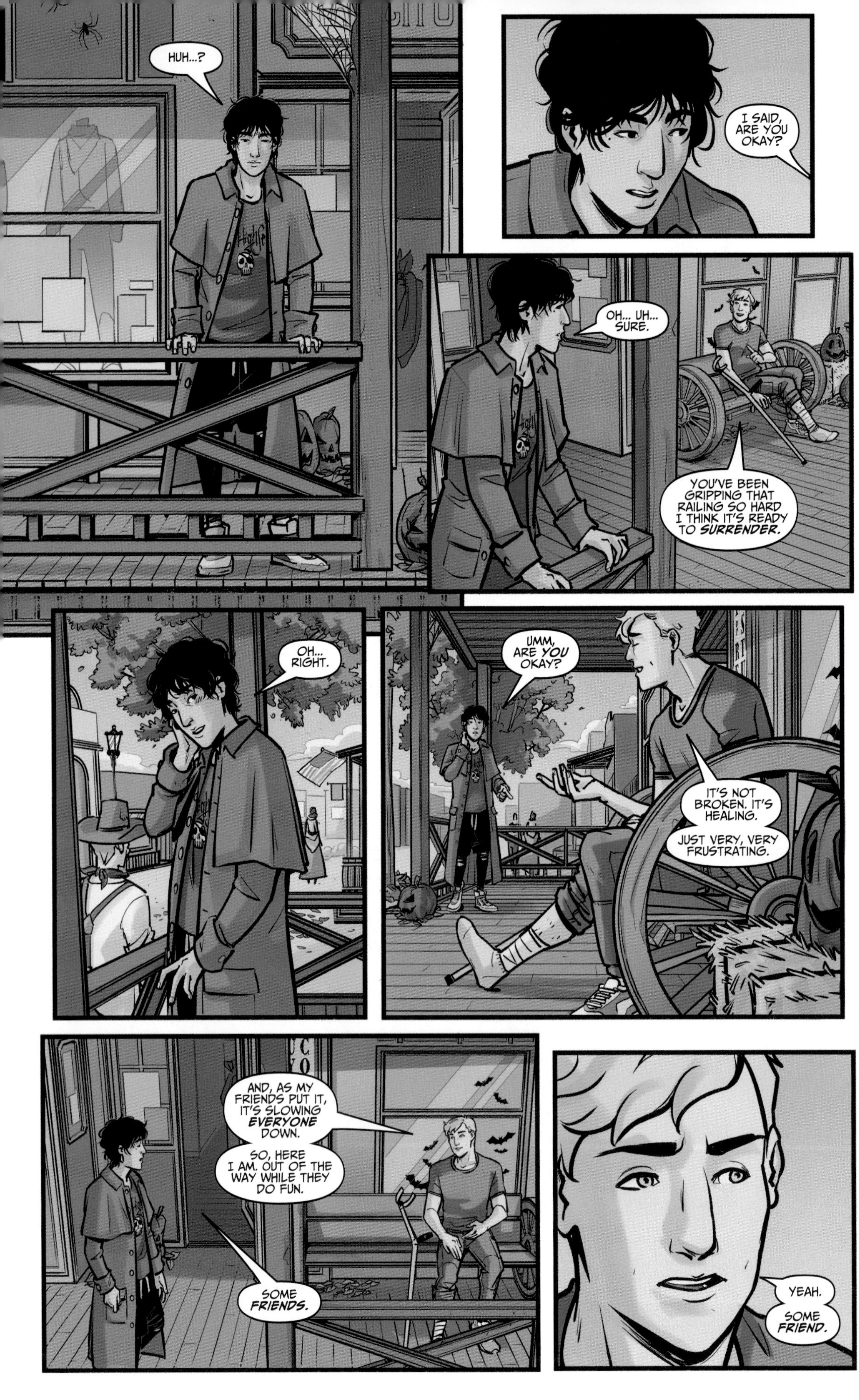
HUH...?
I SAID, ARE YOU OKAY?
OH... UH... SURE.
YOU'VE BEEN GRIPPING THAT RAILING SO HARD I THINK IT'S READY TO *SURRENDER*.
OH... RIGHT.
UMM, ARE *YOU* OKAY?
IT'S NOT BROKEN. IT'S HEALING.
JUST VERY, VERY FRUSTRATING.
AND, AS MY FRIENDS PUT IT, IT'S SLOWING *EVERYONE* DOWN.
SO, HERE I AM. OUT OF THE WAY WHILE THEY DO FUN.
SOME *FRIENDS*.
YEAH.
SOME *FRIEND*.

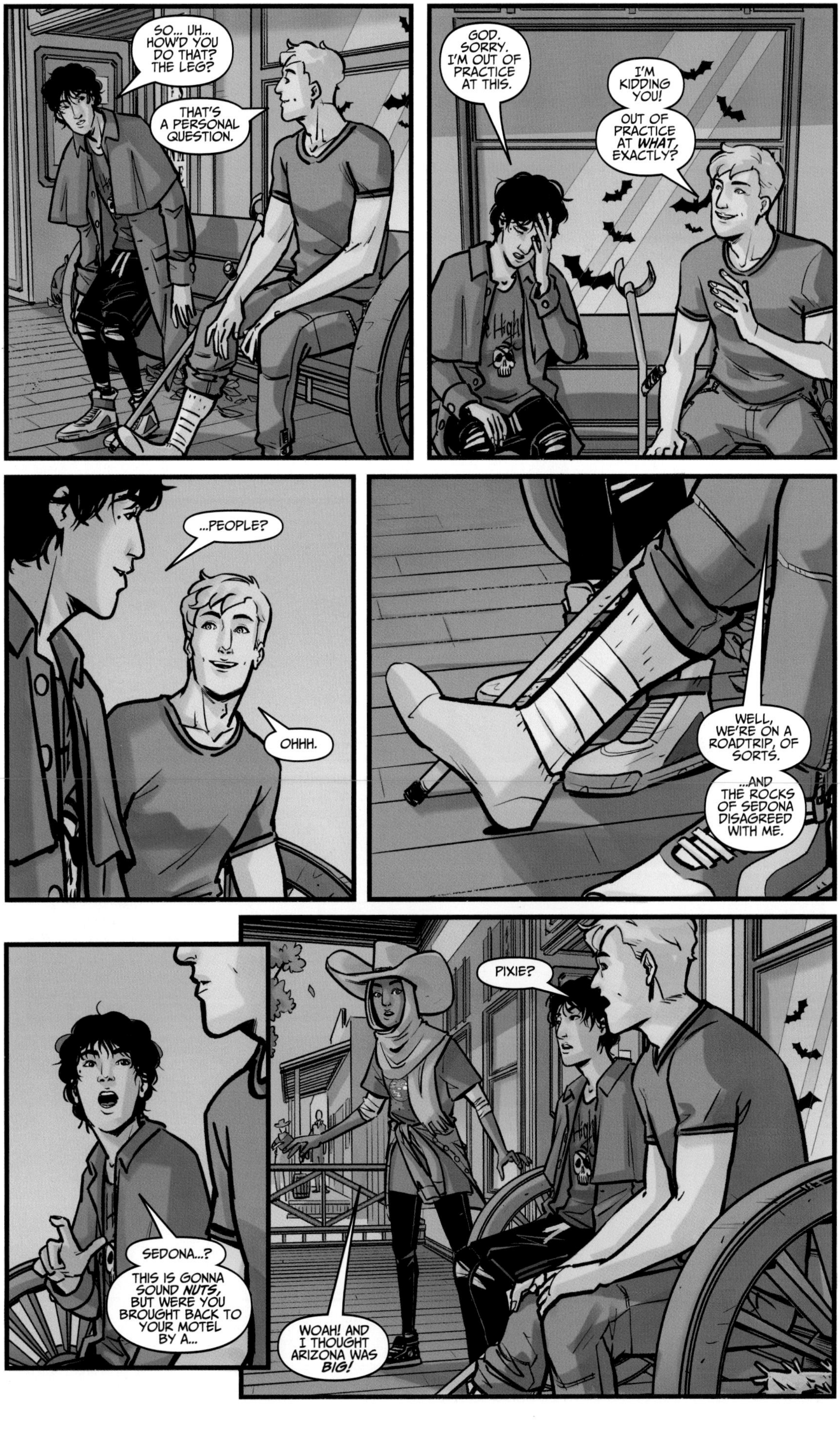
SO... UH... HOW'D YOU DO THAT? THE LEG?
THAT'S A PERSONAL QUESTION.
GOD. SORRY. I'M OUT OF PRACTICE AT THIS.
I'M KIDDING YOU!
OUT OF PRACTICE AT *WHAT*, EXACTLY?
...PEOPLE?
OHHH.
WELL, WE'RE ON A ROADTRIP, OF SORTS.
...AND THE ROCKS OF SEDONA DISAGREED WITH ME.
SEDONA...?
THIS IS GONNA SOUND *NUTS*, BUT WERE YOU BROUGHT BACK TO YOUR MOTEL BY A...
PIXIE?
WOAH! AND I THOUGHT ARIZONA WAS *BIG*!

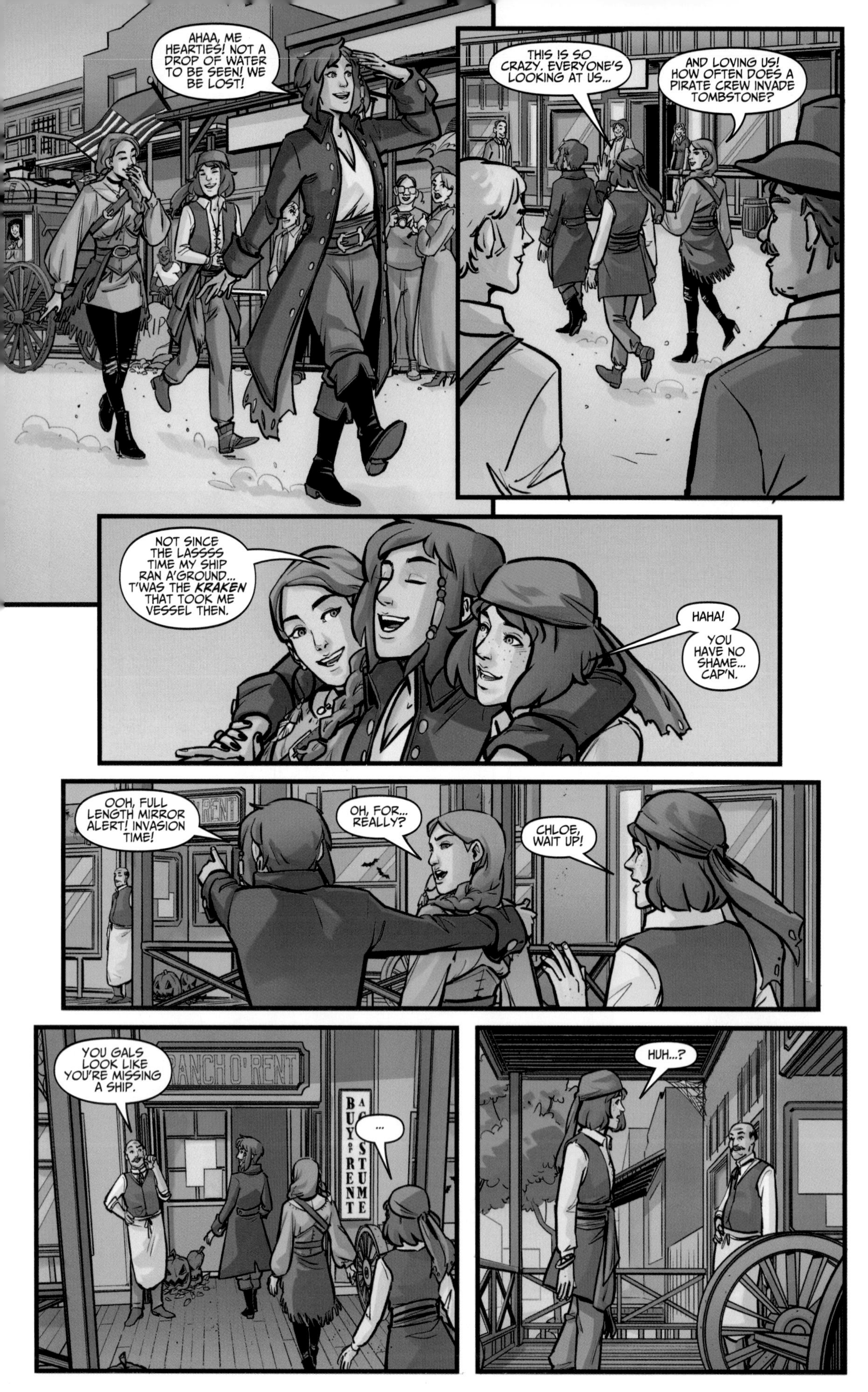
AHAA, ME HEARTIES! NOT A DROP OF WATER TO BE SEEN! WE BE LOST!
THIS IS SO CRAZY. EVERYONE'S LOOKING AT US...
AND LOVING US! HOW OFTEN DOES A PIRATE CREW INVADE TOMBSTONE?
NOT SINCE THE LASSSS TIME MY SHIP RAN A'GROUND... T'WAS THE *KRAKEN* THAT TOOK ME VESSEL THEN.
HAHA!
YOU HAVE NO SHAME... CAP'N.
OOH, FULL LENGTH MIRROR ALERT! INVASION TIME!
RENT
OH, FOR... REALLY?
CHLOE, WAIT UP!
YOU GALS LOOK LIKE YOU'RE MISSING A SHIP.
RANCH O' RENT
BUY or RENT A COSTUME
...
HUH...?

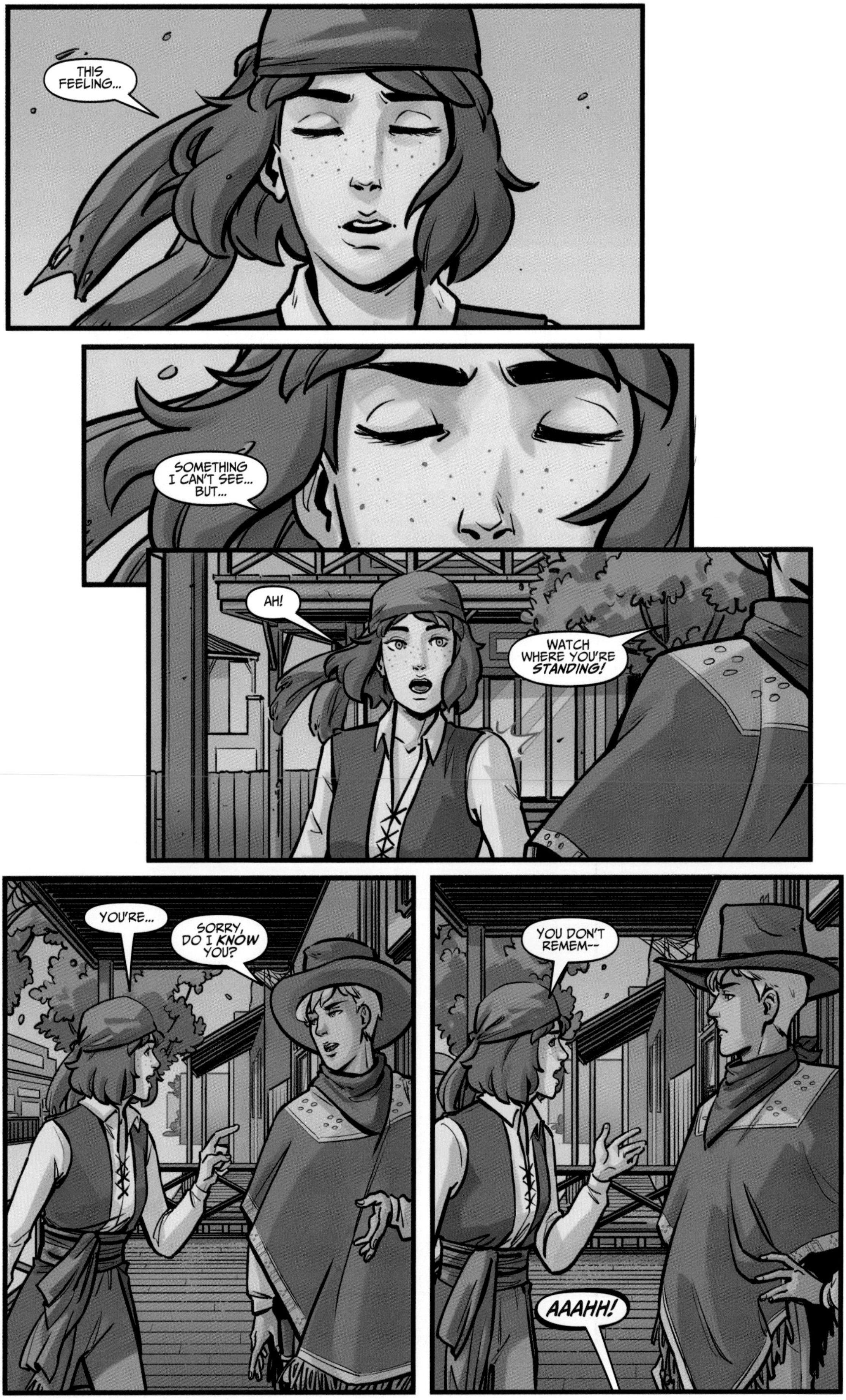
THIS FEELING...
SOMETHING I CAN'T SEE... BUT...
AH!
WATCH WHERE YOU'RE STANDING!
YOU'RE...
SORRY, DO I KNOW YOU?
YOU DON'T REMEM--
AAAHH!

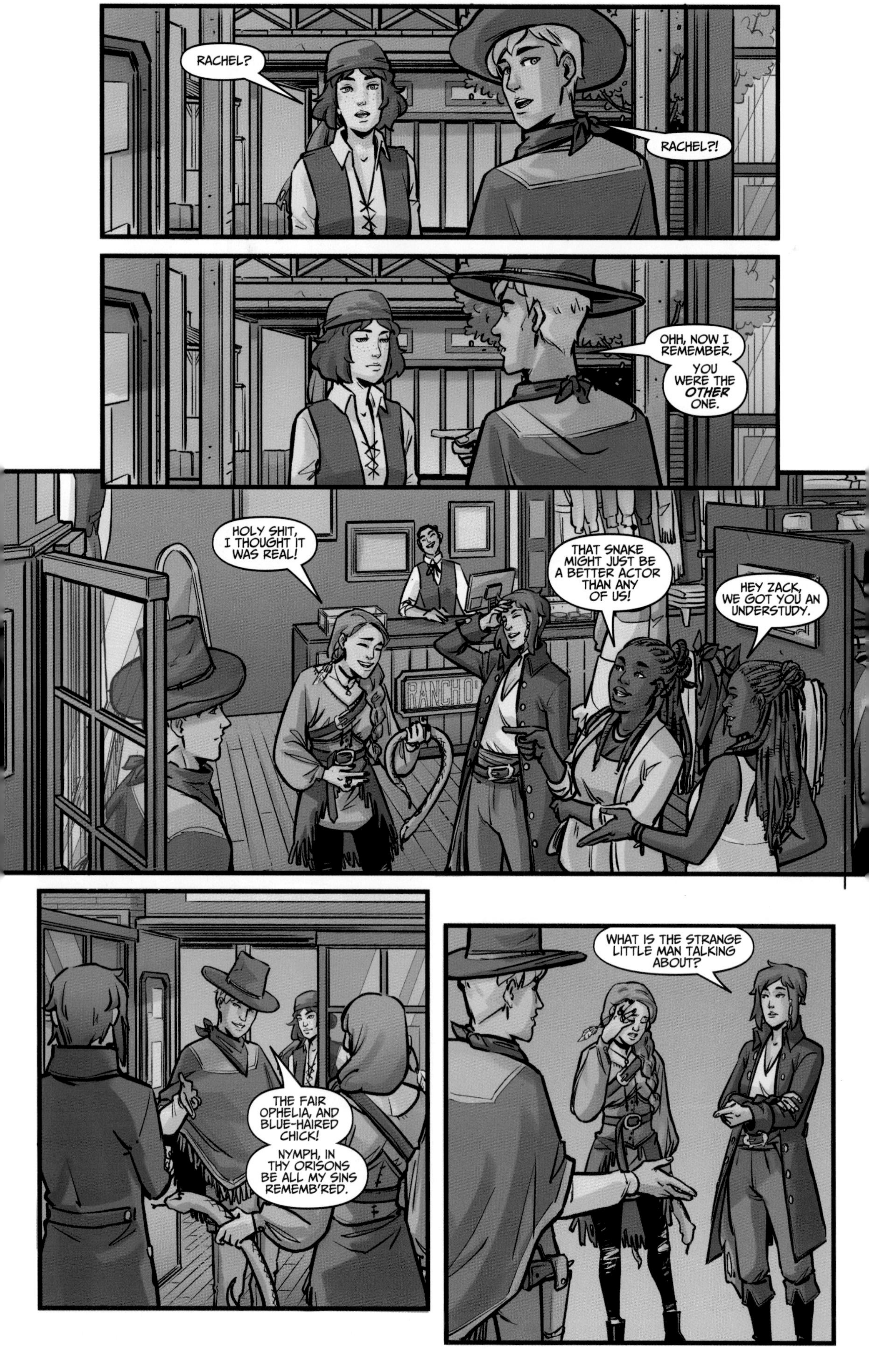
RACHEL?
RACHEL?!
OHH, NOW I REMEMBER.
YOU WERE THE *OTHER* ONE.
HOLY SHIT, I THOUGHT IT WAS REAL!
THAT SNAKE MIGHT JUST BE A BETTER ACTOR THAN ANY OF US!
HEY ZACK, WE GOT YOU AN UNDERSTUDY.
RANCHO'
THE FAIR OPHELIA, AND BLUE-HAIRED CHICK!
NYMPH, IN THY ORISONS BE ALL MY SINS REMEMB'RED.
WHAT IS THE STRANGE LITTLE MAN TALKING ABOUT?

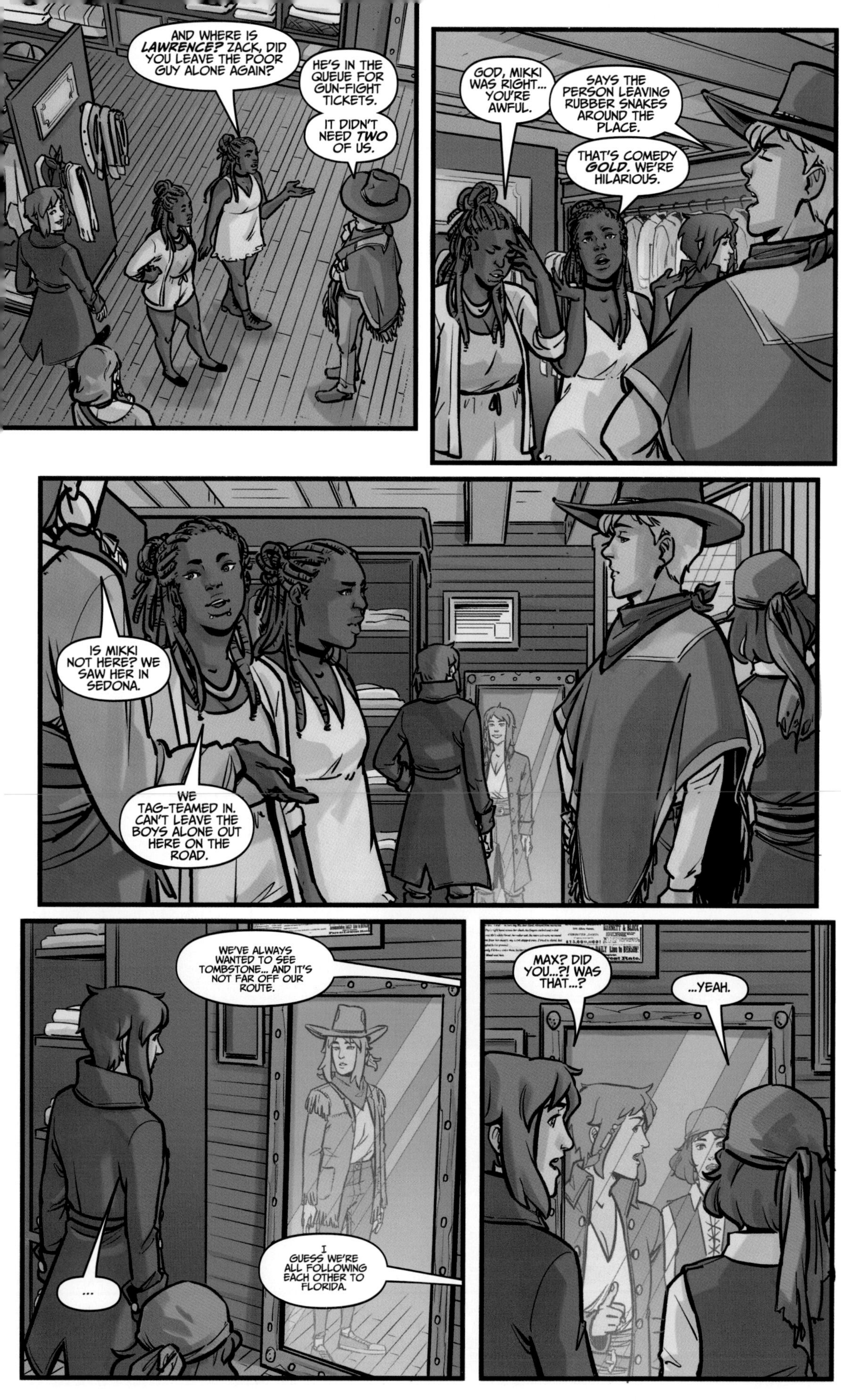
AND WHERE IS LAWRENCE? ZACK, DID YOU LEAVE THE POOR GUY ALONE AGAIN?
HE'S IN THE QUEUE FOR GUN-FIGHT TICKETS.
IT DIDN'T NEED TWO OF US.
GOD, MIKKI WAS RIGHT... YOU'RE AWFUL.
SAYS THE PERSON LEAVING RUBBER SNAKES AROUND THE PLACE.
THAT'S COMEDY GOLD. WE'RE HILARIOUS.
IS MIKKI NOT HERE? WE SAW HER IN SEDONA.
WE TAG-TEAMED IN. CAN'T LEAVE THE BOYS ALONE OUT HERE ON THE ROAD.
WE'VE ALWAYS WANTED TO SEE TOMBSTONE... AND IT'S NOT FAR OFF OUR ROUTE.
...
I GUESS WE'RE ALL FOLLOWING EACH OTHER TO FLORIDA.
MAX? DID YOU...?! WAS THAT...?
...YEAH.

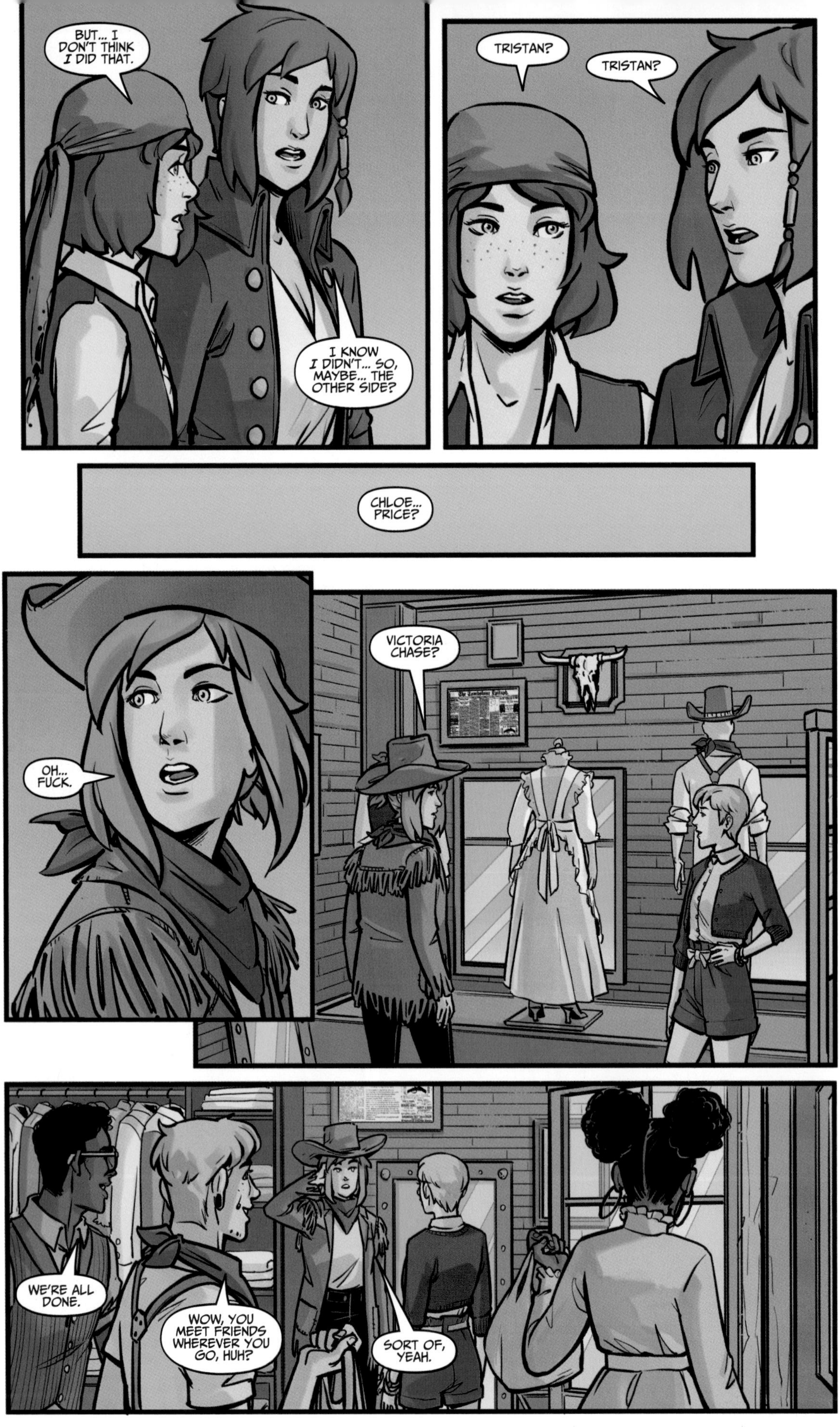
BUT... I DON'T THINK I DID THAT.
I KNOW I DIDN'T... SO, MAYBE... THE OTHER SIDE?
TRISTAN?
TRISTAN?
CHLOE... PRICE?
VICTORIA CHASE?
OH... FUCK.
WE'RE ALL DONE.
WOW, YOU MEET FRIENDS WHEREVER YOU GO, HUH?
SORT OF, YEAH.

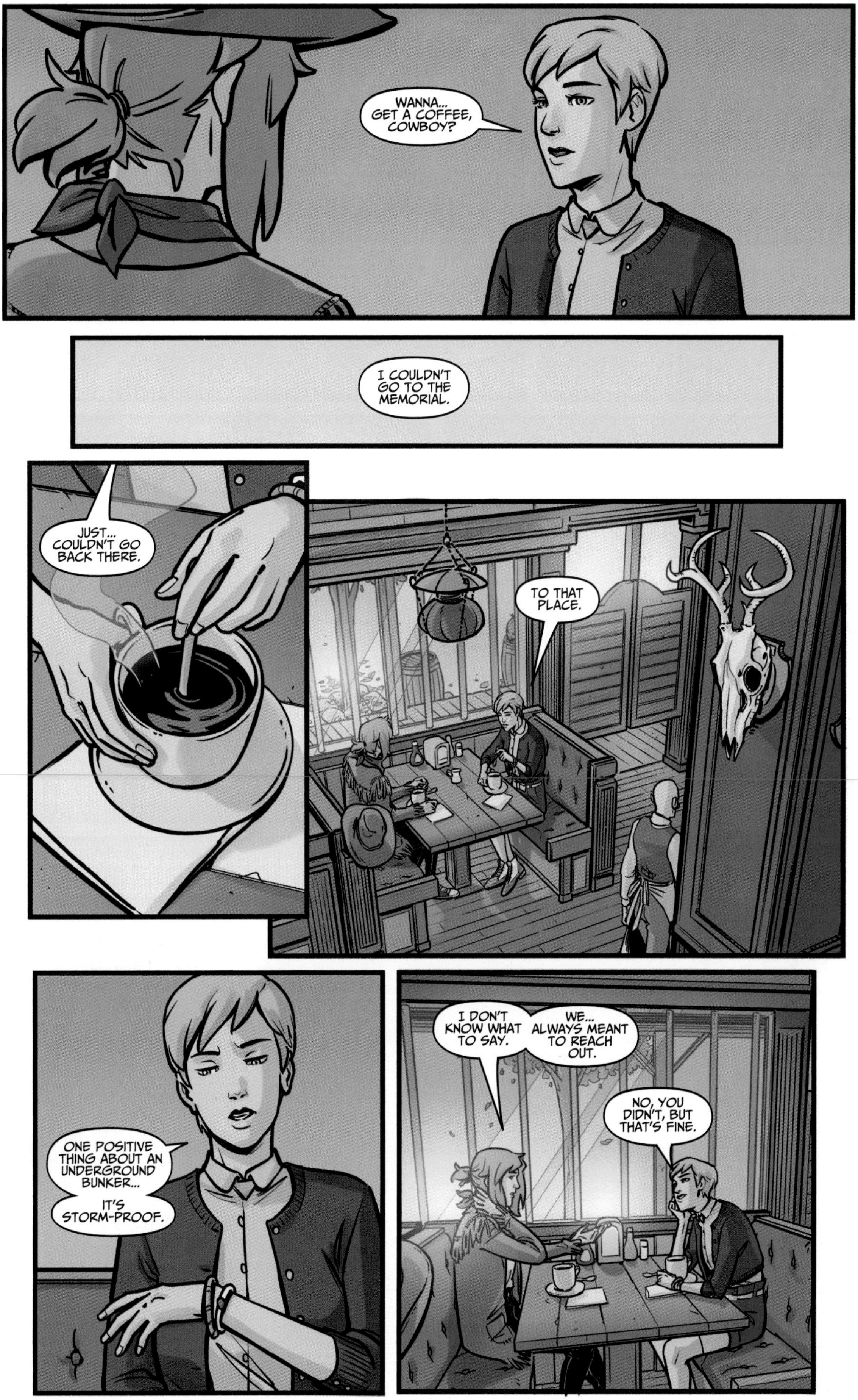

WANNA... GET A COFFEE, COWBOY?
I COULDN'T GO TO THE MEMORIAL.
JUST... COULDN'T GO BACK THERE.
TO THAT PLACE.
ONE POSITIVE THING ABOUT AN UNDERGROUND BUNKER...
IT'S STORM-PROOF.
I DON'T KNOW WHAT TO SAY.
WE... ALWAYS MEANT TO REACH OUT.
NO, YOU DIDN'T, BUT THAT'S FINE.

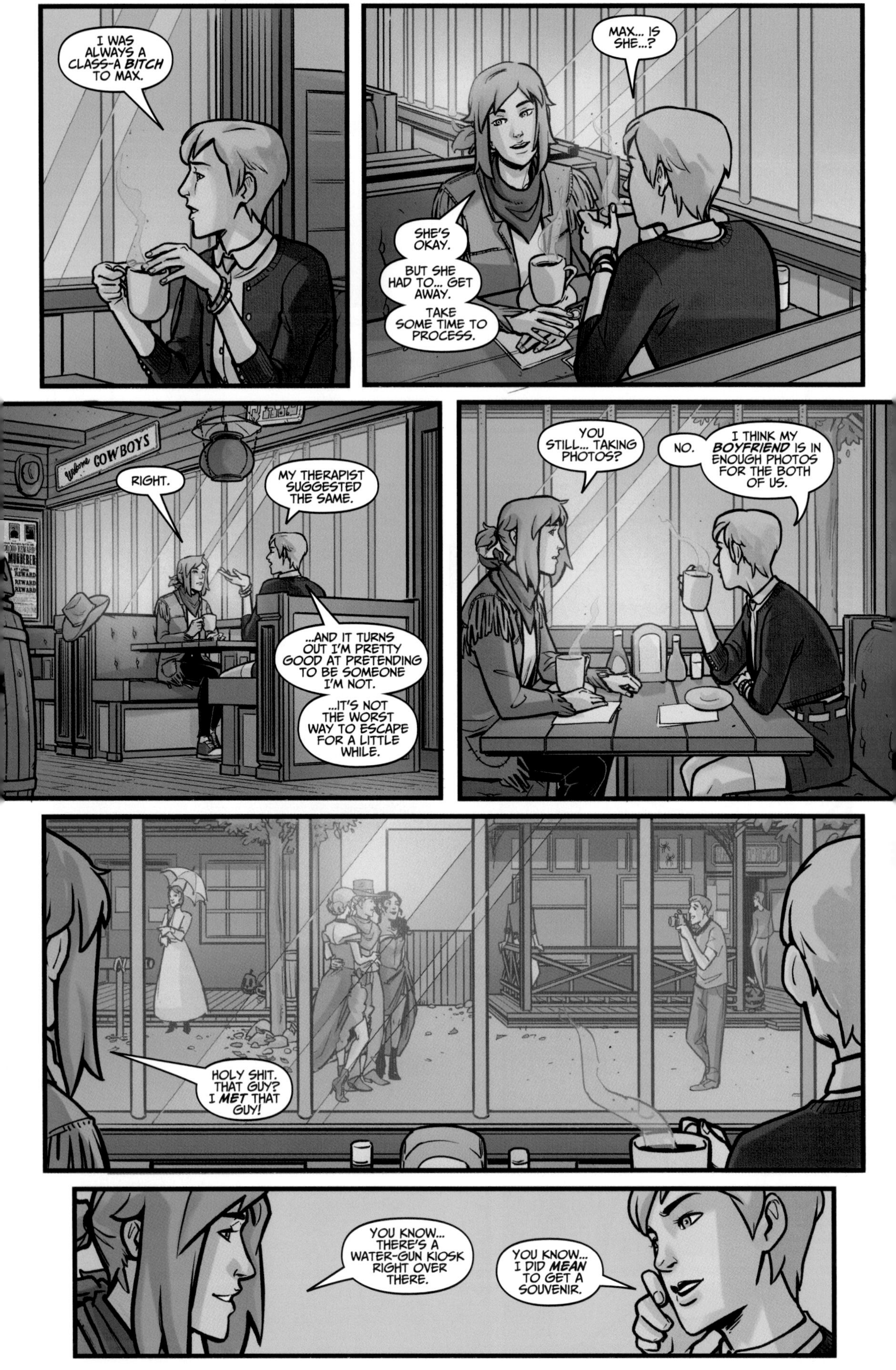
I WAS ALWAYS A CLASS-A *BITCH* TO MAX.
MAX... IS SHE...?
SHE'S OKAY.
BUT SHE HAD TO... GET AWAY.
TAKE SOME TIME TO PROCESS.
Welcome COWBOYS
RIGHT.
MY THERAPIST SUGGESTED THE SAME.
...AND IT TURNS OUT I'M PRETTY GOOD AT PRETENDING TO BE SOMEONE I'M NOT.
...IT'S NOT THE WORST WAY TO ESCAPE FOR A LITTLE WHILE.
YOU STILL... TAKING PHOTOS?
NO.
I THINK MY *BOYFRIEND* IS IN ENOUGH PHOTOS FOR THE BOTH OF US.
HOLY SHIT. THAT GUY? I *MET* THAT GUY!
YOU KNOW... THERE'S A WATER-GUN KIOSK RIGHT OVER THERE.
YOU KNOW... I DID *MEAN* TO GET A SOUVENIR.

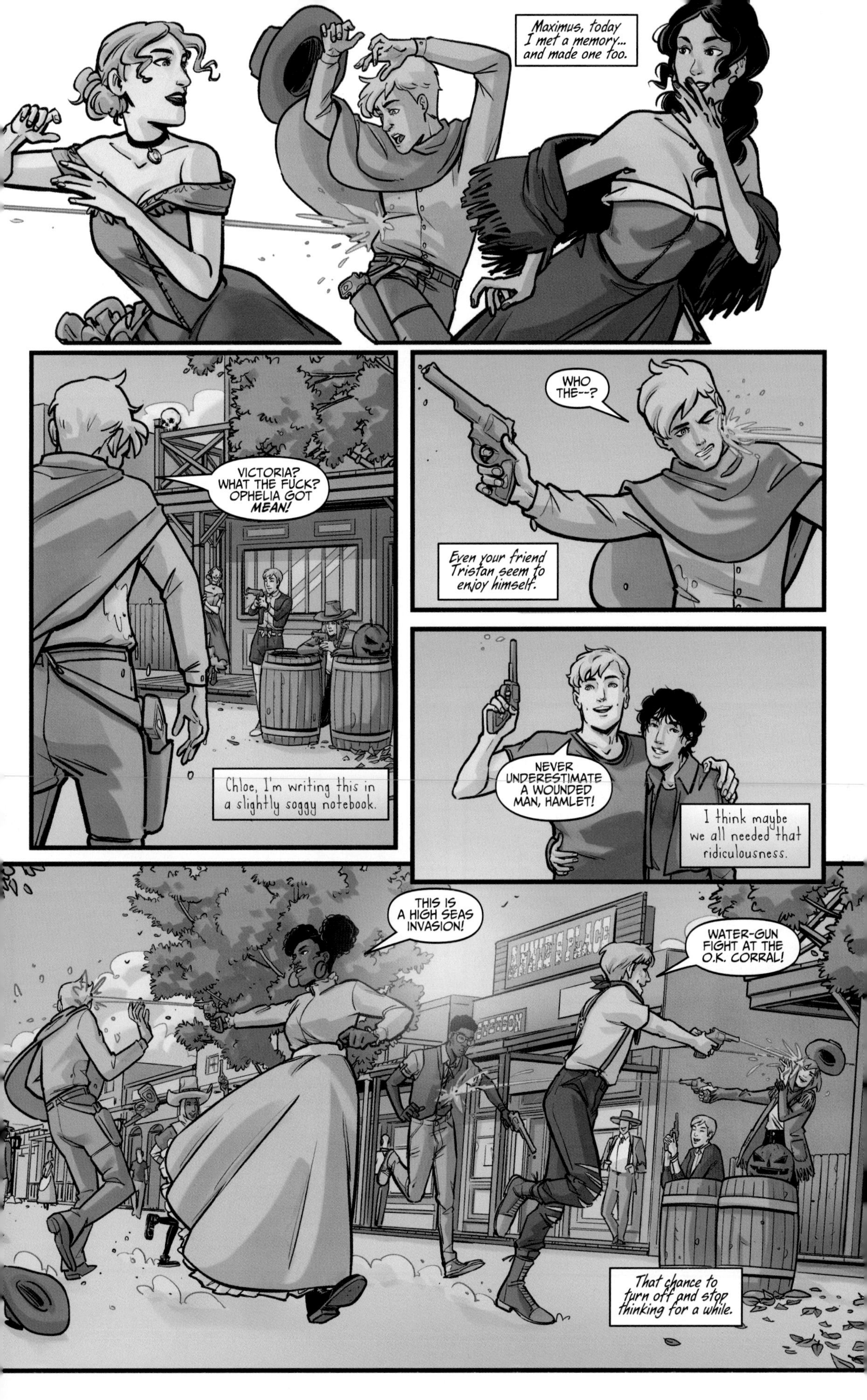
Maximus, today I met a memory... and made one too.
VICTORIA? WHAT THE FUCK? OPHELIA GOT MEAN!
Chloe, I'm writing this in a slightly soggy notebook.
WHO THE--?
Even your friend Tristan seem to enjoy himself.
NEVER UNDERESTIMATE A WOUNDED MAN, HAMLET!
I think maybe we all needed that ridiculousness.
THIS IS A HIGH SEAS INVASION!
WATER-GUN FIGHT AT THE O.K. CORRAL!
That chance to turn off and stop thinking for a while.

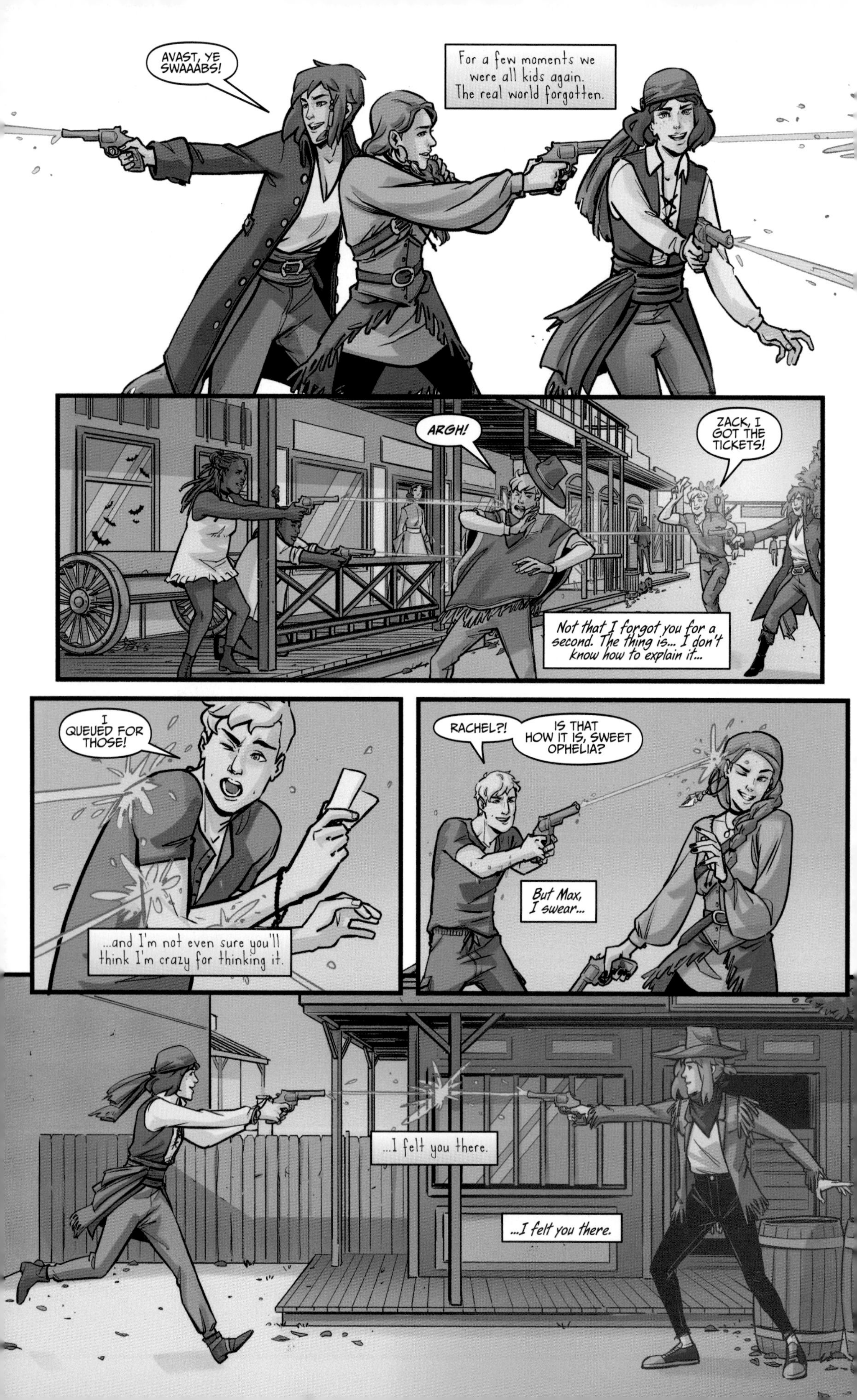
AVAST, YE SWAAABS!
For a few moments we were all kids again. The real world forgotten.
ARGH!
ZACK, I GOT THE TICKETS!
Not that I forgot you for a second. The thing is... I don't know how to explain it...
I QUEUED FOR THOSE!
...and I'm not even sure you'll think I'm crazy for thinking it.
RACHEL?!
IS THAT HOW IT IS, SWEET OPHELIA?
But Max, I swear...
...I felt you there.
...I felt you there.

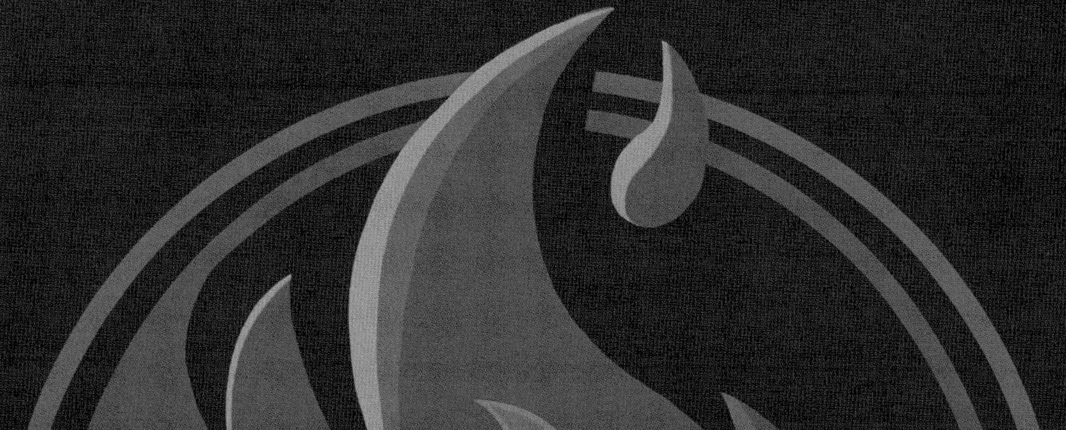

City on Fire

CHAPTER 3

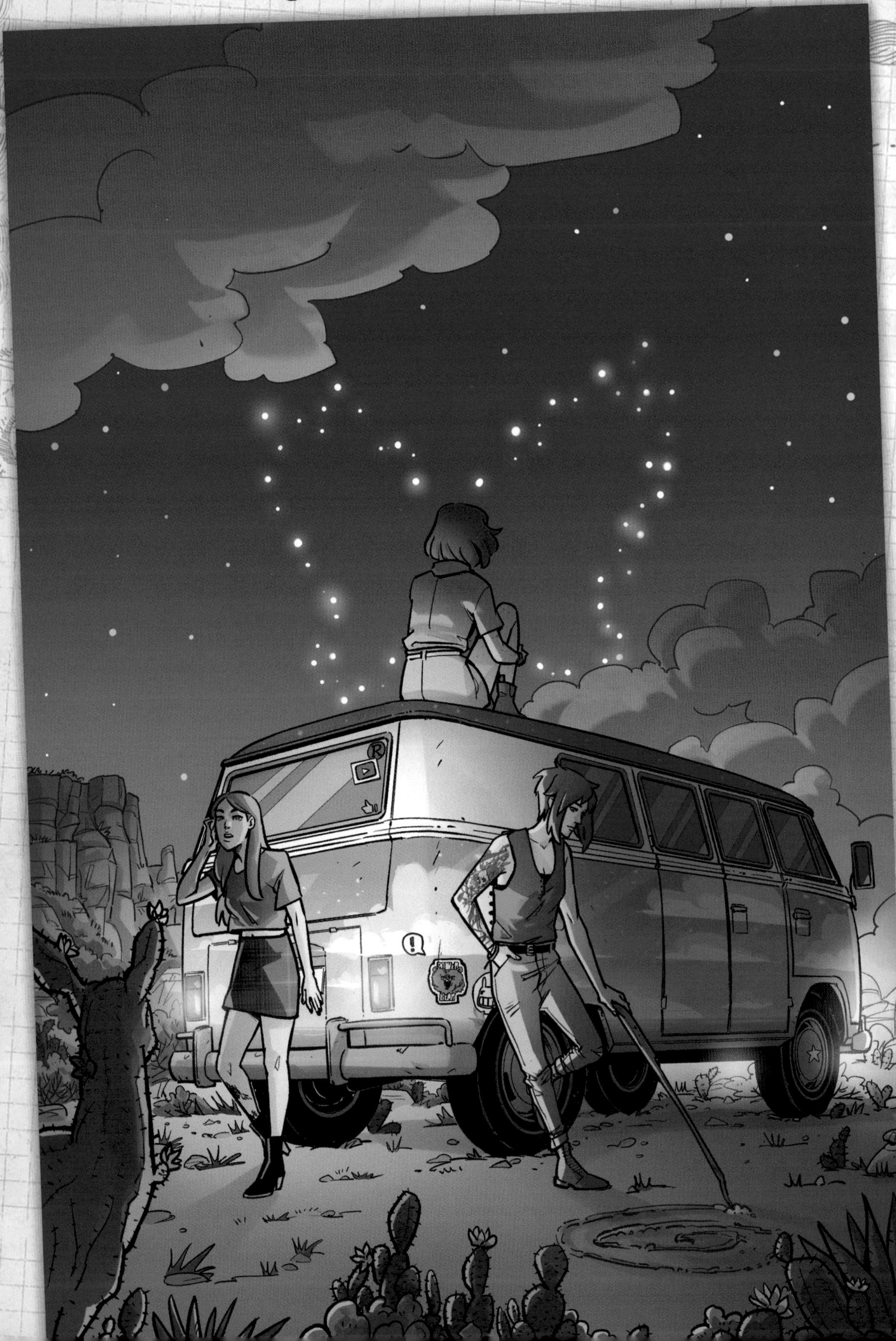

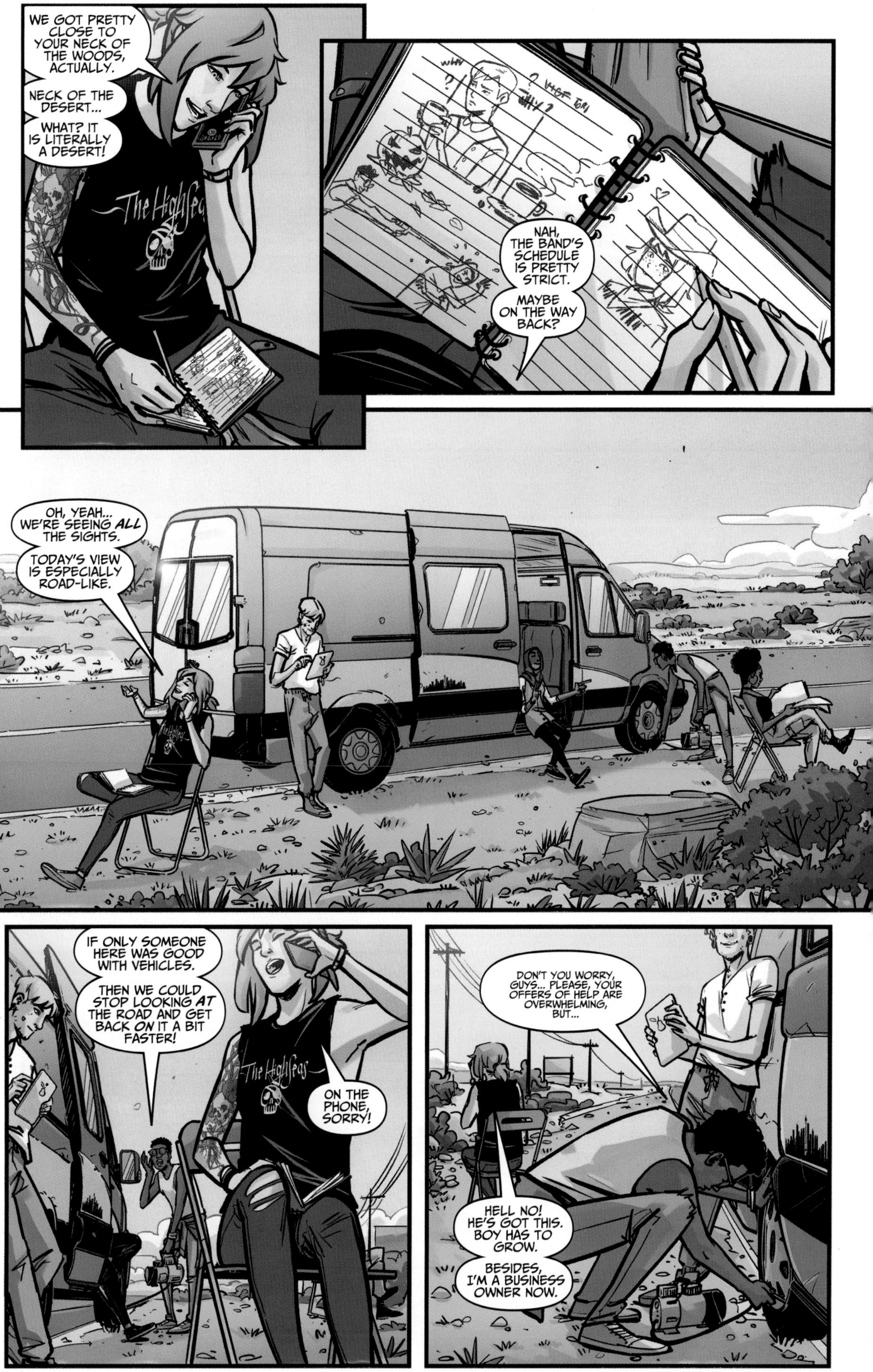
WE GOT PRETTY CLOSE TO YOUR NECK OF THE WOODS, ACTUALLY.
NECK OF THE DESERT...
WHAT? IT IS LITERALLY A DESERT!
The High Seas
NAH, THE BAND'S SCHEDULE IS PRETTY STRICT.
MAYBE ON THE WAY BACK?
OH, YEAH... WE'RE SEEING ALL THE SIGHTS.
TODAY'S VIEW IS ESPECIALLY ROAD-LIKE.
IF ONLY SOMEONE HERE WAS GOOD WITH VEHICLES.
THEN WE COULD STOP LOOKING AT THE ROAD AND GET BACK ON IT A BIT FASTER!
The High Seas
ON THE PHONE, SORRY!
DON'T YOU WORRY, GUYS... PLEASE, YOUR OFFERS OF HELP ARE OVERWHELMING, BUT...
HELL NO! HE'S GOT THIS. BOY HAS TO GROW.
BESIDES, I'M A BUSINESS OWNER NOW.

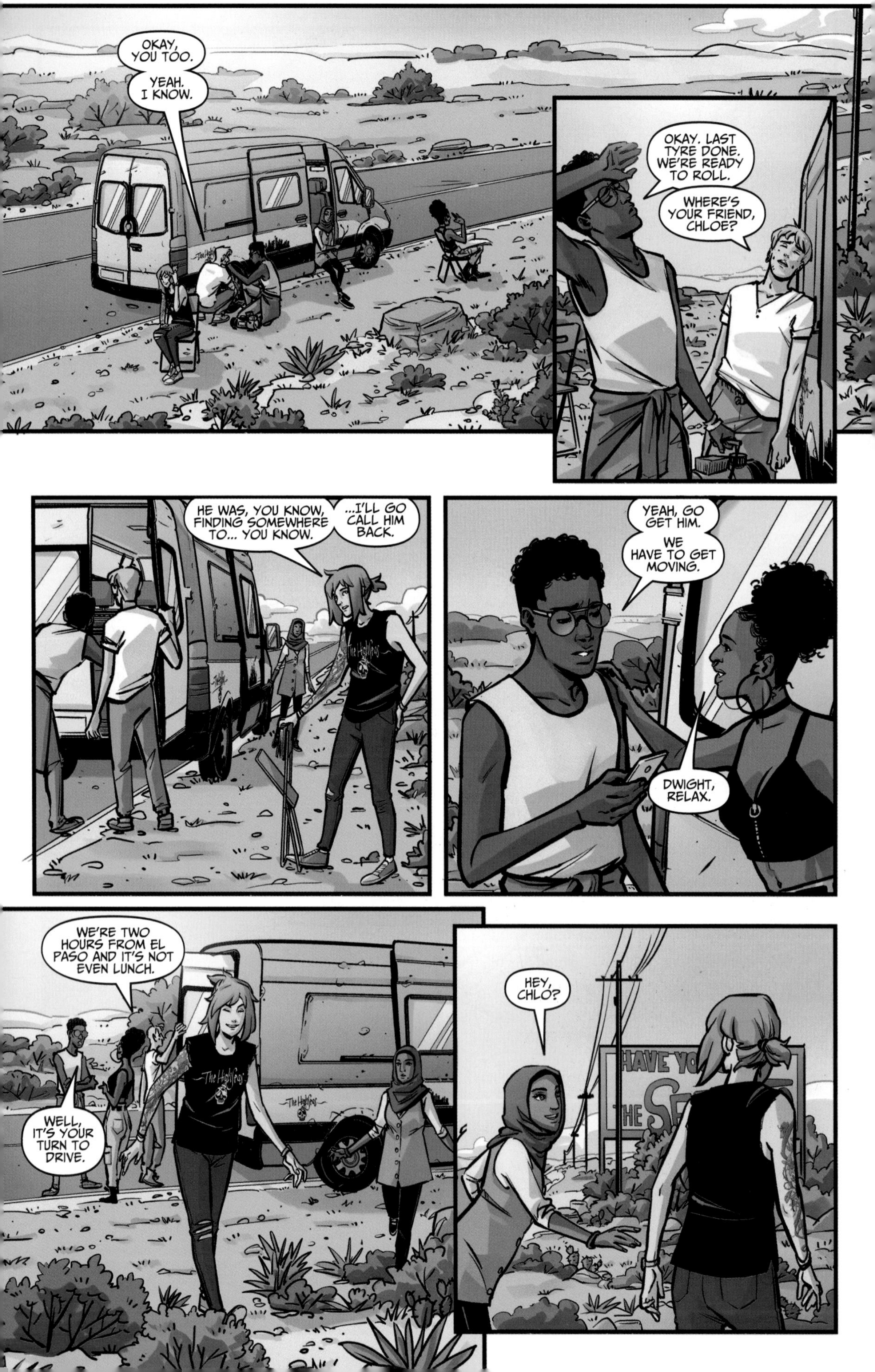
OKAY, YOU TOO.
YEAH. I KNOW.
OKAY. LAST TYRE DONE. WE'RE READY TO ROLL.
WHERE'S YOUR FRIEND, CHLOE?
HE WAS, YOU KNOW, FINDING SOMEWHERE TO... YOU KNOW.
...I'LL GO CALL HIM BACK.
YEAH, GO GET HIM.
WE HAVE TO GET MOVING.
DWIGHT, RELAX.
WE'RE TWO HOURS FROM EL PASO AND IT'S NOT EVEN LUNCH.
WELL, IT'S YOUR TURN TO DRIVE.
HEY, CHLO?

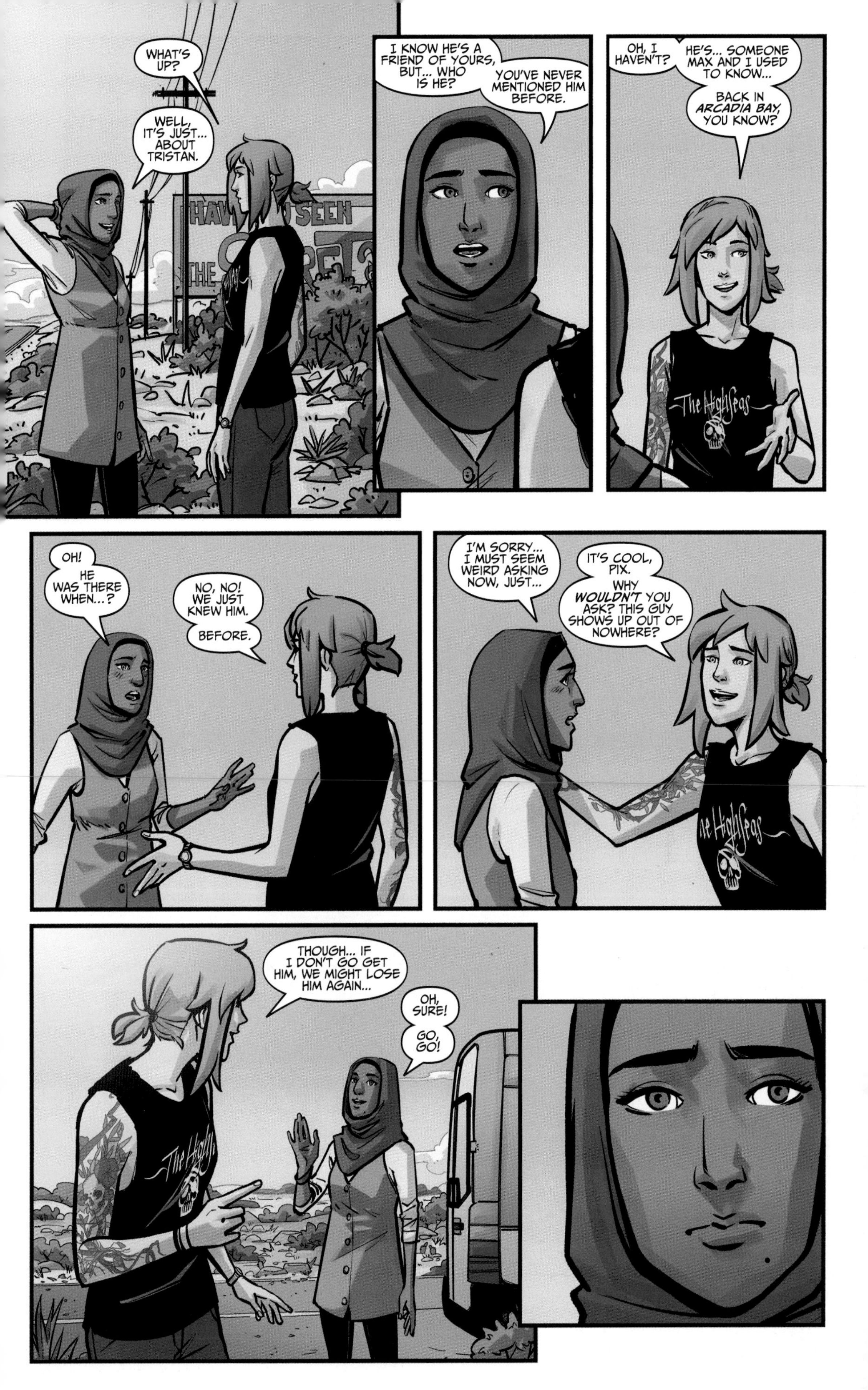
WHAT'S UP?
WELL, IT'S JUST... ABOUT TRISTAN.
I KNOW HE'S A FRIEND OF YOURS, BUT... WHO IS HE?
YOU'VE NEVER MENTIONED HIM BEFORE.
OH, I HAVEN'T?
HE'S... SOMEONE MAX AND I USED TO KNOW...
BACK IN *ARCADIA BAY*, YOU KNOW?
The HighSeas
OH! HE WAS THERE WHEN...?
NO, NO! WE JUST KNEW HIM.
BEFORE.
I'M SORRY... I MUST SEEM WEIRD ASKING NOW, JUST...
IT'S COOL, PIX.
WHY ***WOULDN'T*** YOU ASK? THIS GUY SHOWS UP OUT OF NOWHERE?
THOUGH... IF I DON'T GO GET HIM, WE MIGHT LOSE HIM AGAIN...
OH, SURE!
GO, GO!

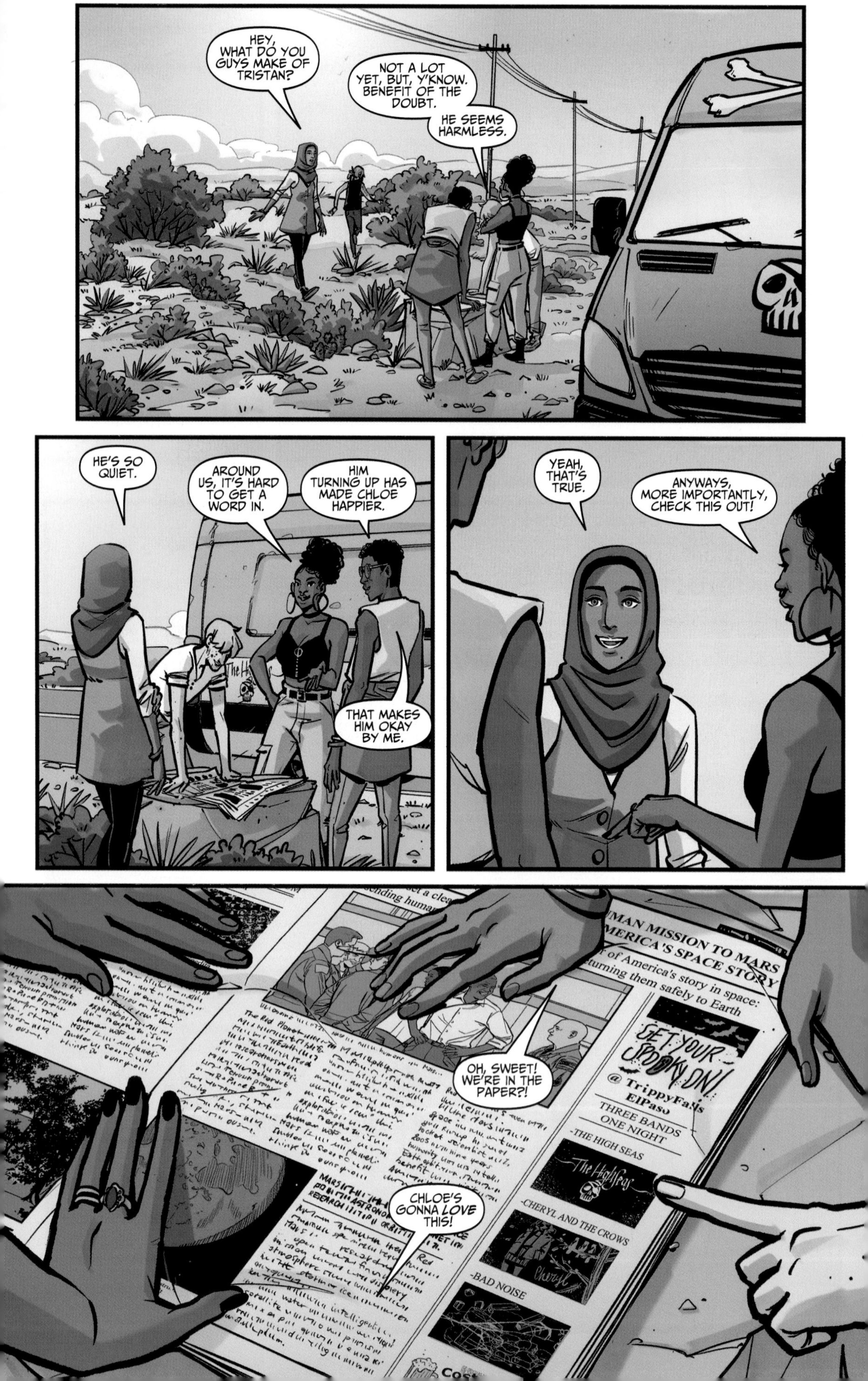
HEY, WHAT DO YOU GUYS MAKE OF TRISTAN?
NOT A LOT YET, BUT, Y'KNOW. BENEFIT OF THE DOUBT.
HE SEEMS HARMLESS.
HE'S SO QUIET.
AROUND US, IT'S HARD TO GET A WORD IN.
HIM TURNING UP HAS MADE CHLOE HAPPIER.
THAT MAKES HIM OKAY BY ME.
YEAH, THAT'S TRUE.
ANYWAYS, MORE IMPORTANTLY, CHECK THIS OUT!
OH, SWEET! WE'RE IN THE PAPER?!
CHLOE'S GONNA *LOVE* THIS!
GET YOUR SPOOKY ON!
@ TrippyFalls ElPaso
THREE BANDS ONE NIGHT
-THE HIGH SEAS
-CHERYL AND THE CROWS
-BAD NOISE

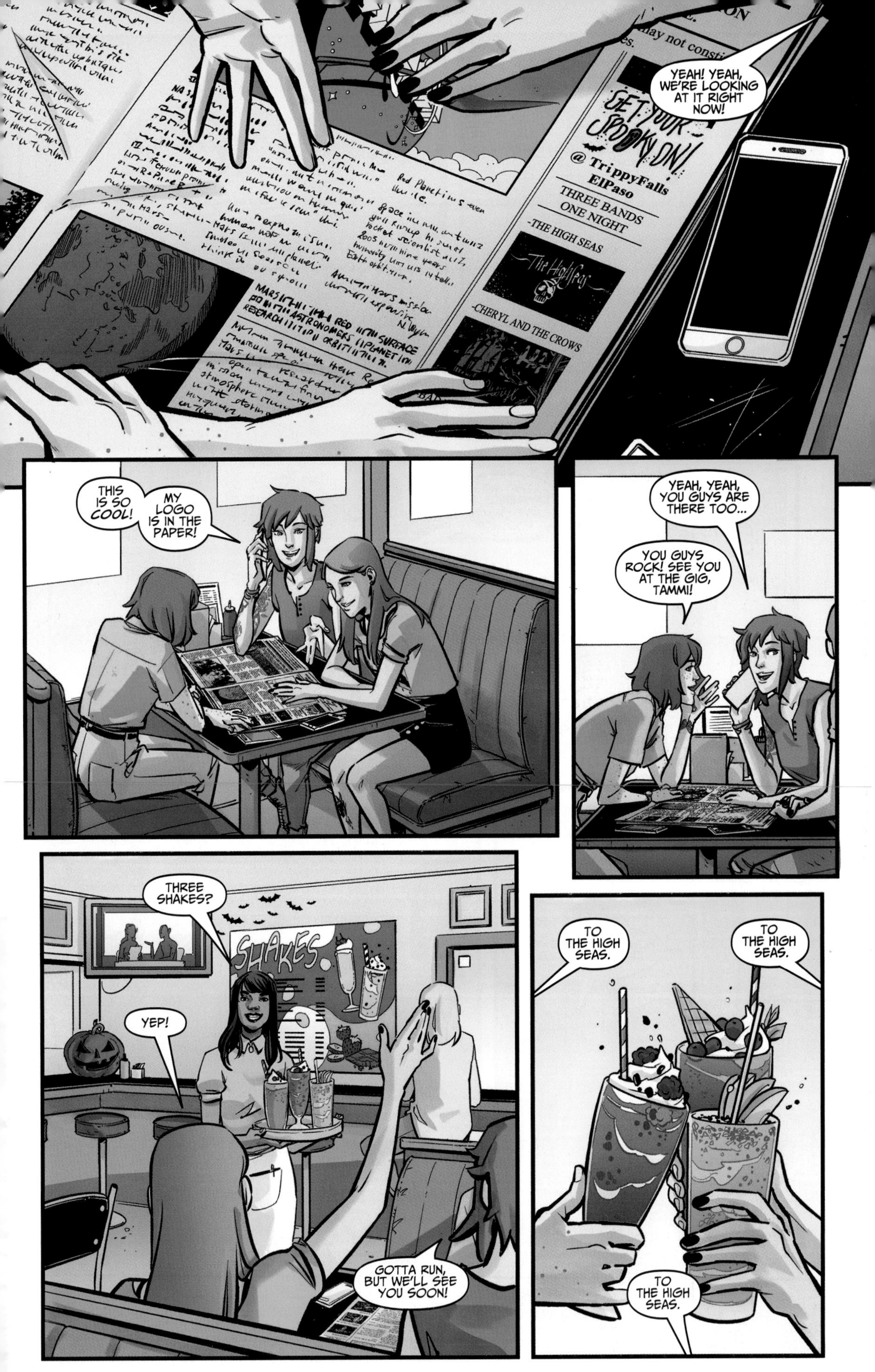
GET YOUR SPOOKY ON!
@ TrippyFalls ElPaso
THREE BANDS ONE NIGHT
-THE HIGH SEAS
-CHERYL AND THE CROWS
YEAH! YEAH, WE'RE LOOKING AT IT RIGHT NOW!
THIS IS SO COOL!
MY LOGO IS IN THE PAPER!
YEAH, YEAH, YOU GUYS ARE THERE TOO...
YOU GUYS ROCK! SEE YOU AT THE GIG, TAMMI!
THREE SHAKES?
SHAKES
YEP!
GOTTA RUN, BUT WE'LL SEE YOU SOON!
TO THE HIGH SEAS.
TO THE HIGH SEAS.
TO THE HIGH SEAS.

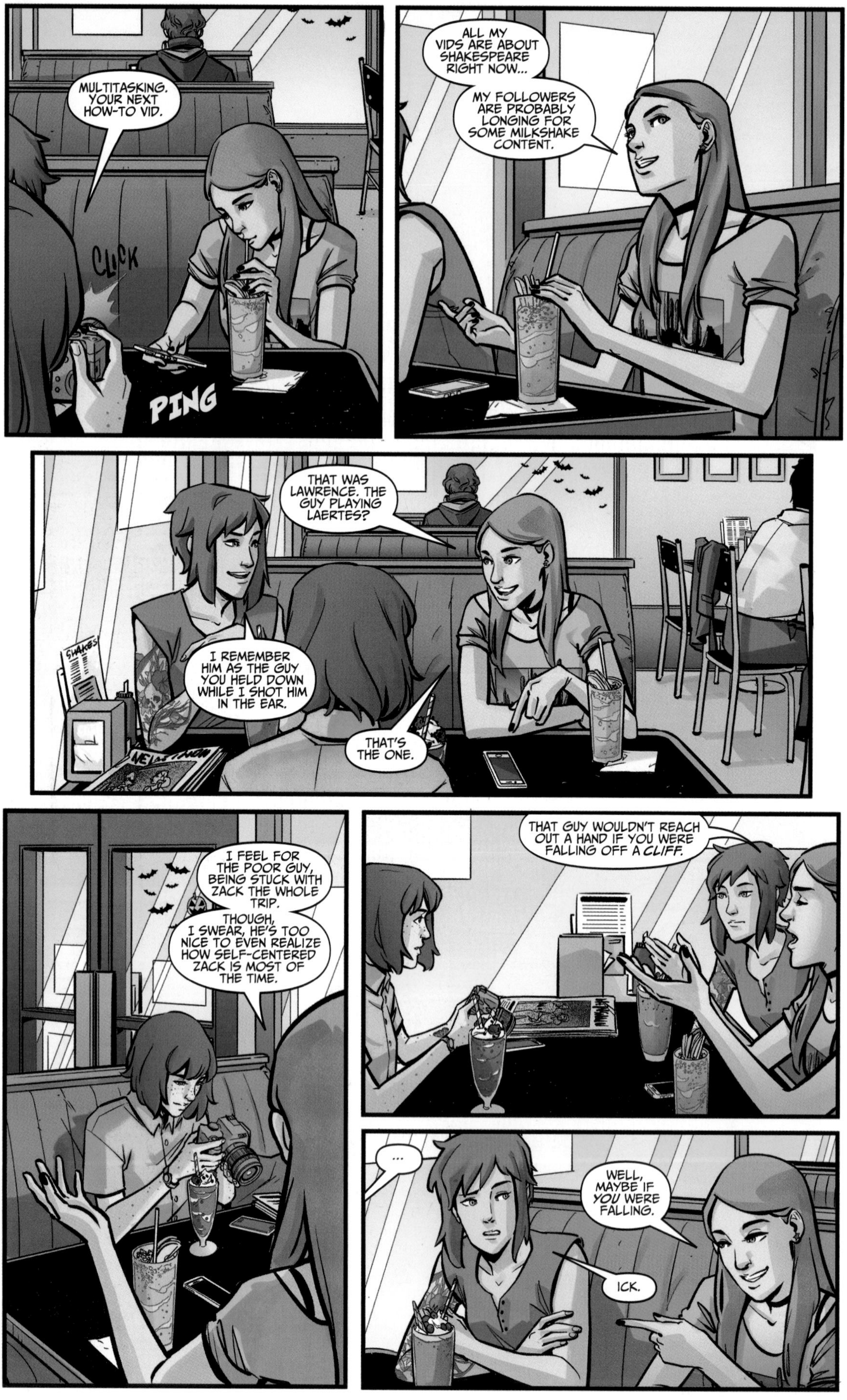
MULTITASKING. YOUR NEXT HOW-TO VID.
CLICK
PING
ALL MY VIDS ARE ABOUT SHAKESPEARE RIGHT NOW...
MY FOLLOWERS ARE PROBABLY LONGING FOR SOME MILKSHAKE CONTENT.
THAT WAS LAWRENCE. THE GUY PLAYING LAERTES?
I REMEMBER HIM AS THE GUY YOU HELD DOWN WHILE I SHOT HIM IN THE EAR.
THAT'S THE ONE.
SHAKES
I FEEL FOR THE POOR GUY, BEING STUCK WITH ZACK THE WHOLE TRIP.
THOUGH, I SWEAR, HE'S TOO NICE TO EVEN REALIZE HOW SELF-CENTERED ZACK IS MOST OF THE TIME.
THAT GUY WOULDN'T REACH OUT A HAND IF YOU WERE FALLING OFF A *CLIFF*.
...
WELL, MAYBE IF *YOU* WERE FALLING.
ICK.

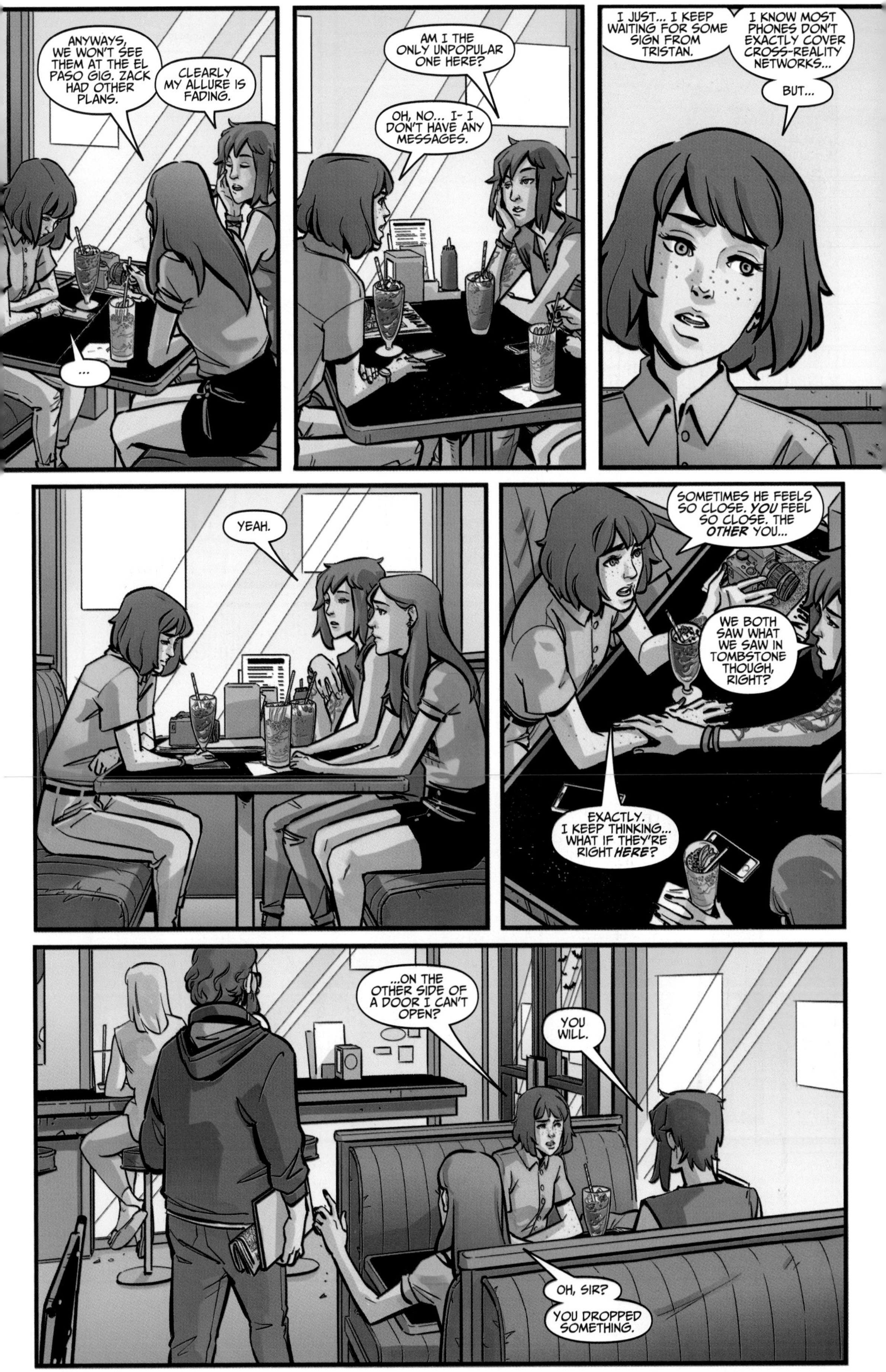
ANYWAYS, WE WON'T SEE THEM AT THE EL PASO GIG. ZACK HAD OTHER PLANS.
CLEARLY MY ALLURE IS FADING.
...
AM I THE ONLY UNPOPULAR ONE HERE?
OH, NO... I- I DON'T HAVE ANY MESSAGES.
I JUST... I KEEP WAITING FOR SOME SIGN FROM TRISTAN.
I KNOW MOST PHONES DON'T EXACTLY COVER CROSS-REALITY NETWORKS...
BUT...
YEAH.
SOMETIMES HE FEELS SO CLOSE. *YOU* FEEL SO CLOSE. THE *OTHER* YOU...
WE BOTH SAW WHAT WE SAW IN TOMBSTONE THOUGH, RIGHT?
EXACTLY. I KEEP THINKING... WHAT IF THEY'RE RIGHT *HERE*?
...ON THE OTHER SIDE OF A DOOR I CAN'T OPEN?
YOU WILL.
OH, SIR?
YOU DROPPED SOMETHING.

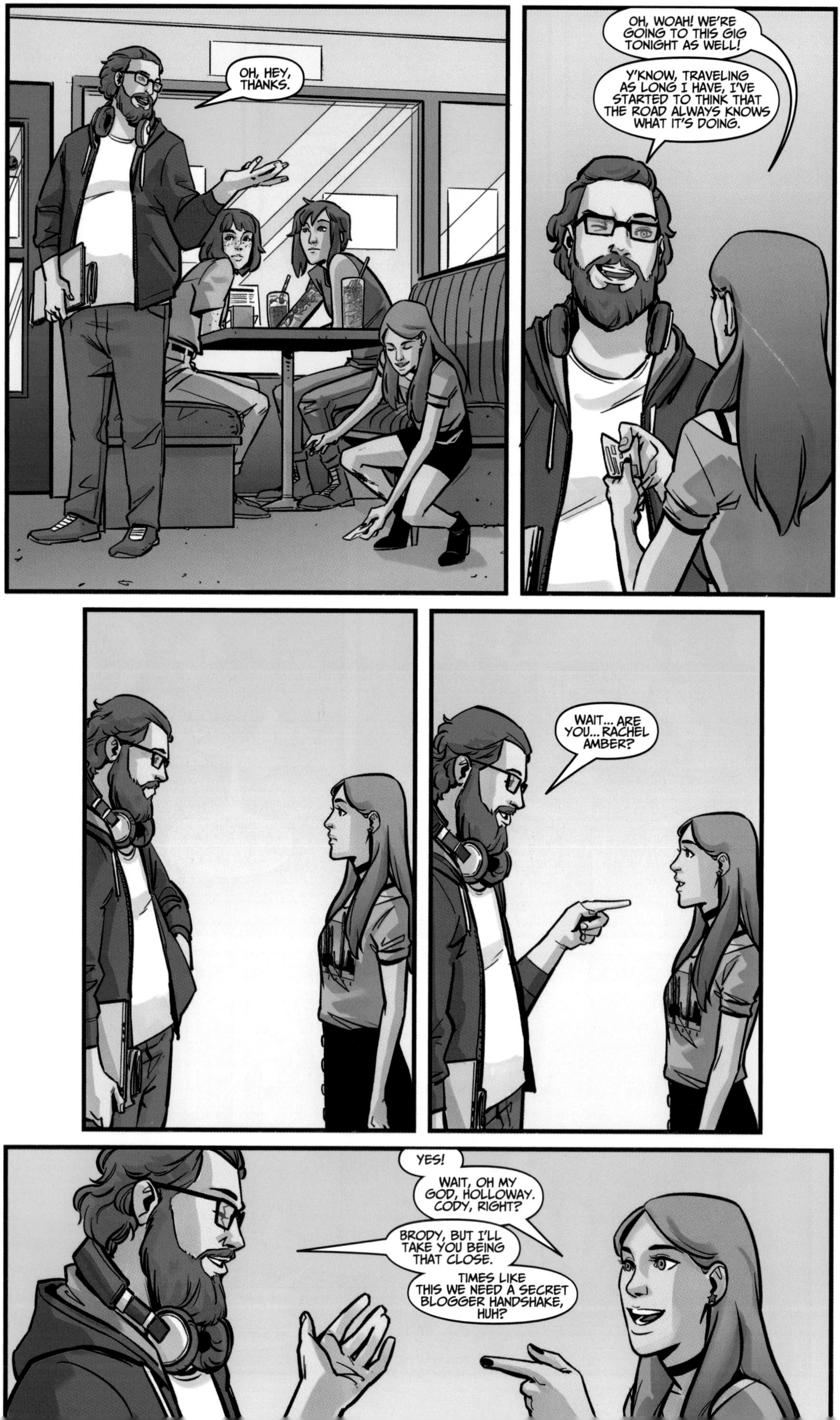
OH, HEY, THANKS.
OH, WOAH! WE'RE GOING TO THIS GIG TONIGHT AS WELL!
Y'KNOW, TRAVELING AS LONG I HAVE, I'VE STARTED TO THINK THAT THE ROAD ALWAYS KNOWS WHAT IT'S DOING.
WAIT... ARE YOU... RACHEL AMBER?
YES!
WAIT, OH MY GOD, HOLLOWAY. CODY, RIGHT?
BRODY, BUT I'LL TAKE YOU BEING THAT CLOSE.
TIMES LIKE THIS WE NEED A SECRET BLOGGER HANDSHAKE, HUH?

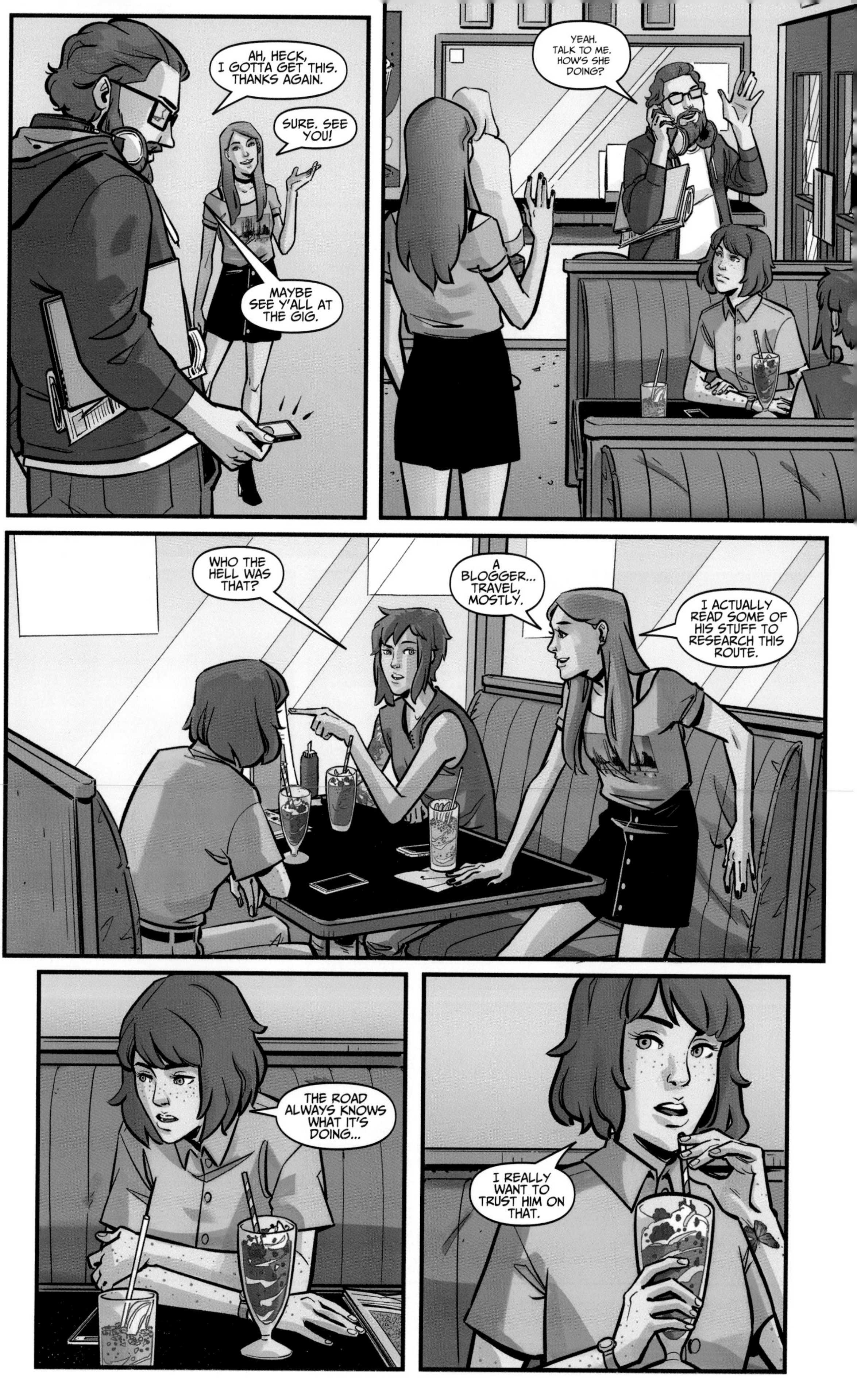
AH, HECK, I GOTTA GET THIS. THANKS AGAIN.
SURE. SEE YOU!
MAYBE SEE Y'ALL AT THE GIG.
YEAH. TALK TO ME. HOW'S SHE DOING?
WHO THE HELL WAS THAT?
A BLOGGER... TRAVEL, MOSTLY.
I ACTUALLY READ SOME OF HIS STUFF TO RESEARCH THIS ROUTE.
THE ROAD ALWAYS KNOWS WHAT IT'S DOING...
I REALLY WANT TO TRUST HIM ON THAT.

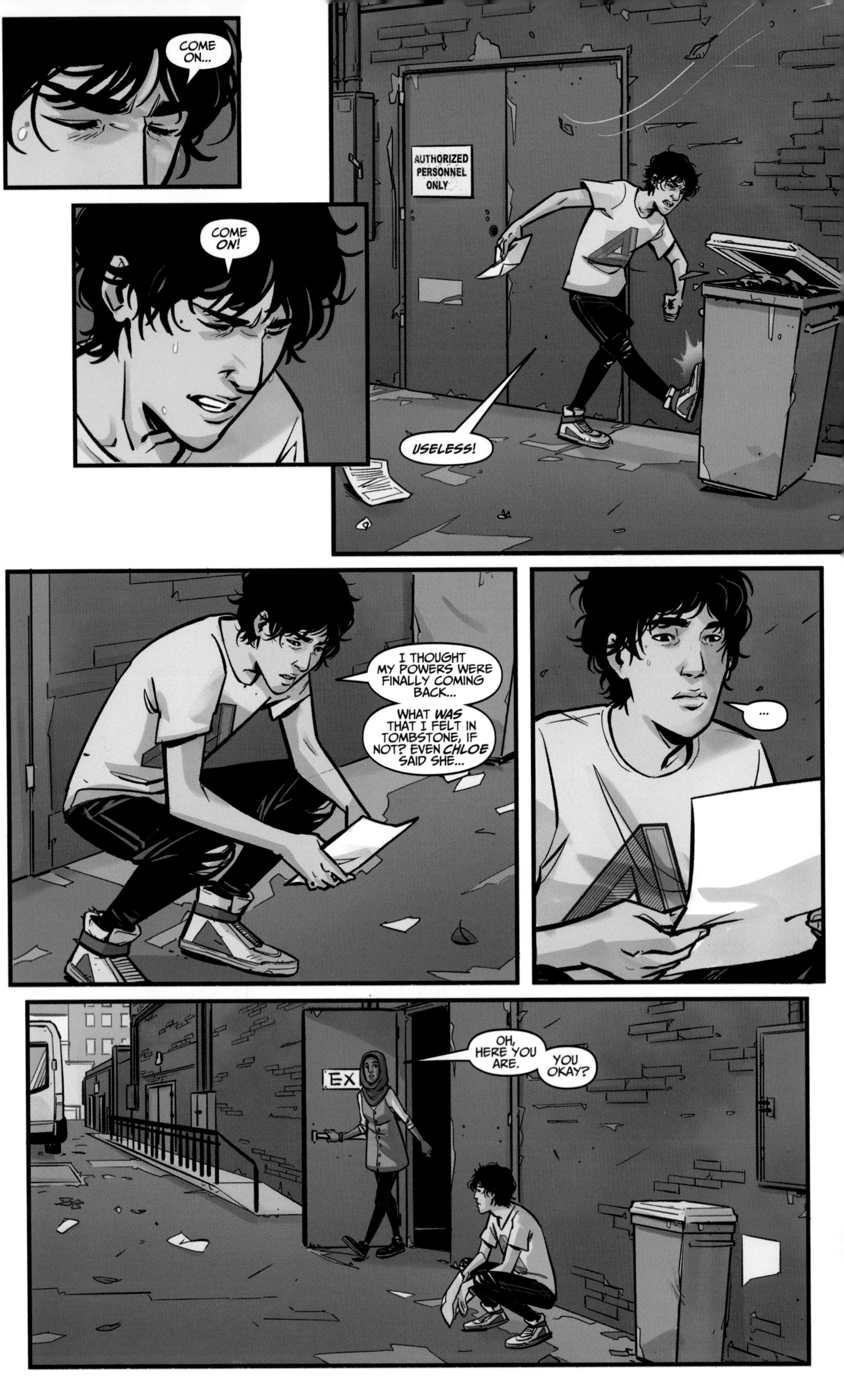
COME ON...
COME ON!
AUTHORIZED PERSONNEL ONLY
USELESS!
I THOUGHT MY POWERS WERE FINALLY COMING BACK...
WHAT WAS THAT I FELT IN TOMBSTONE, IF NOT? EVEN CHLOE SAID SHE...
...
EX
OH, HERE YOU ARE.
YOU OKAY?

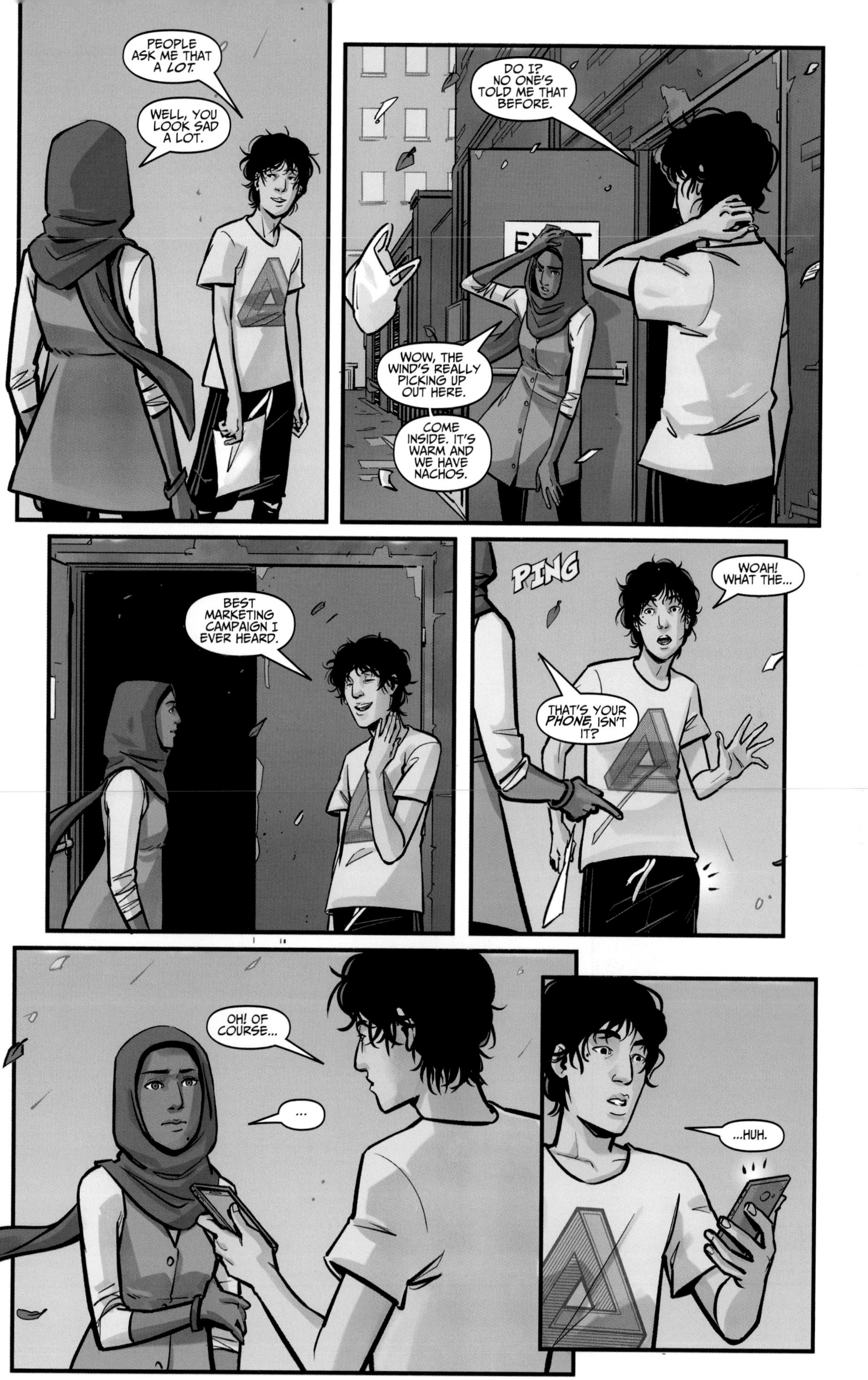
PEOPLE ASK ME THAT A *LOT.*
WELL, YOU LOOK SAD A LOT.
DO I? NO ONE'S TOLD ME THAT BEFORE.
EXIT
WOW, THE WIND'S REALLY PICKING UP OUT HERE.
COME INSIDE. IT'S WARM AND WE HAVE NACHOS.
BEST MARKETING CAMPAIGN I EVER HEARD.
PING
WOAH! WHAT THE...
THAT'S YOUR *PHONE*, ISN'T IT?
OH! OF COURSE...
...
...HUH.

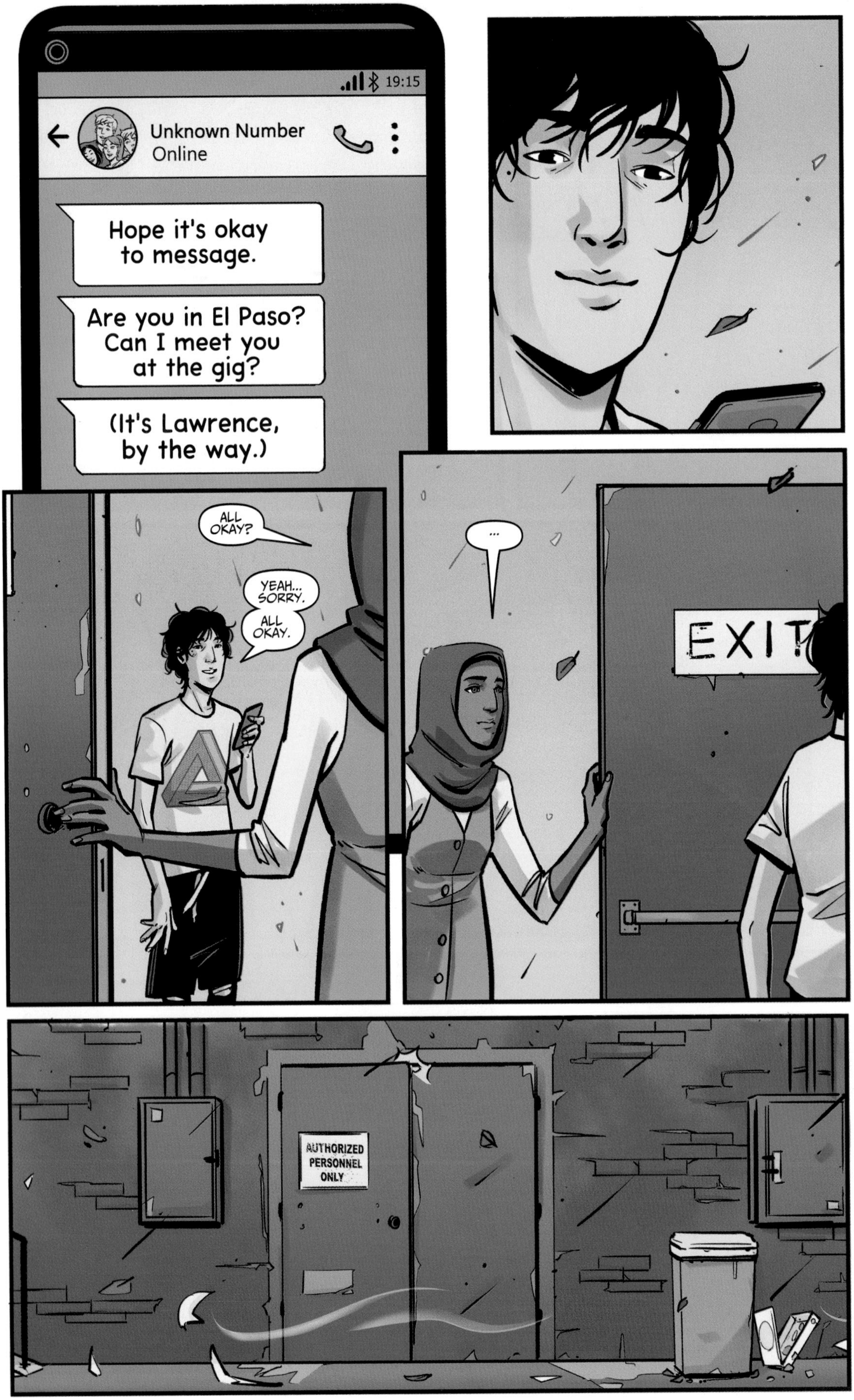

19:15
Unknown Number
Online
Hope it's okay to message.
Are you in El Paso? Can I meet you at the gig?
(It's Lawrence, by the way.)
ALL OKAY?
YEAH... SORRY.
ALL OKAY.
...
EXIT
AUTHORIZED PERSONNEL ONLY

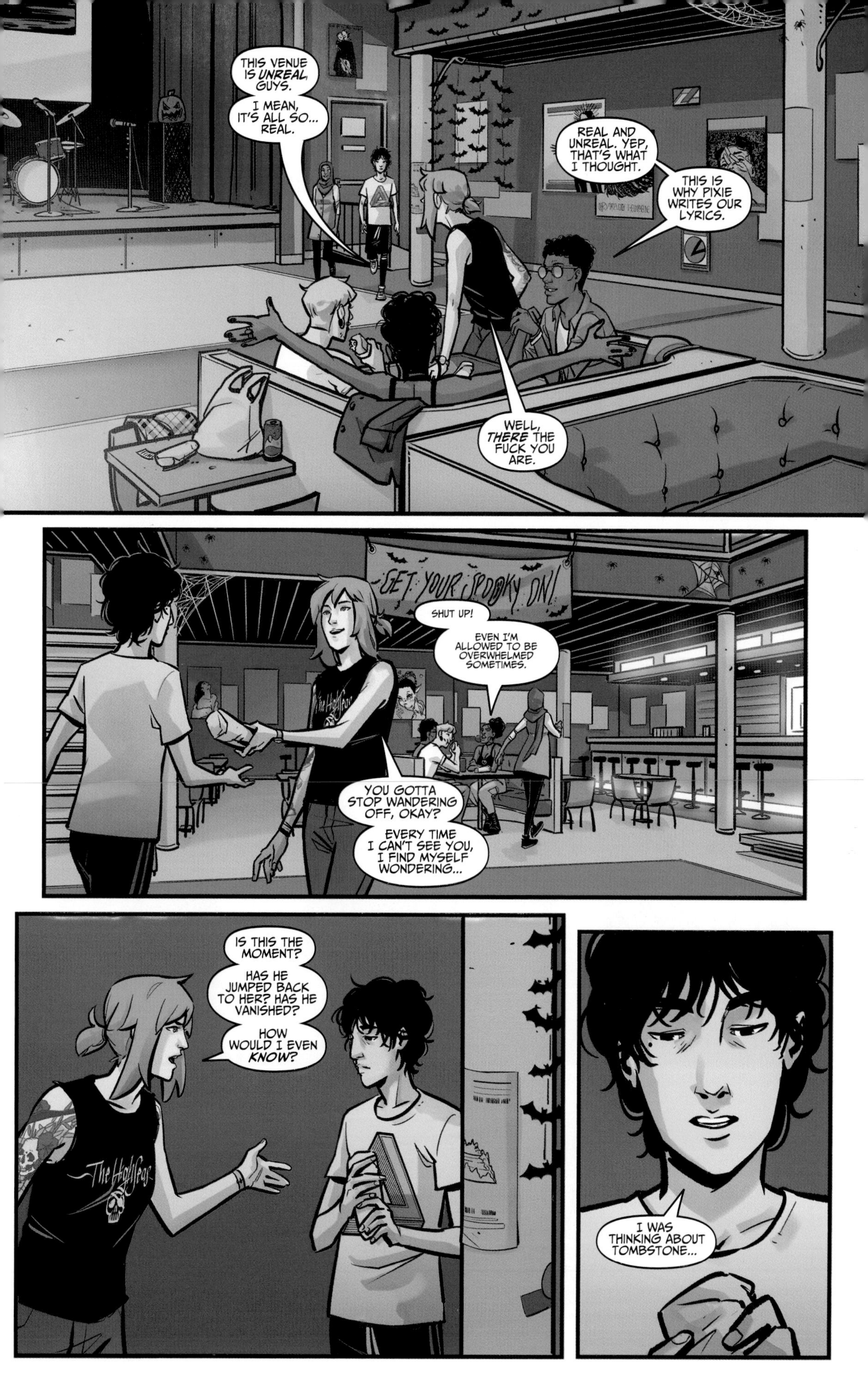

THIS VENUE IS *UNREAL*, GUYS.
I MEAN, IT'S ALL SO... REAL.
REAL AND UNREAL. YEP, THAT'S WHAT I THOUGHT.
THIS IS WHY PIXIE WRITES OUR LYRICS.
WELL, *THERE* THE FUCK YOU ARE.
GET YOUR SPOOKY ON!
SHUT UP!
EVEN I'M ALLOWED TO BE OVERWHELMED SOMETIMES.
YOU GOTTA STOP WANDERING OFF, OKAY?
EVERY TIME I CAN'T SEE YOU, I FIND MYSELF WONDERING...
IS THIS THE MOMENT?
HAS HE JUMPED BACK TO HER? HAS HE VANISHED?
HOW WOULD I EVEN *KNOW*?
The High Fears
I WAS THINKING ABOUT TOMBSTONE...

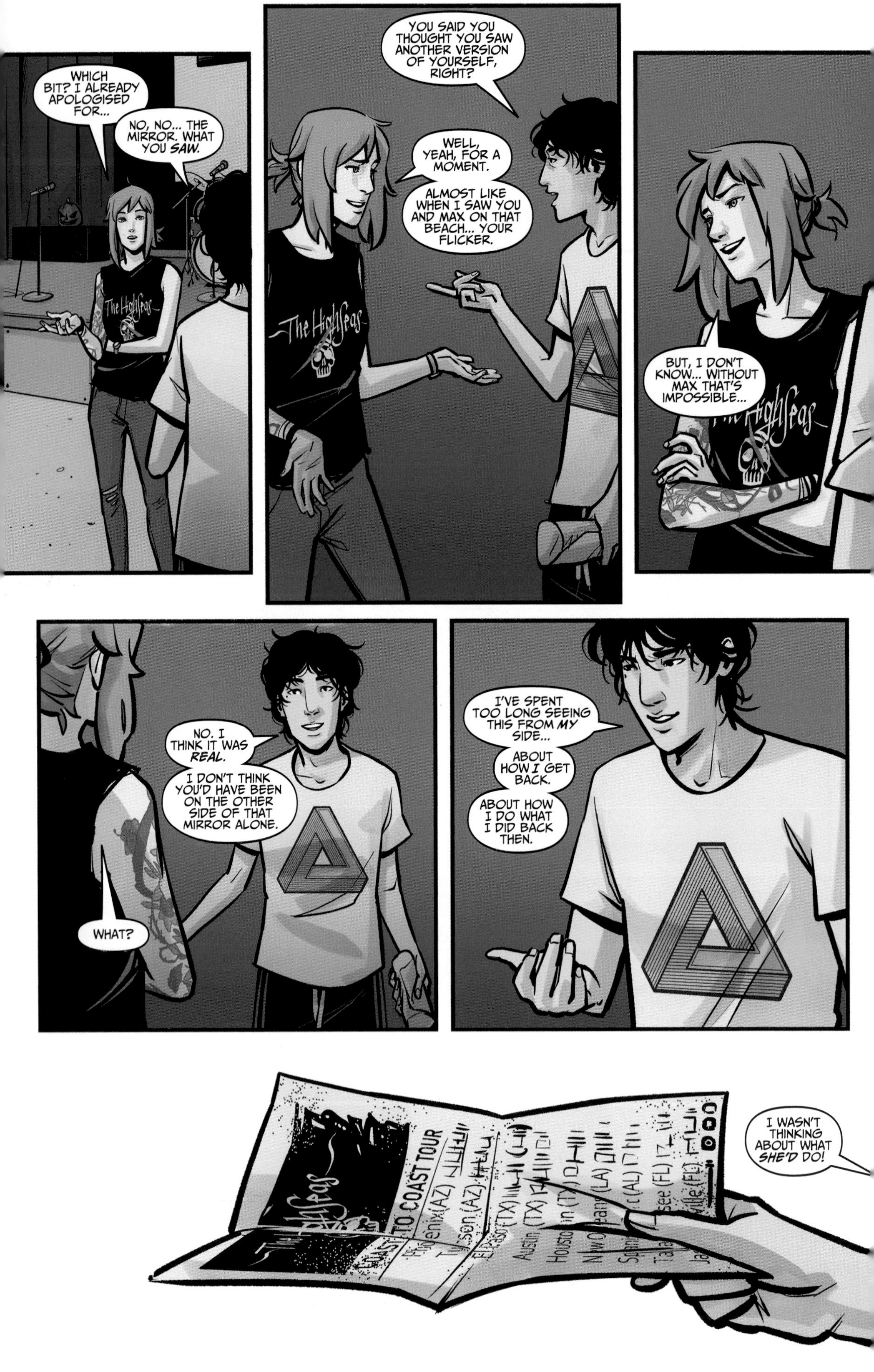

WHICH BIT? I ALREADY APOLOGISED FOR...
NO, NO... THE MIRROR. WHAT YOU *SAW.*
YOU SAID YOU THOUGHT YOU SAW ANOTHER VERSION OF YOURSELF, RIGHT?
WELL, YEAH, FOR A MOMENT.
ALMOST LIKE WHEN I SAW YOU AND MAX ON THAT BEACH... YOUR FLICKER.
BUT, I DON'T KNOW... WITHOUT MAX THAT'S IMPOSSIBLE...
NO. I THINK IT WAS ***REAL.***
I DON'T THINK YOU'D HAVE BEEN ON THE OTHER SIDE OF THAT MIRROR ALONE.
WHAT?
I'VE SPENT TOO LONG SEEING THIS FROM *MY* SIDE...
ABOUT HOW *I* GET BACK.
ABOUT HOW I DO WHAT I DID BACK THEN.
TO COAST TOUR
I WASN'T THINKING ABOUT WHAT ***SHE'D*** DO!

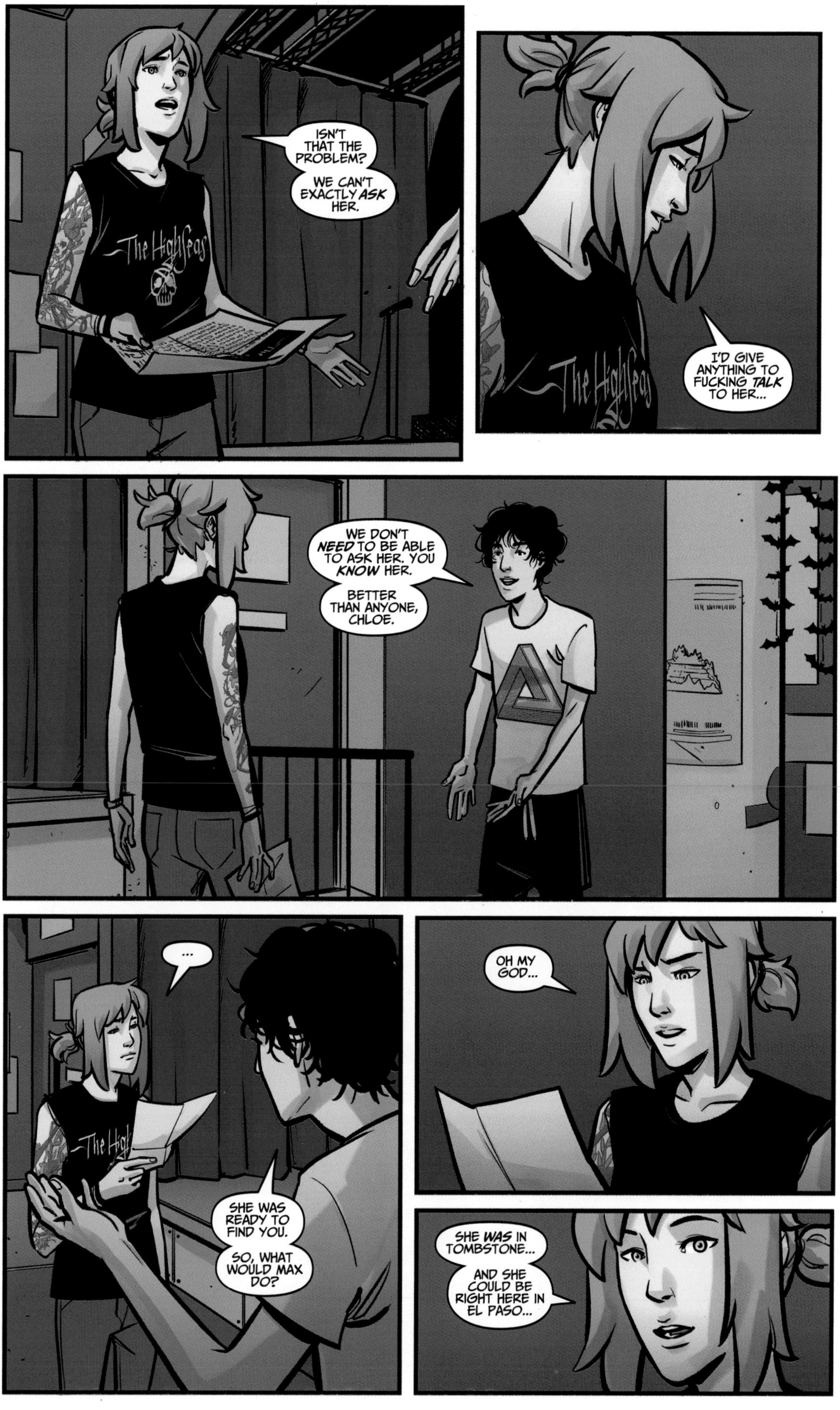
ISN'T THAT THE PROBLEM?
WE CAN'T EXACTLY *ASK* HER.
The HighSeas
I'D GIVE ANYTHING TO FUCKING *TALK* TO HER...
WE DON'T *NEED* TO BE ABLE TO ASK HER. YOU *KNOW* HER.
BETTER THAN ANYONE, CHLOE.
...
SHE WAS READY TO FIND YOU.
SO, WHAT WOULD MAX DO?
OH MY GOD...
SHE *WAS* IN TOMBSTONE...
AND SHE COULD BE RIGHT HERE IN EL PASO...

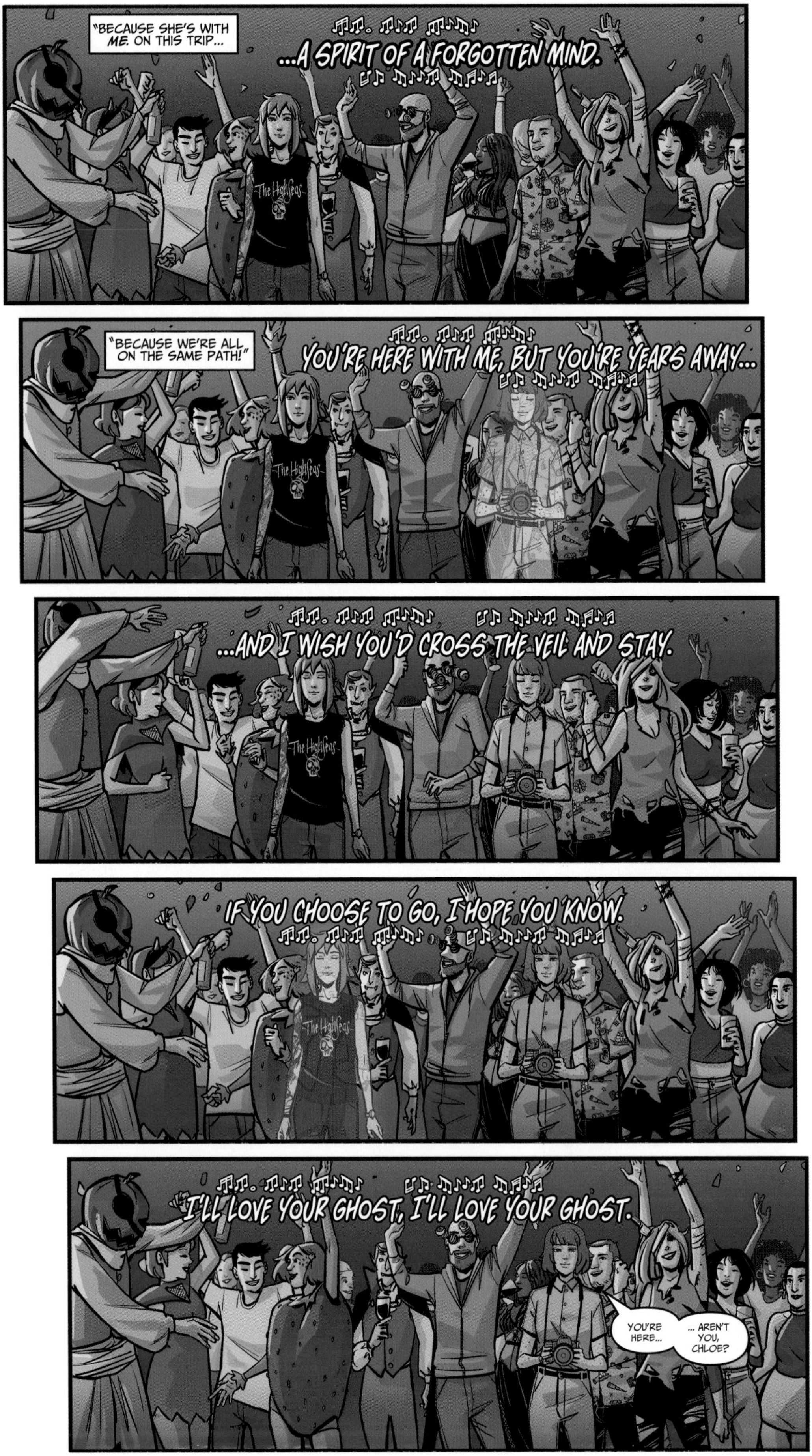
"BECAUSE SHE'S WITH *ME*. ON THIS TRIP...
...A SPIRIT OF A FORGOTTEN MIND.
"BECAUSE WE'RE ALL ON THE SAME PATH!"
YOU'RE HERE WITH ME, BUT YOU'RE YEARS AWAY...
...AND I WISH YOU'D CROSS THE VEIL AND STAY.
IF YOU CHOOSE TO GO, I HOPE YOU KNOW.
I'LL LOVE YOUR GHOST, I'LL LOVE YOUR GHOST.
YOU'RE HERE...
... AREN'T YOU, CHLOE?

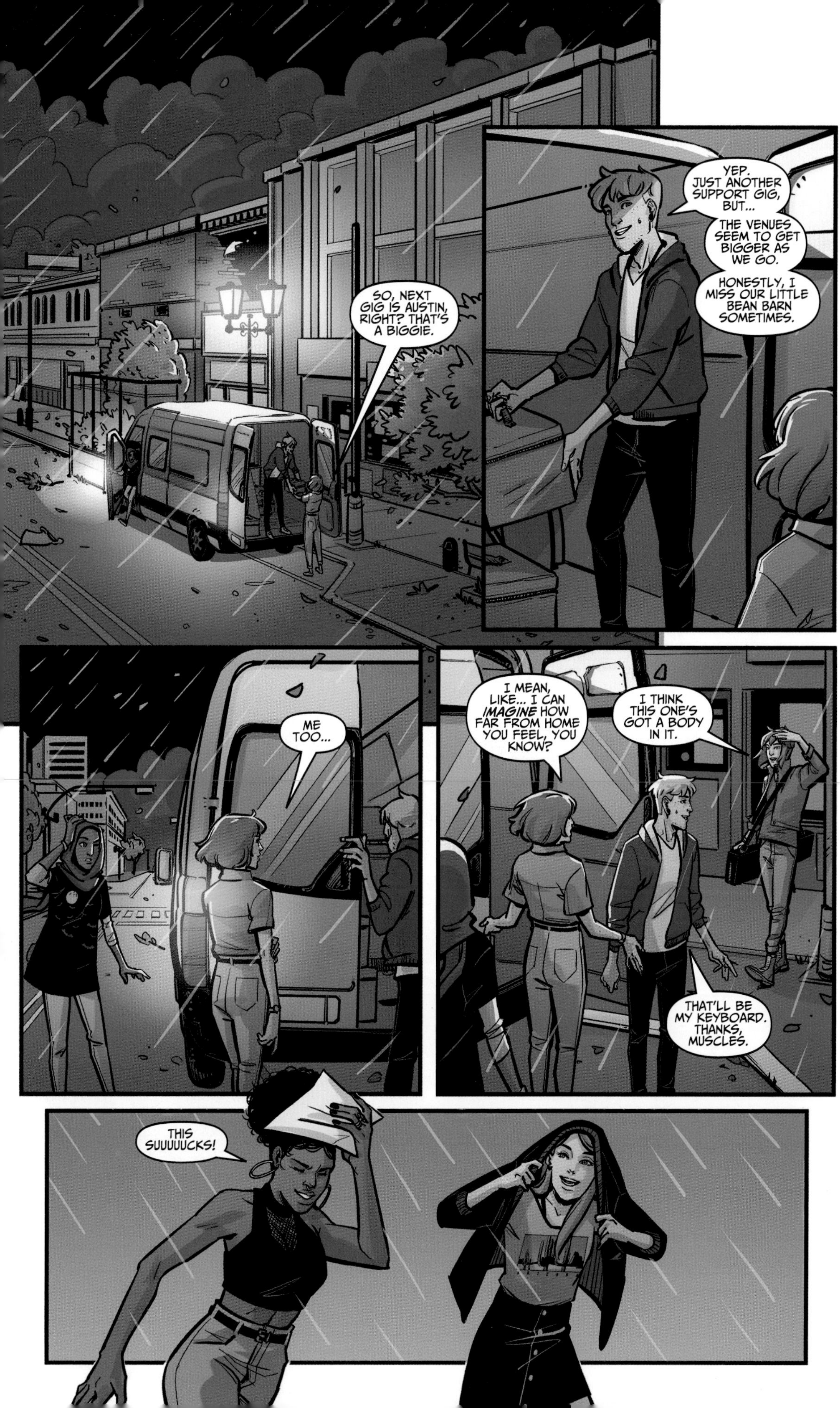
SO, NEXT GIG IS AUSTIN, RIGHT? THAT'S A BIGGIE.
YEP. JUST ANOTHER SUPPORT GIG, BUT...
THE VENUES SEEM TO GET BIGGER AS WE GO.
HONESTLY, I MISS OUR LITTLE BEAN BARN SOMETIMES.
ME TOO...
I MEAN, LIKE... I CAN *IMAGINE* HOW FAR FROM HOME YOU FEEL, YOU KNOW?
I THINK THIS ONE'S GOT A BODY IN IT.
THAT'LL BE MY KEYBOARD. THANKS, MUSCLES.
THIS SUUUUUCKS!

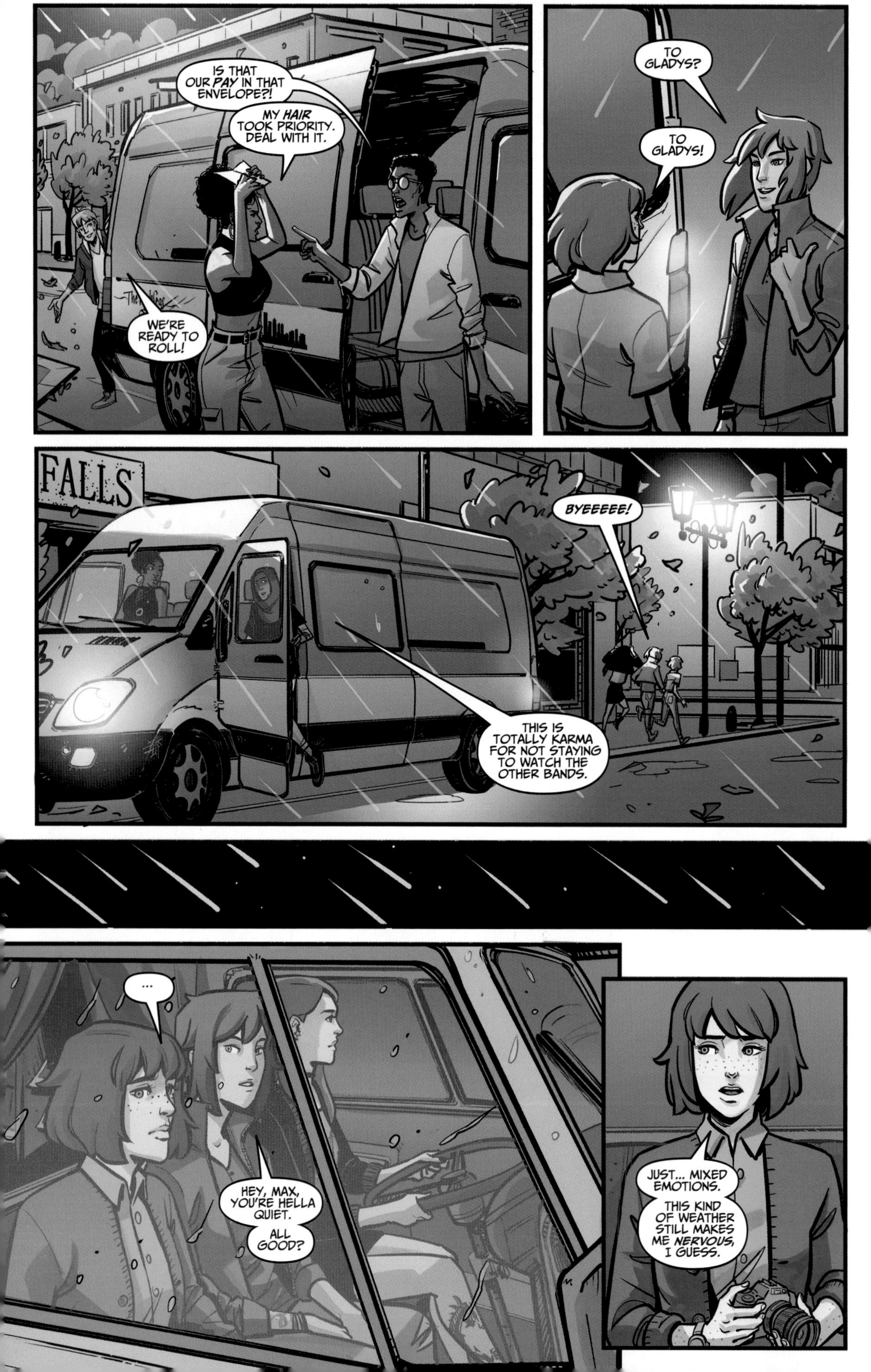
IS THAT OUR *PAY* IN THAT ENVELOPE?!
MY *HAIR* TOOK PRIORITY. DEAL WITH IT.
WE'RE READY TO ROLL!
TO GLADYS?
TO GLADYS!
FALLS
BYEEEEE!
THIS IS TOTALLY KARMA FOR NOT STAYING TO WATCH THE OTHER BANDS.
...
HEY, MAX, YOU'RE HELLA QUIET.
ALL GOOD?
JUST... MIXED EMOTIONS.
THIS KIND OF WEATHER STILL MAKES ME *NERVOUS,* I GUESS.

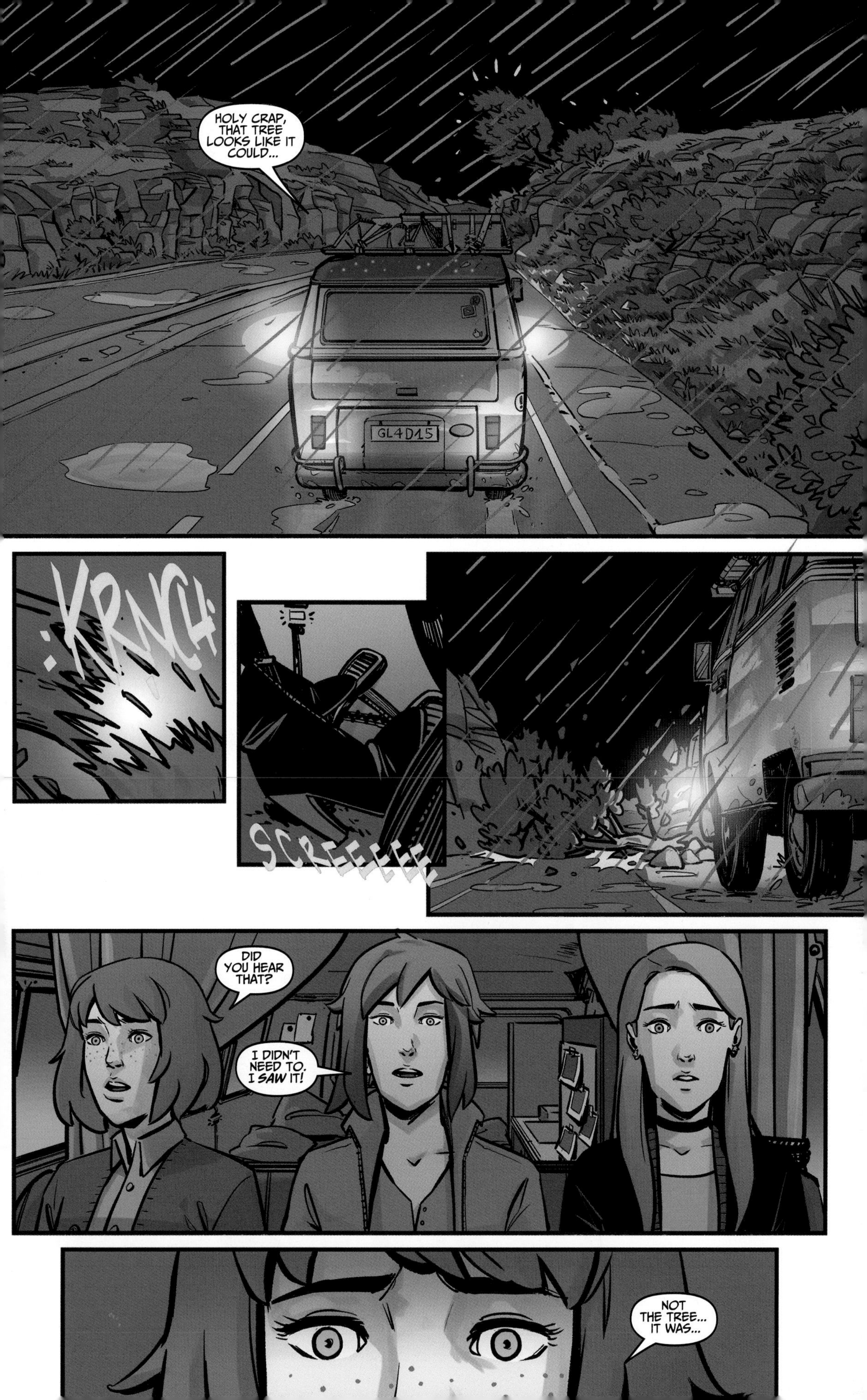
HOLY CRAP, THAT TREE LOOKS LIKE IT COULD...
GL4D15
KRNCH
SCREEEEE
DID YOU HEAR THAT?
I DIDN'T NEED TO. I *SAW* IT!
NOT THE TREE... IT WAS...

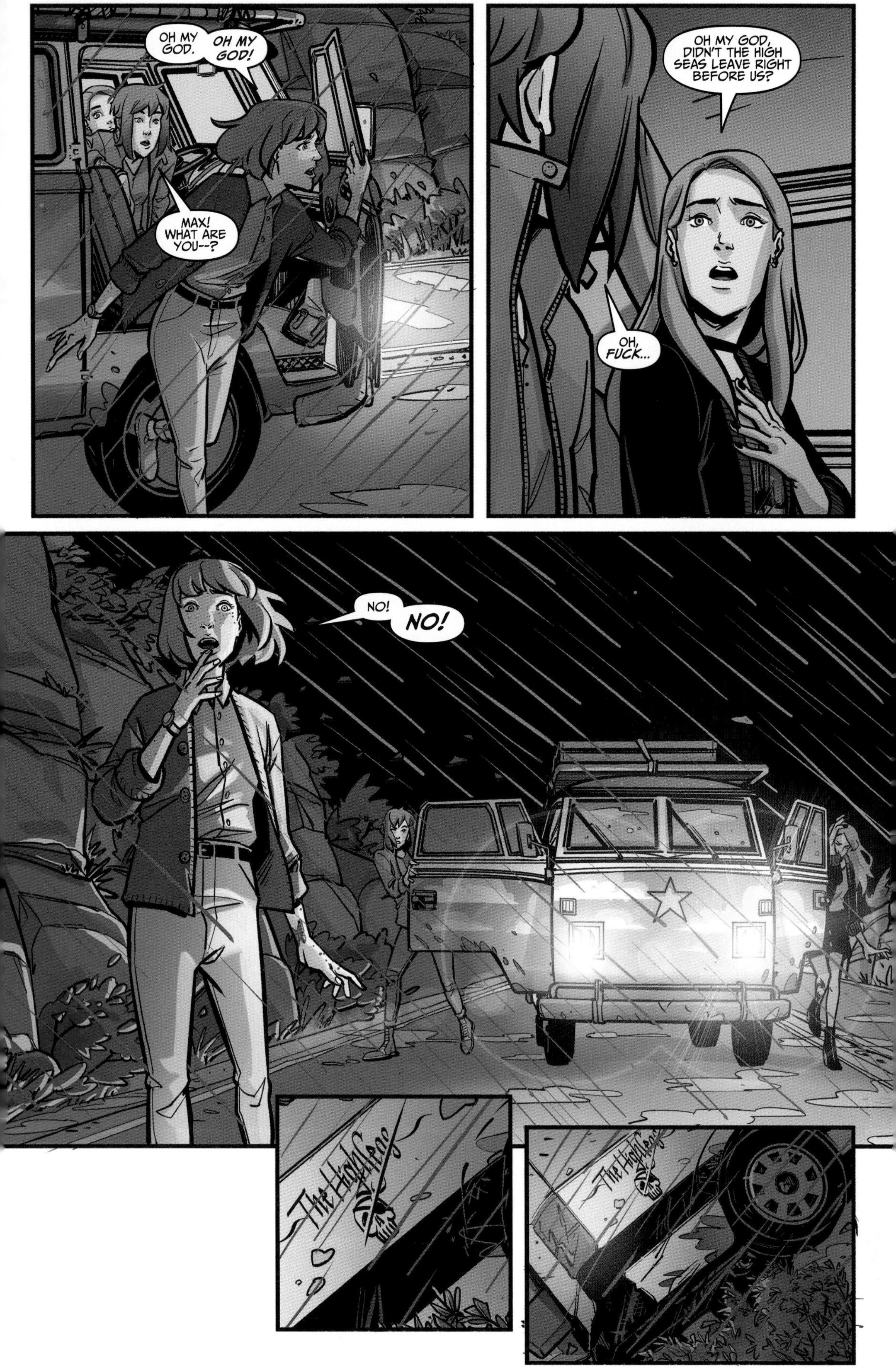
OH MY GOD.
OH MY GOD!
MAX! WHAT ARE YOU--?
OH MY GOD, DIDN'T THE HIGH SEAS LEAVE RIGHT BEFORE US?
OH, FUCK...
NO!
NO!
The High Seas
The High Seas

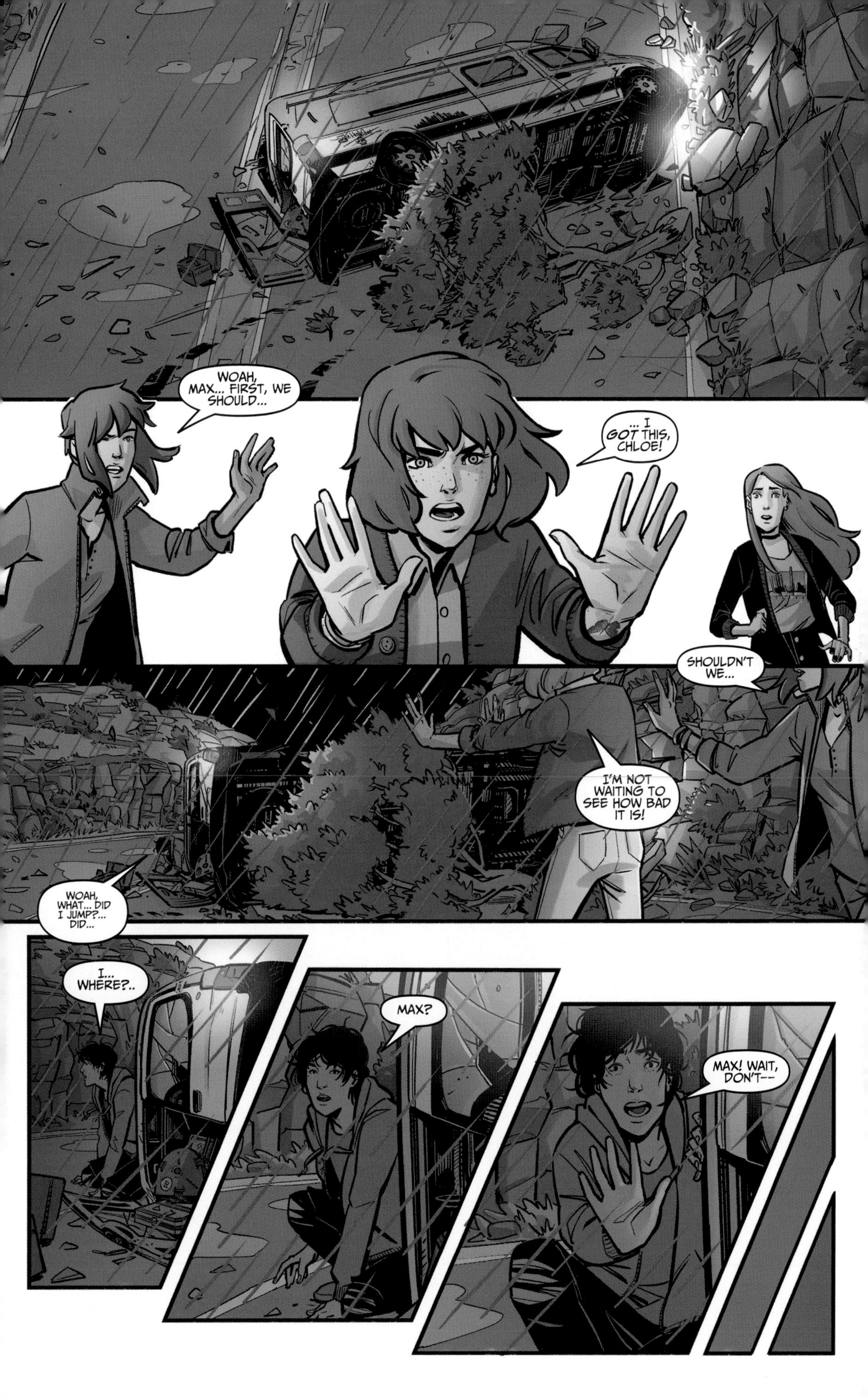
WOAH, MAX... FIRST, WE SHOULD...
... I GOT THIS, CHLOE!
SHOULDN'T WE...
I'M NOT WAITING TO SEE HOW BAD IT IS!
WOAH, WHAT... DID I JUMP?... DID...
I... WHERE?..
MAX?
MAX! WAIT, DON'T--

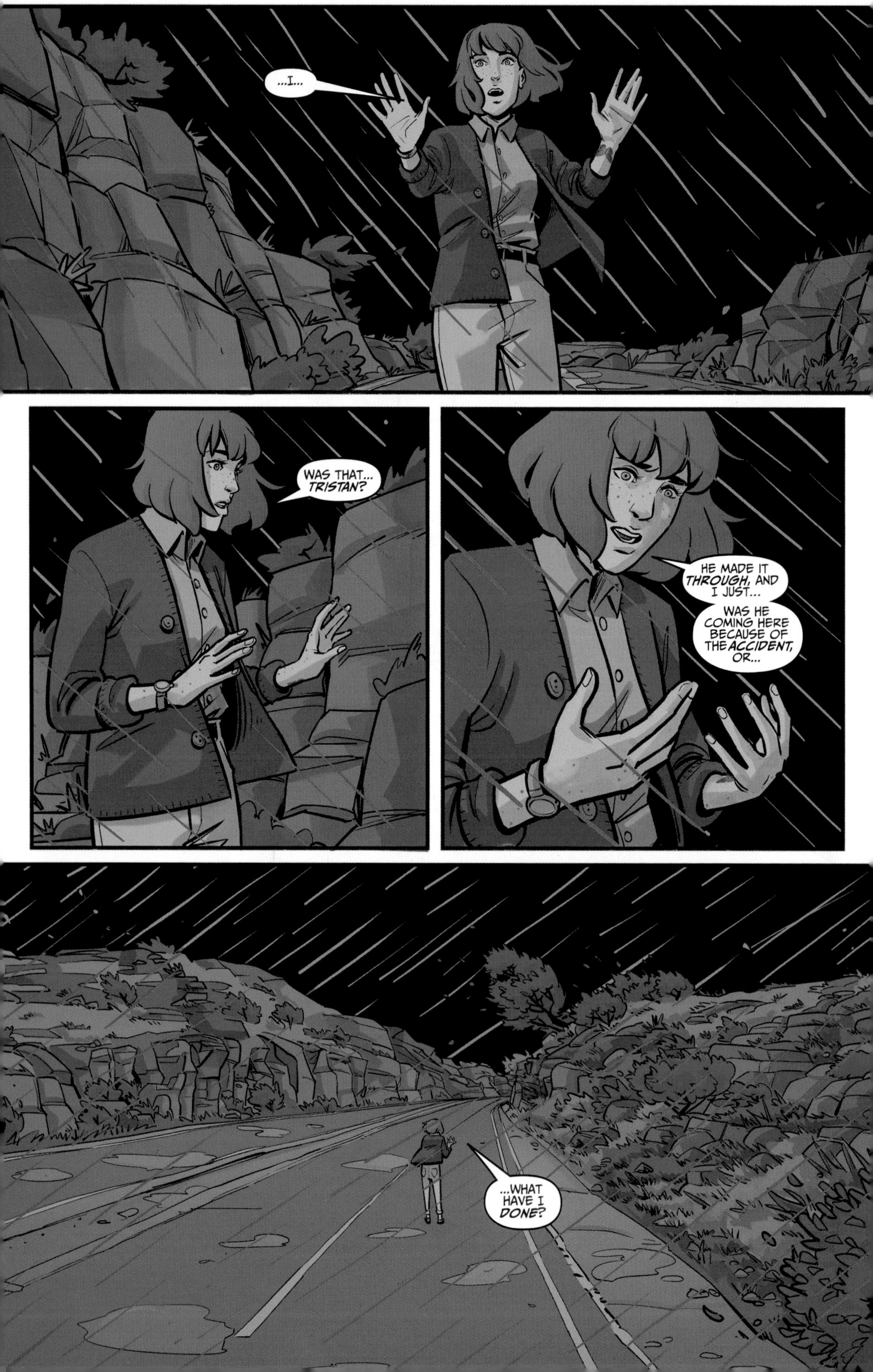
...I...
WAS THAT... *TRISTAN?*
HE MADE IT *THROUGH,* AND I JUST...
WAS HE COMING HERE BECAUSE OF THE *ACCIDENT,* OR...
...WHAT HAVE I *DONE?*

CHAPTER 4

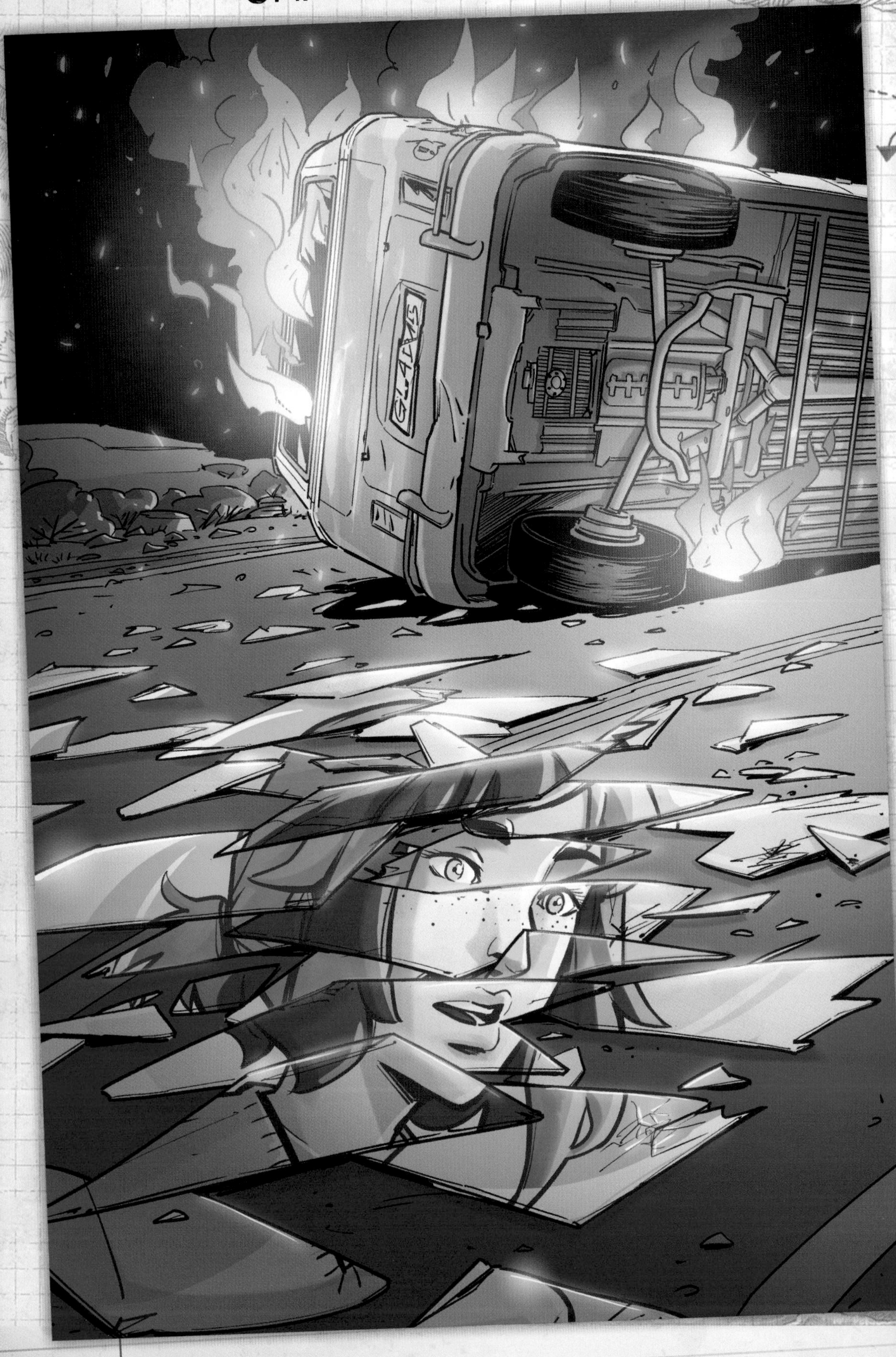

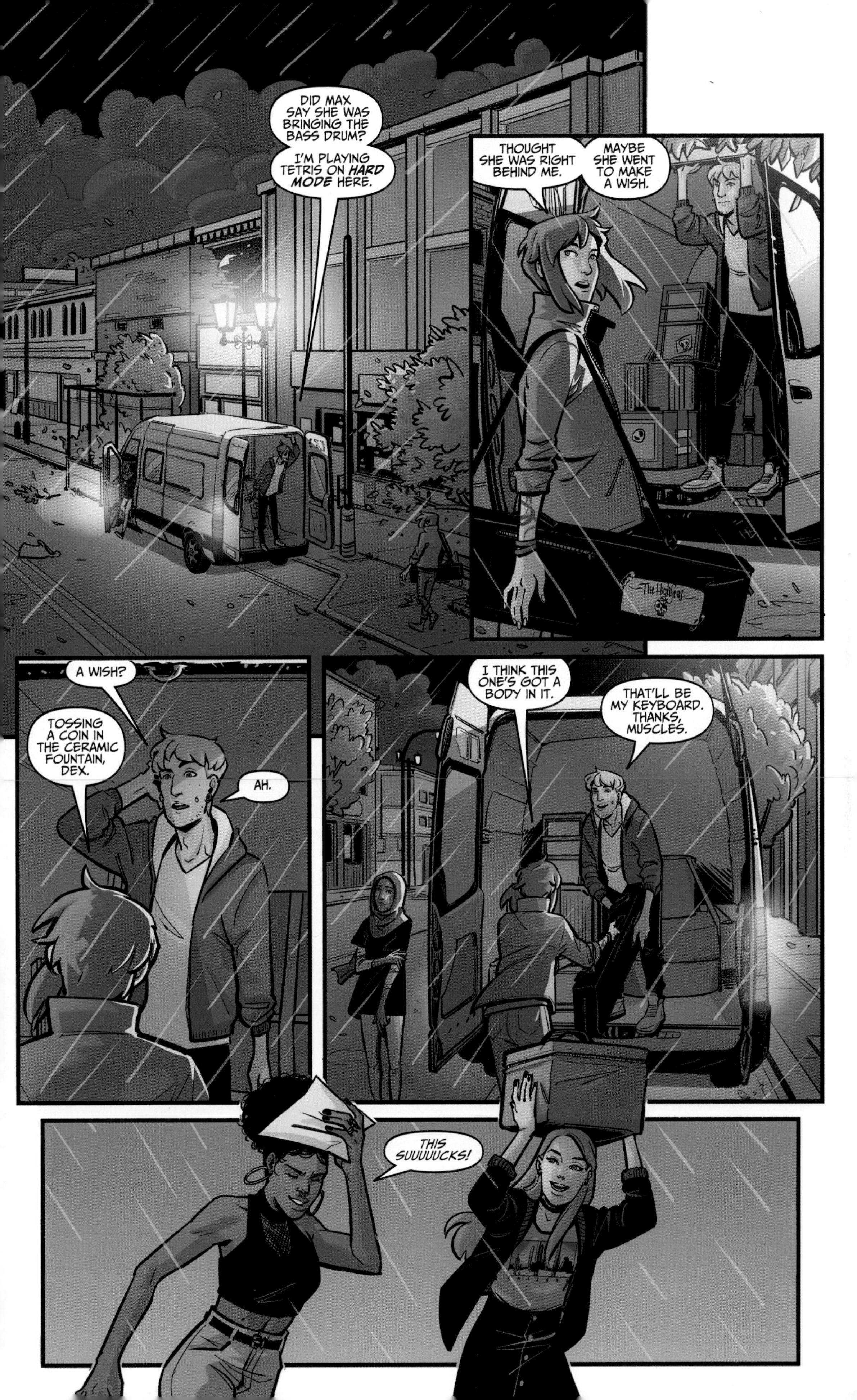
DID MAX SAY SHE WAS BRINGING THE BASS DRUM?
I'M PLAYING TETRIS ON **HARD MODE** HERE.
THOUGHT SHE WAS RIGHT BEHIND ME.
MAYBE SHE WENT TO MAKE A WISH.
The High Seas
A WISH?
TOSSING A COIN IN THE CERAMIC FOUNTAIN, DEX.
AH.
I THINK THIS ONE'S GOT A BODY IN IT.
THAT'LL BE MY KEYBOARD. THANKS, MUSCLES.
THIS SUUUUUCKS!

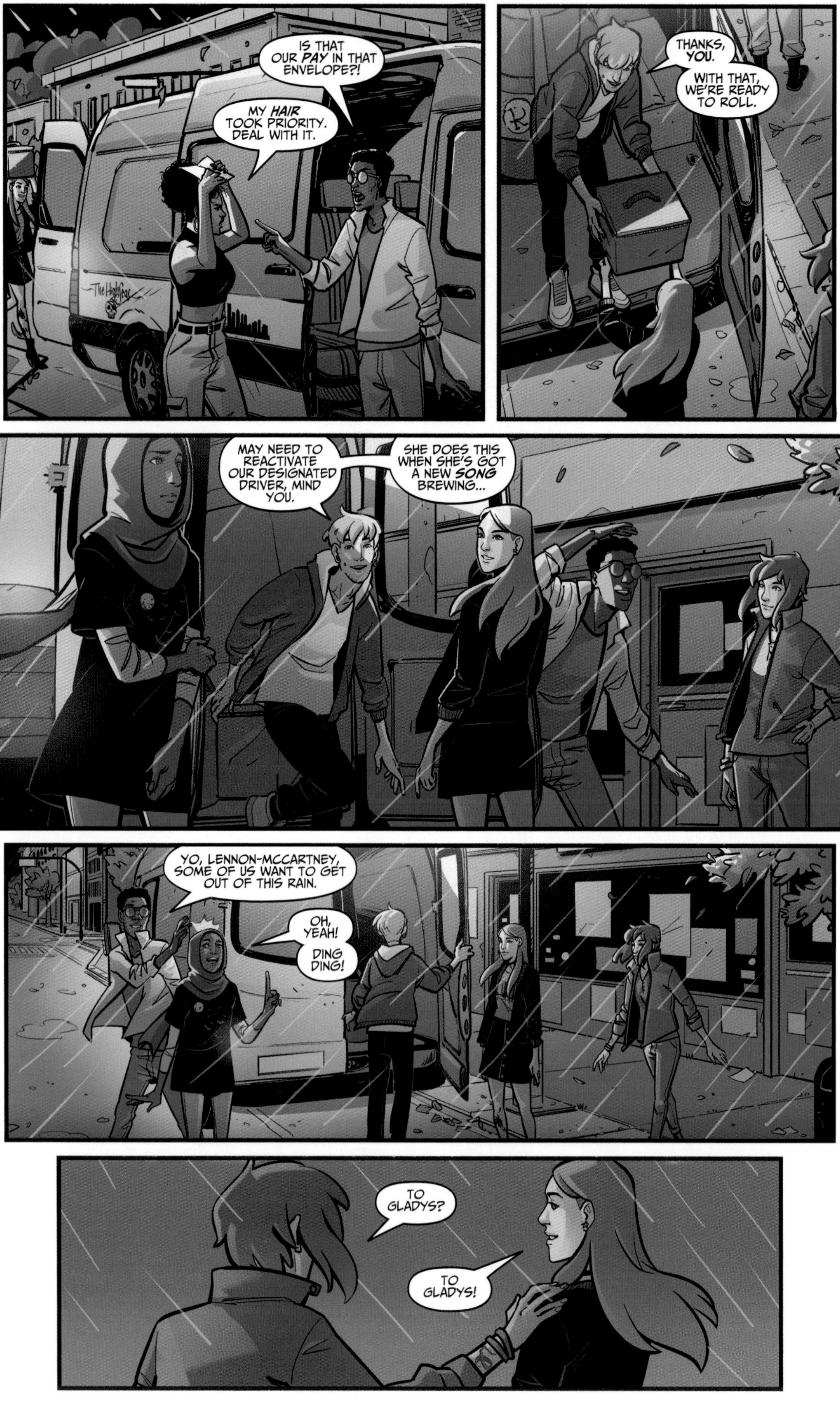
IS THAT OUR PAY IN THAT ENVELOPE?!
MY HAIR TOOK PRIORITY. DEAL WITH IT.
THANKS, YOU.
WITH THAT, WE'RE READY TO ROLL.
MAY NEED TO REACTIVATE OUR DESIGNATED DRIVER, MIND YOU.
SHE DOES THIS WHEN SHE'S GOT A NEW SONG BREWING...
YO, LENNON-MCCARTNEY, SOME OF US WANT TO GET OUT OF THIS RAIN.
OH, YEAH!
DING DING!
TO GLADYS?
TO GLADYS!

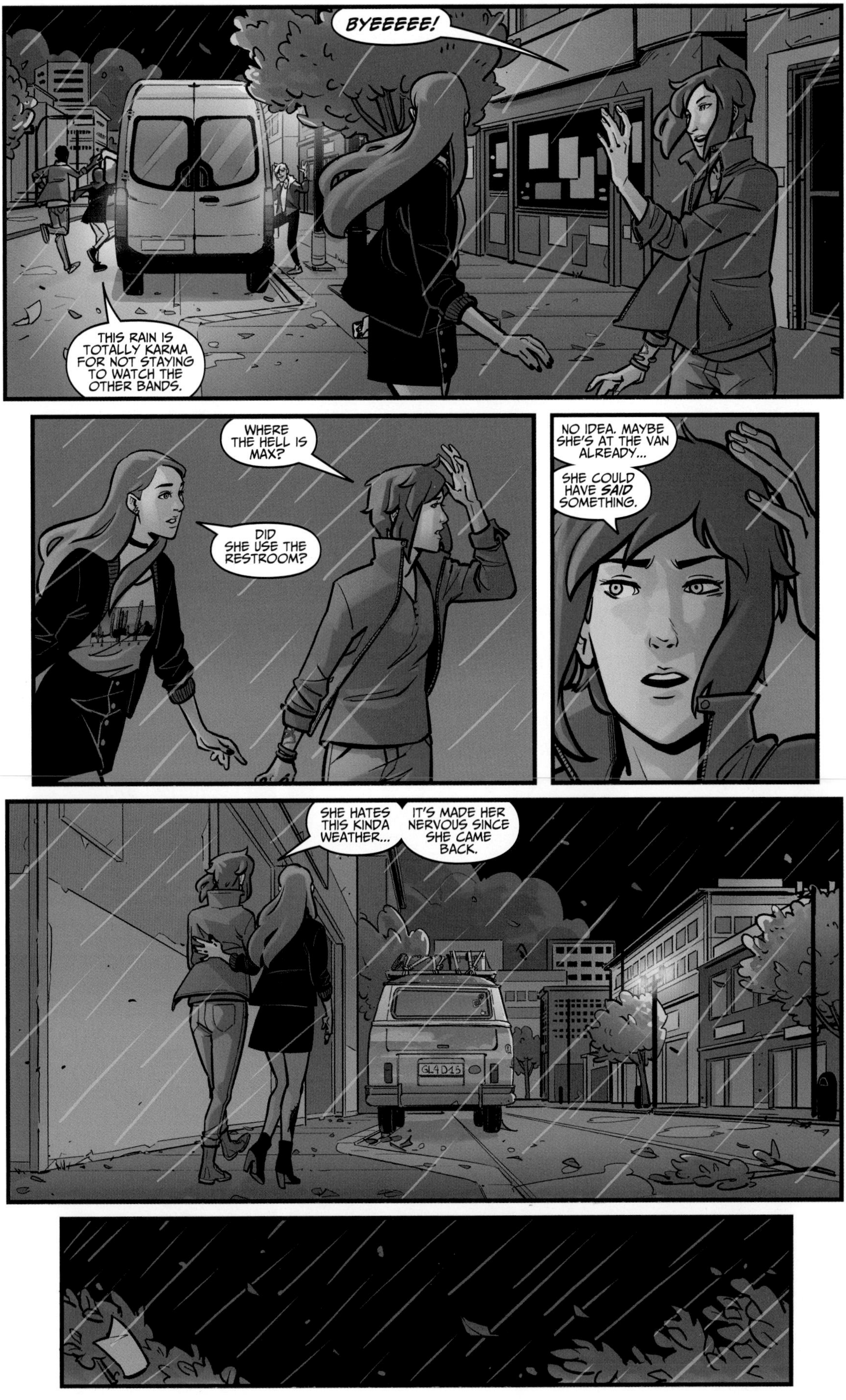
BYEEEEE!
THIS RAIN IS TOTALLY KARMA FOR NOT STAYING TO WATCH THE OTHER BANDS.
WHERE THE HELL IS MAX?
DID SHE USE THE RESTROOM?
NO IDEA. MAYBE SHE'S AT THE VAN ALREADY...
SHE COULD HAVE *SAID* SOMETHING.
SHE HATES THIS KINDA WEATHER...
IT'S MADE HER NERVOUS SINCE SHE CAME BACK.
GL4D15

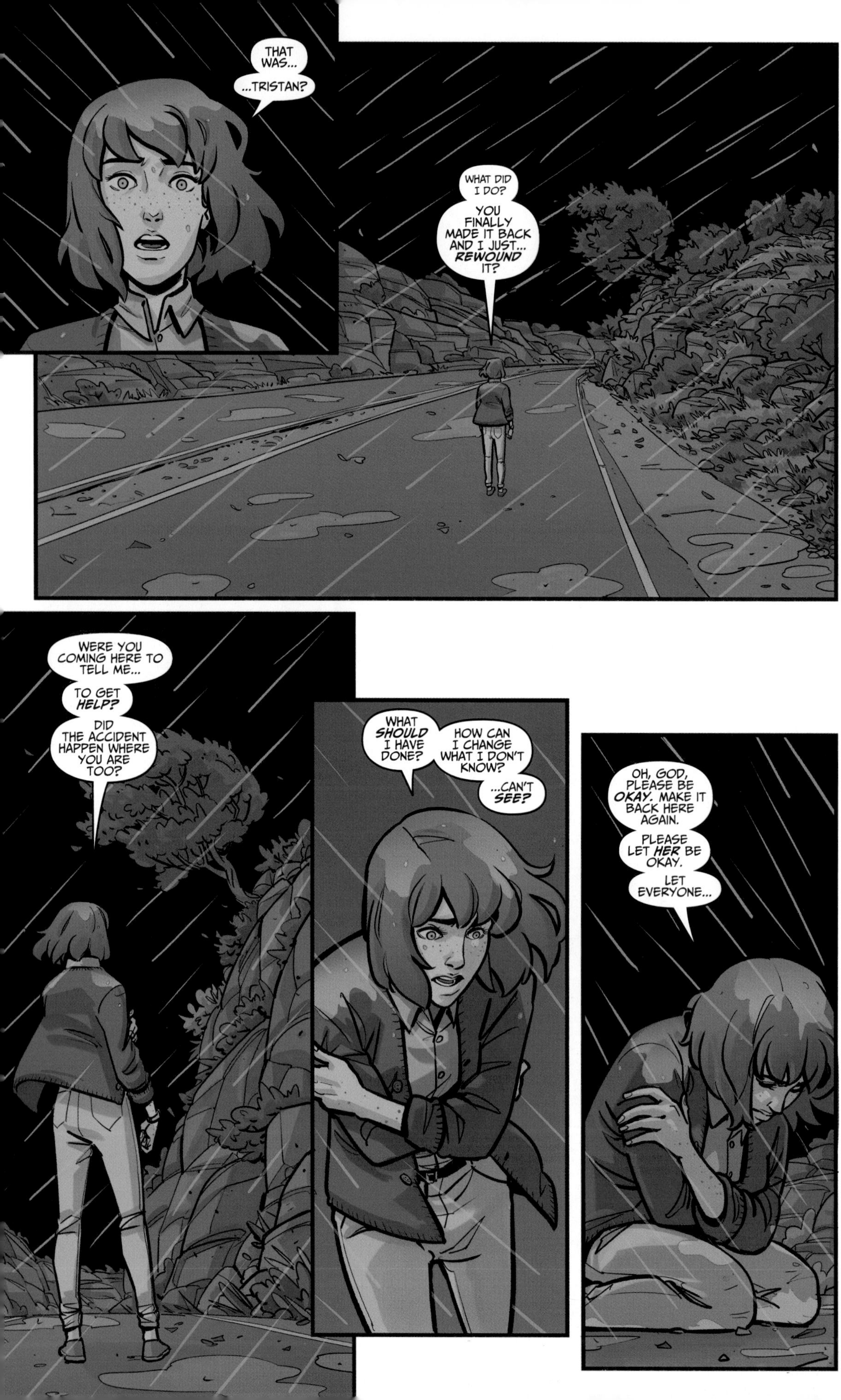
THAT WAS...
...TRISTAN?
WHAT DID I DO?
YOU FINALLY MADE IT BACK AND I JUST... REWOUND IT?
WERE YOU COMING HERE TO TELL ME...
TO GET HELP?
DID THE ACCIDENT HAPPEN WHERE YOU ARE TOO?
WHAT SHOULD I HAVE DONE?
HOW CAN I CHANGE WHAT I DON'T KNOW?
...CAN'T SEE?
OH, GOD, PLEASE BE OKAY. MAKE IT BACK HERE AGAIN.
PLEASE LET HER BE OKAY.
LET EVERYONE...

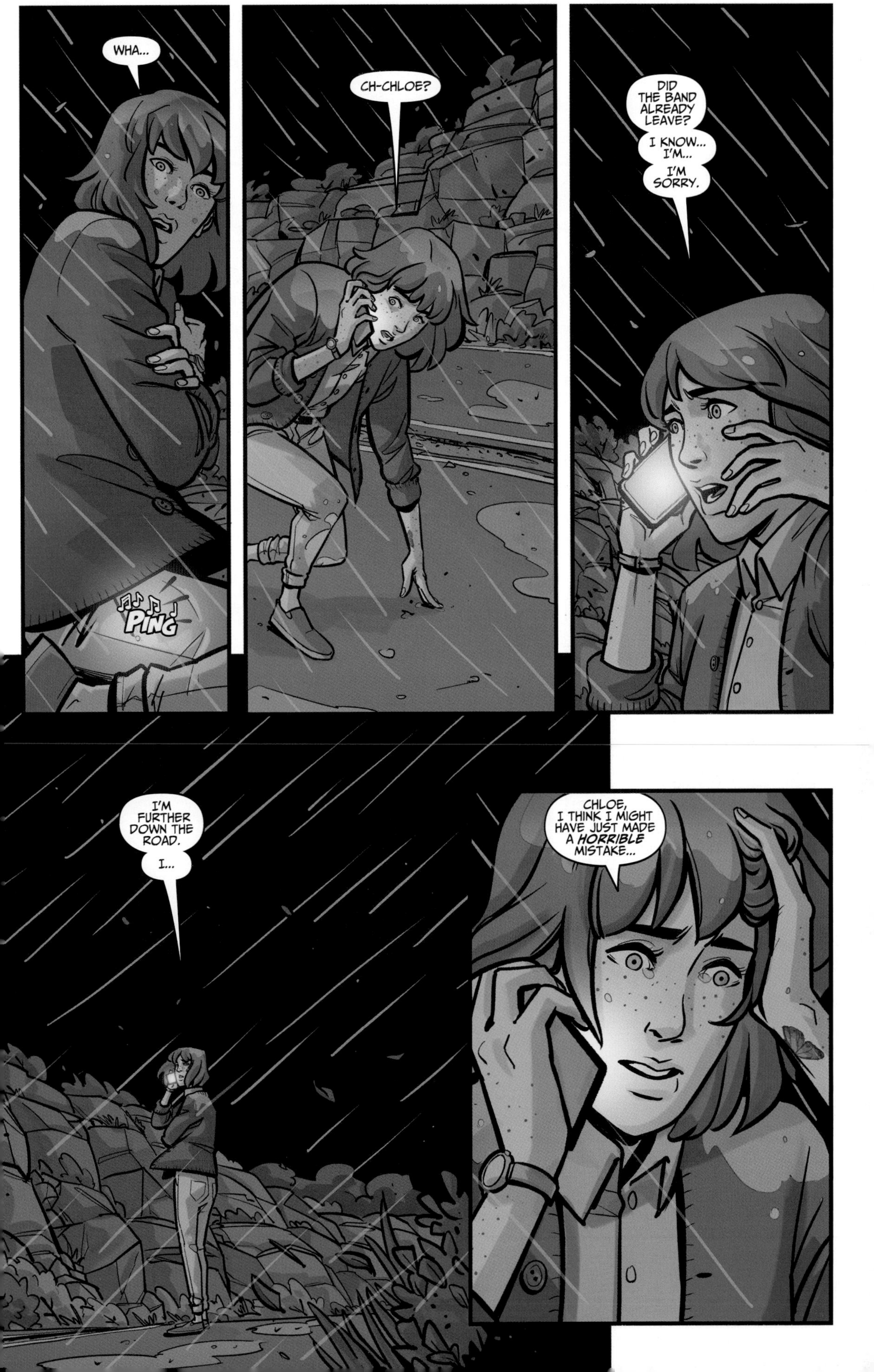
WHA...
PING
CH-CHLOE?
DID THE BAND ALREADY LEAVE?
I KNOW... I'M...
I'M SORRY.
I'M FURTHER DOWN THE ROAD.
I...
CHLOE, I THINK I MIGHT HAVE JUST MADE A *HORRIBLE* MISTAKE...

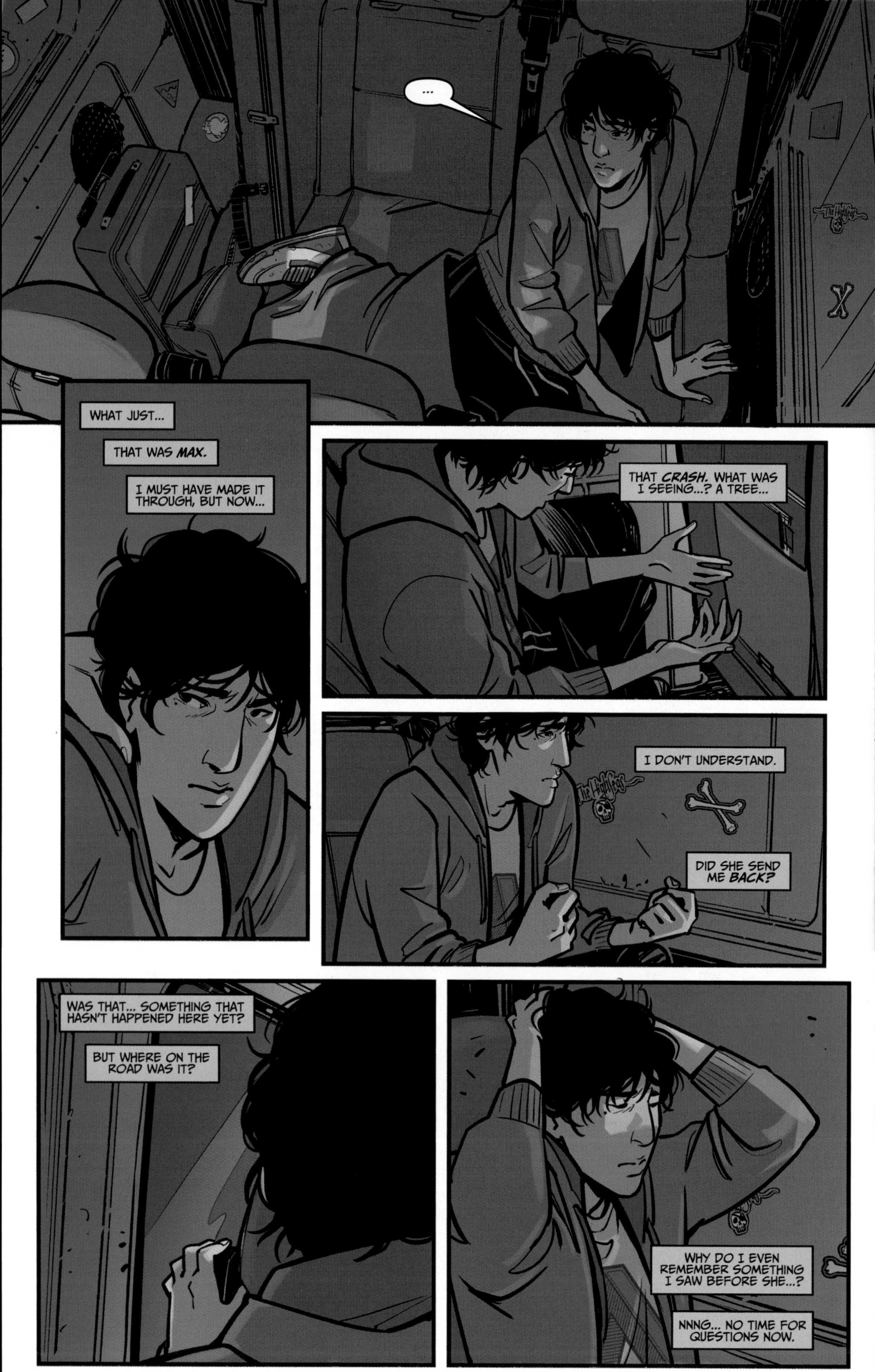
...
WHAT JUST...
THAT WAS MAX.
I MUST HAVE MADE IT THROUGH, BUT NOW...
THAT CRASH. WHAT WAS I SEEING...? A TREE...
I DON'T UNDERSTAND.
DID SHE SEND ME BACK?
WAS THAT... SOMETHING THAT HASN'T HAPPENED HERE YET?
BUT WHERE ON THE ROAD WAS IT?
WHY DO I EVEN REMEMBER SOMETHING I SAW BEFORE SHE...?
NNNG... NO TIME FOR QUESTIONS NOW.

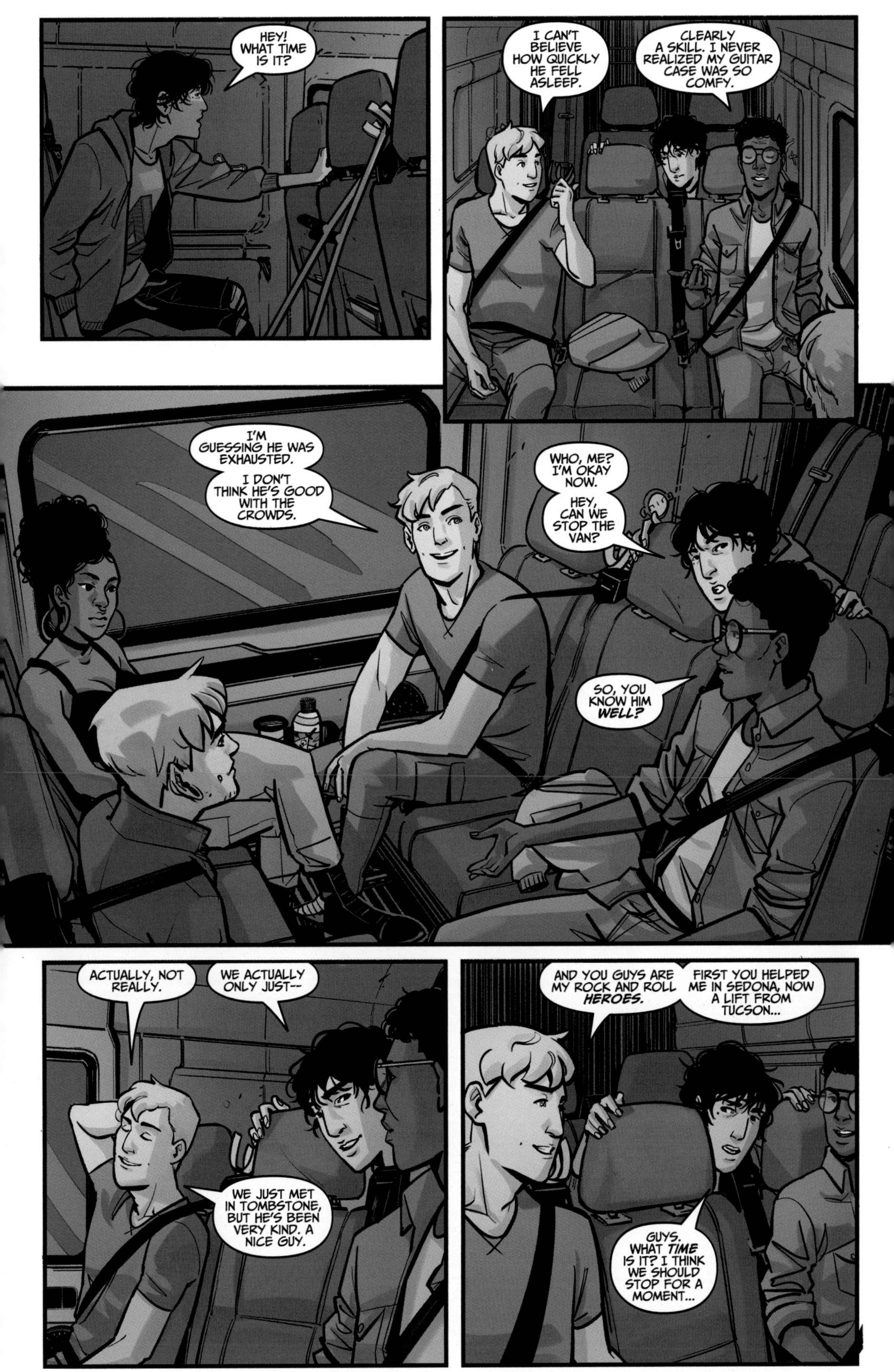
HEY! WHAT TIME IS IT?
I CAN'T BELIEVE HOW QUICKLY HE FELL ASLEEP.
CLEARLY A SKILL. I NEVER REALIZED MY GUITAR CASE WAS SO COMFY.
I'M GUESSING HE WAS EXHAUSTED.
I DON'T THINK HE'S GOOD WITH THE CROWDS.
WHO, ME? I'M OKAY NOW.
HEY, CAN WE STOP THE VAN?
SO, YOU KNOW HIM *WELL?*
ACTUALLY, NOT REALLY.
WE ACTUALLY ONLY JUST--
WE JUST MET IN TOMBSTONE, BUT HE'S BEEN VERY KIND. A NICE GUY.
AND YOU GUYS ARE MY ROCK AND ROLL *HEROES.*
FIRST YOU HELPED ME IN SEDONA, NOW A LIFT FROM TUCSON...
GUYS. WHAT *TIME* IS IT? I THINK WE SHOULD STOP FOR A MOMENT...

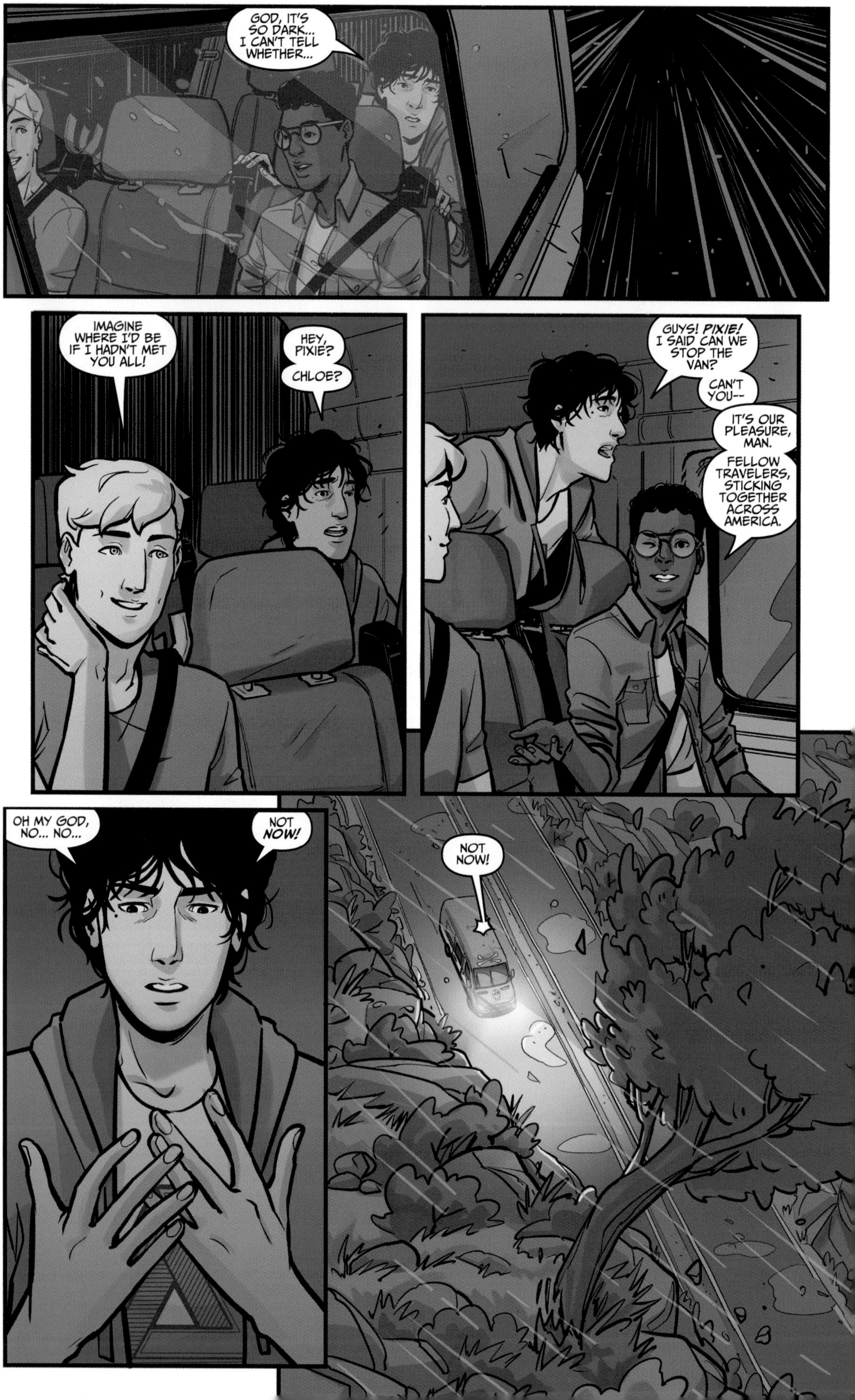
GOD, IT'S SO DARK... I CAN'T TELL WHETHER...
IMAGINE WHERE I'D BE IF I HADN'T MET YOU ALL!
HEY, PIXIE?
CHLOE?
GUYS! *PIXIE!* I SAID CAN WE STOP THE VAN?
CAN'T YOU--
IT'S OUR PLEASURE, MAN.
FELLOW TRAVELERS, STICKING TOGETHER ACROSS AMERICA.
OH MY GOD, NO... NO...
NOT *NOW!*
NOT NOW!

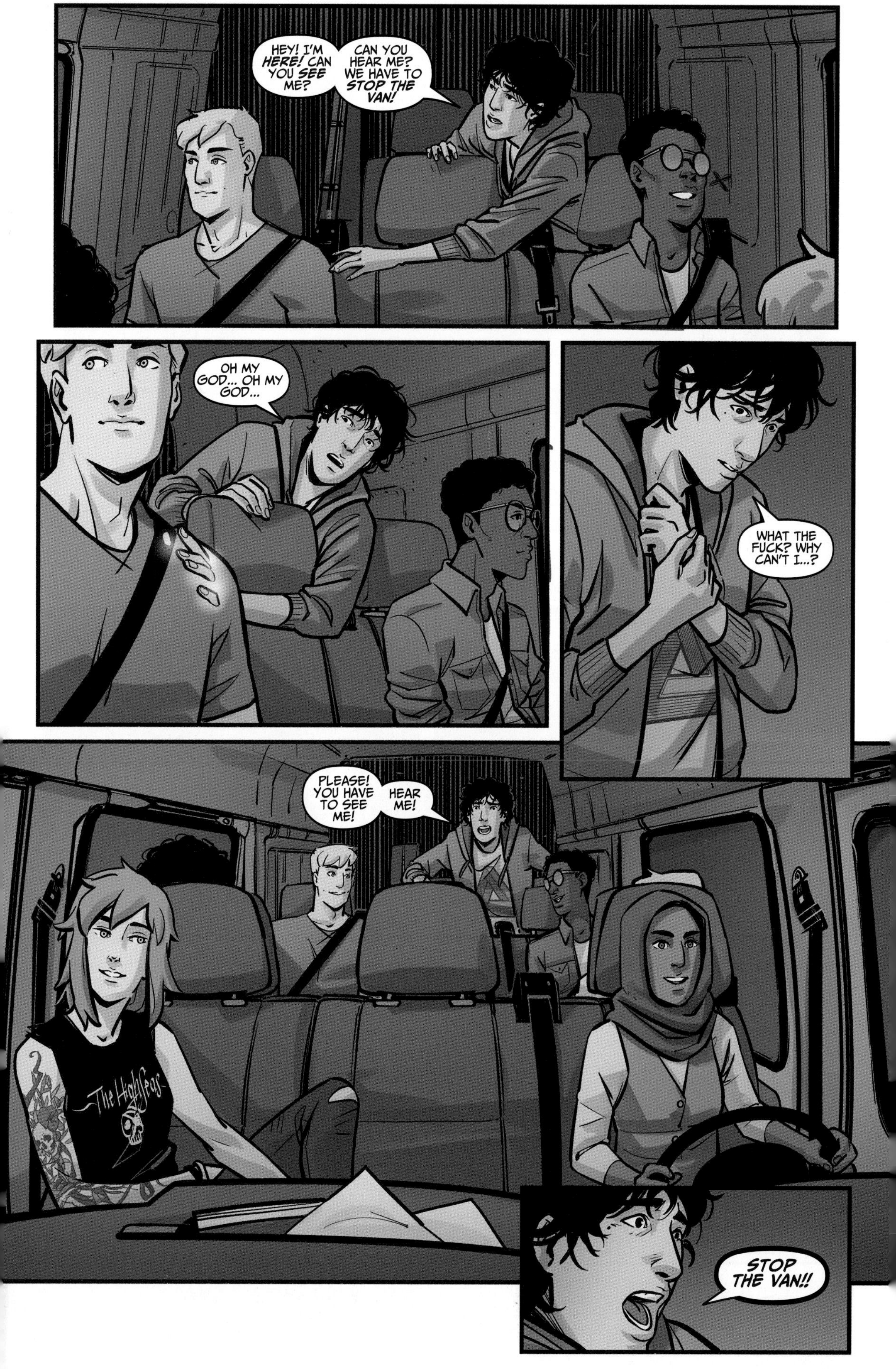

HEY! I'M HERE! CAN YOU SEE ME?
CAN YOU HEAR ME? WE HAVE TO STOP THE VAN!
OH MY GOD... OH MY GOD...
WHAT THE FUCK? WHY CAN'T I...?
PLEASE! YOU HAVE TO SEE ME!
HEAR ME!
The High Seas
STOP THE VAN!!

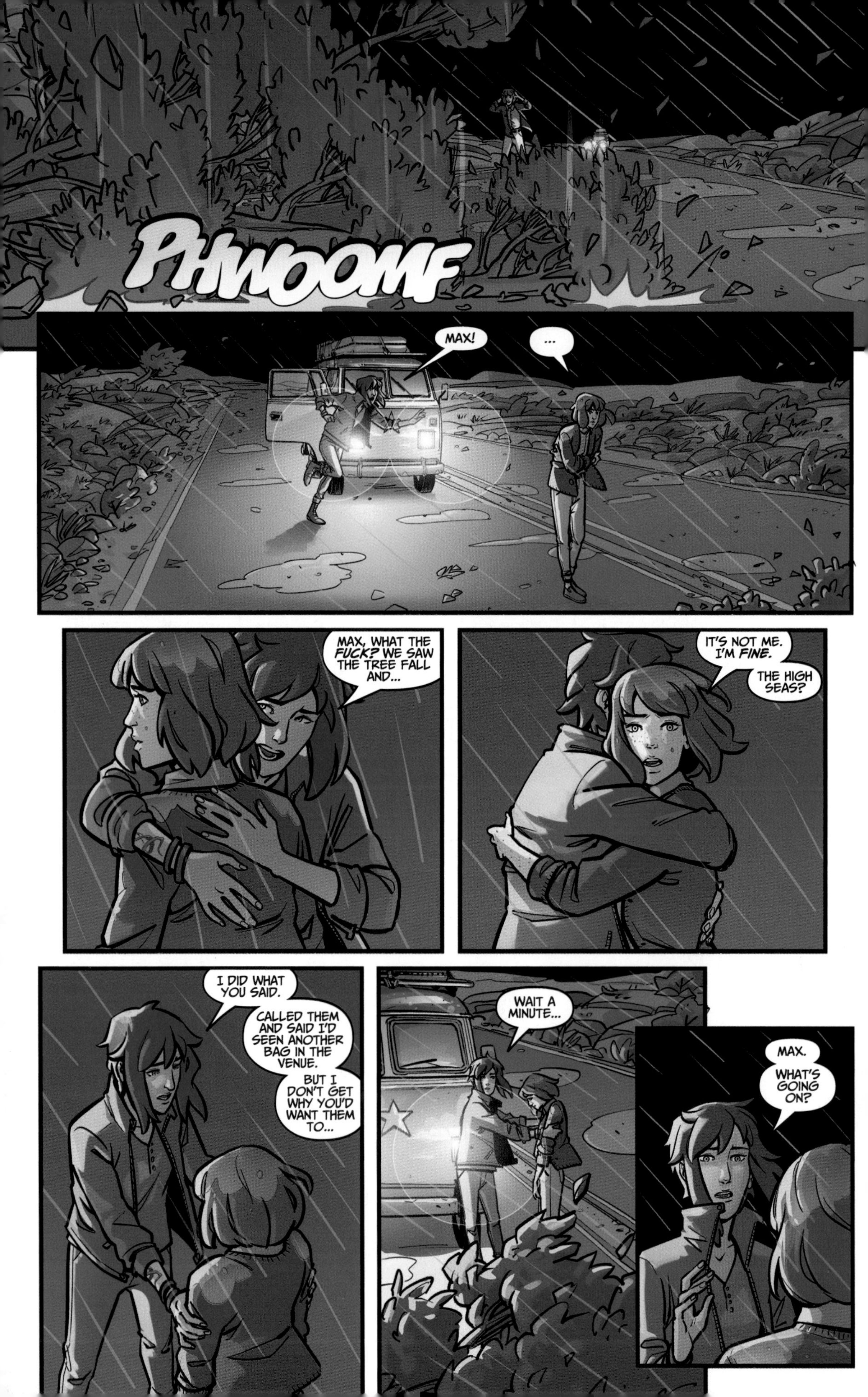
PHWOOMF
MAX!
...
MAX, WHAT THE *FUCK?* WE SAW THE TREE FALL AND...
IT'S NOT ME. I'M *FINE.*
THE HIGH SEAS?
I DID WHAT YOU SAID.
CALLED THEM AND SAID I'D SEEN ANOTHER BAG IN THE VENUE.
BUT I DON'T GET WHY YOU'D WANT THEM TO...
WAIT A MINUTE...
MAX.
WHAT'S GOING ON?

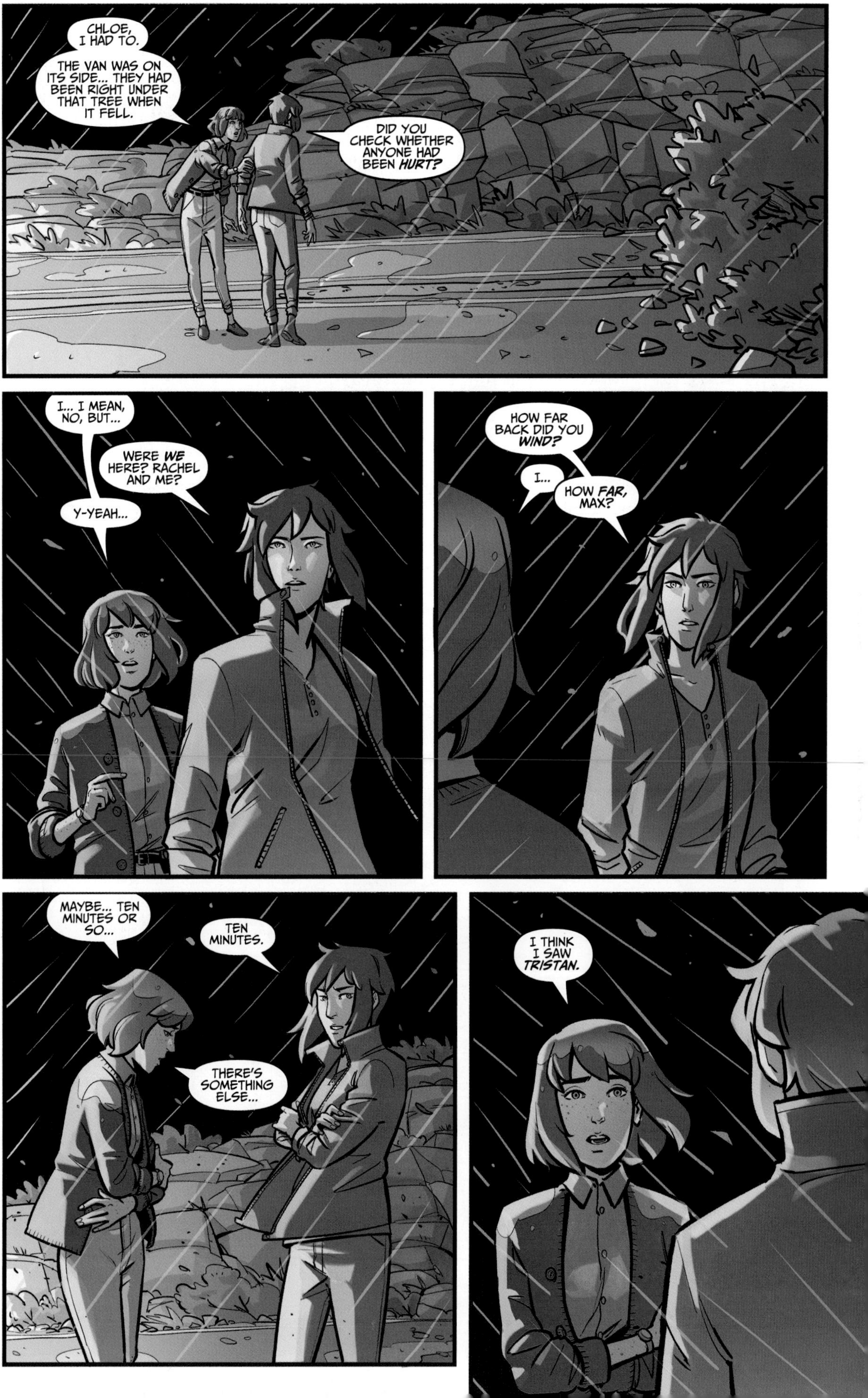
CHLOE, I HAD TO.
THE VAN WAS ON ITS SIDE... THEY HAD BEEN RIGHT UNDER THAT TREE WHEN IT FELL.
DID YOU CHECK WHETHER ANYONE HAD BEEN *HURT?*
I... I MEAN, NO, BUT...
WERE *WE* HERE? RACHEL AND ME?
Y-YEAH...
HOW FAR BACK DID YOU *WIND?*
I...
HOW *FAR,* MAX?
MAYBE... TEN MINUTES OR SO...
TEN MINUTES.
THERE'S SOMETHING ELSE...
I THINK I SAW *TRISTAN.*

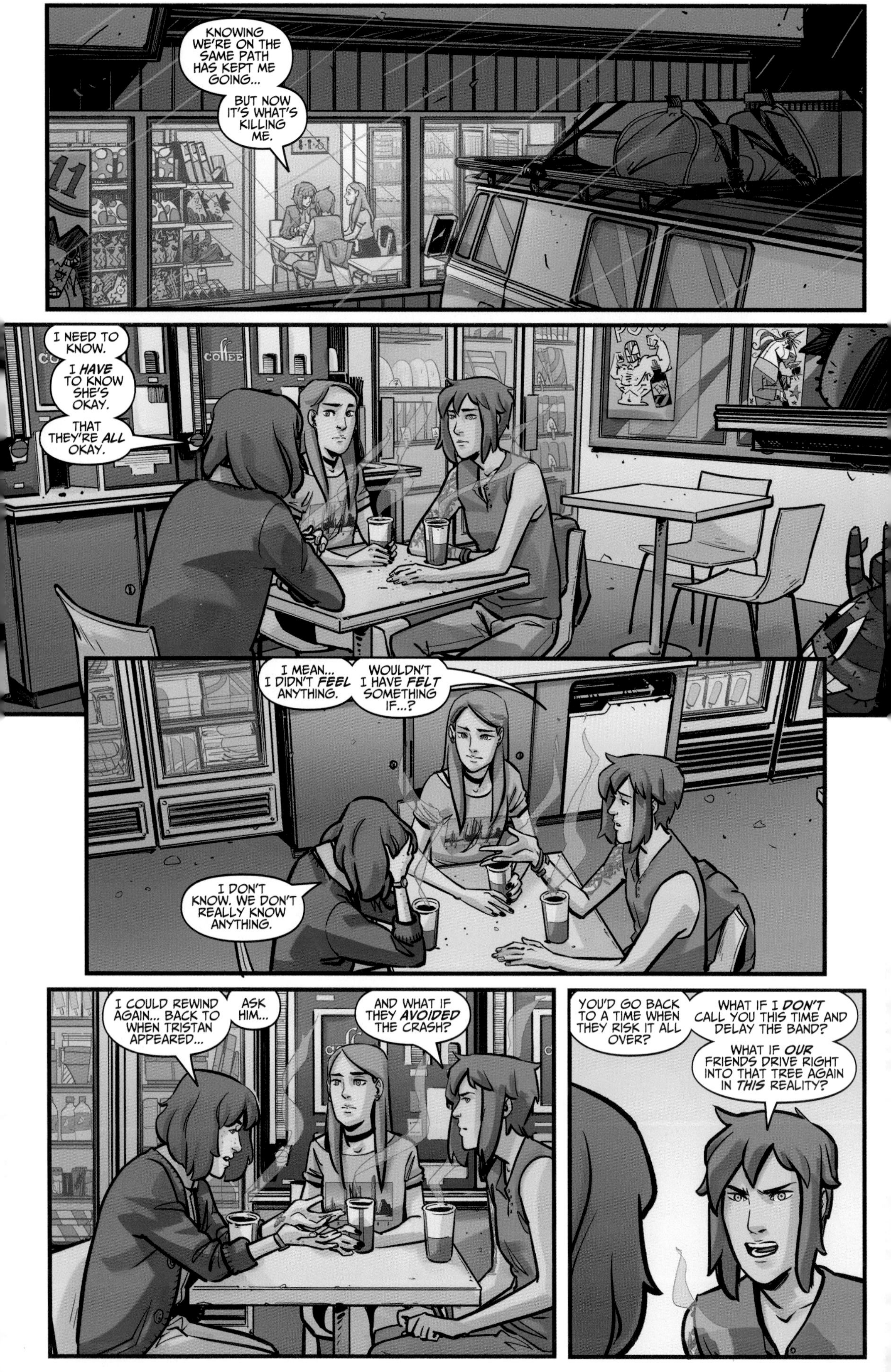
KNOWING WE'RE ON THE SAME PATH HAS KEPT ME GOING...
BUT NOW IT'S WHAT'S KILLING ME.
I NEED TO KNOW.
I *HAVE* TO KNOW SHE'S OKAY.
THAT THEY'RE *ALL* OKAY.
I MEAN... I DIDN'T *FEEL* ANYTHING.
WOULDN'T I HAVE *FELT* SOMETHING IF...?
I DON'T KNOW. WE DON'T REALLY KNOW ANYTHING.
I COULD REWIND AGAIN... BACK TO WHEN TRISTAN APPEARED...
ASK HIM...
AND WHAT IF THEY *AVOIDED* THE CRASH?
YOU'D GO BACK TO A TIME WHEN THEY RISK IT ALL OVER?
WHAT IF I *DON'T* CALL YOU THIS TIME AND DELAY THE BAND?
WHAT IF *OUR* FRIENDS DRIVE RIGHT INTO THAT TREE AGAIN IN *THIS* REALITY?

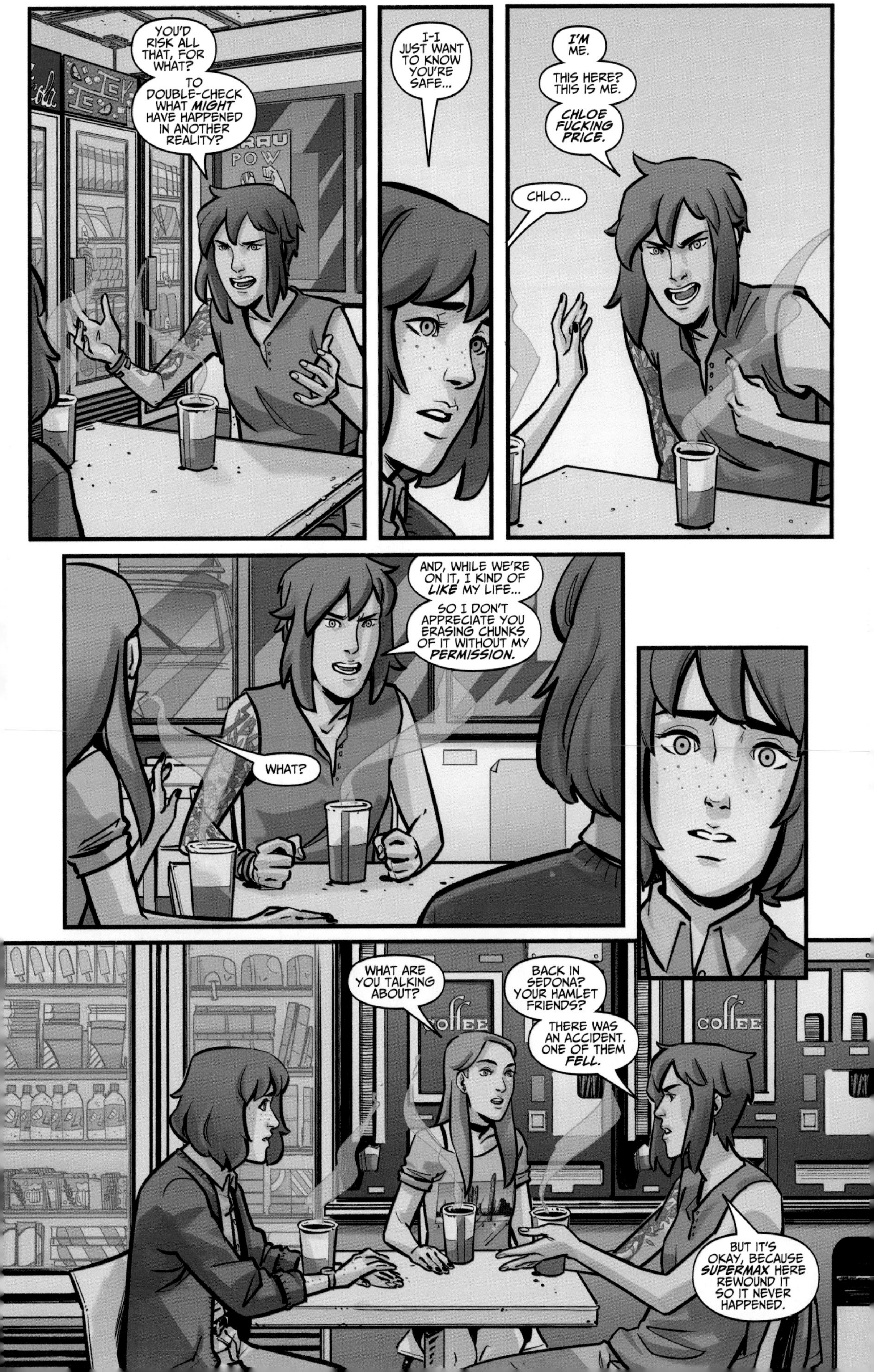

YOU'D RISK ALL THAT, FOR WHAT?
TO DOUBLE-CHECK WHAT MIGHT HAVE HAPPENED IN ANOTHER REALITY?
I-I JUST WANT TO KNOW YOU'RE SAFE...
I'M ME.
THIS HERE? THIS IS ME.
CHLOE FUCKING PRICE.
CHLO...
AND, WHILE WE'RE ON IT, I KIND OF LIKE MY LIFE...
SO I DON'T APPRECIATE YOU ERASING CHUNKS OF IT WITHOUT MY PERMISSION.
WHAT?
WHAT ARE YOU TALKING ABOUT?
BACK IN SEDONA? YOUR HAMLET FRIENDS?
THERE WAS AN ACCIDENT. ONE OF THEM FELL.
BUT IT'S OKAY, BECAUSE SUPERMAX HERE REWOUND IT SO IT NEVER HAPPENED.

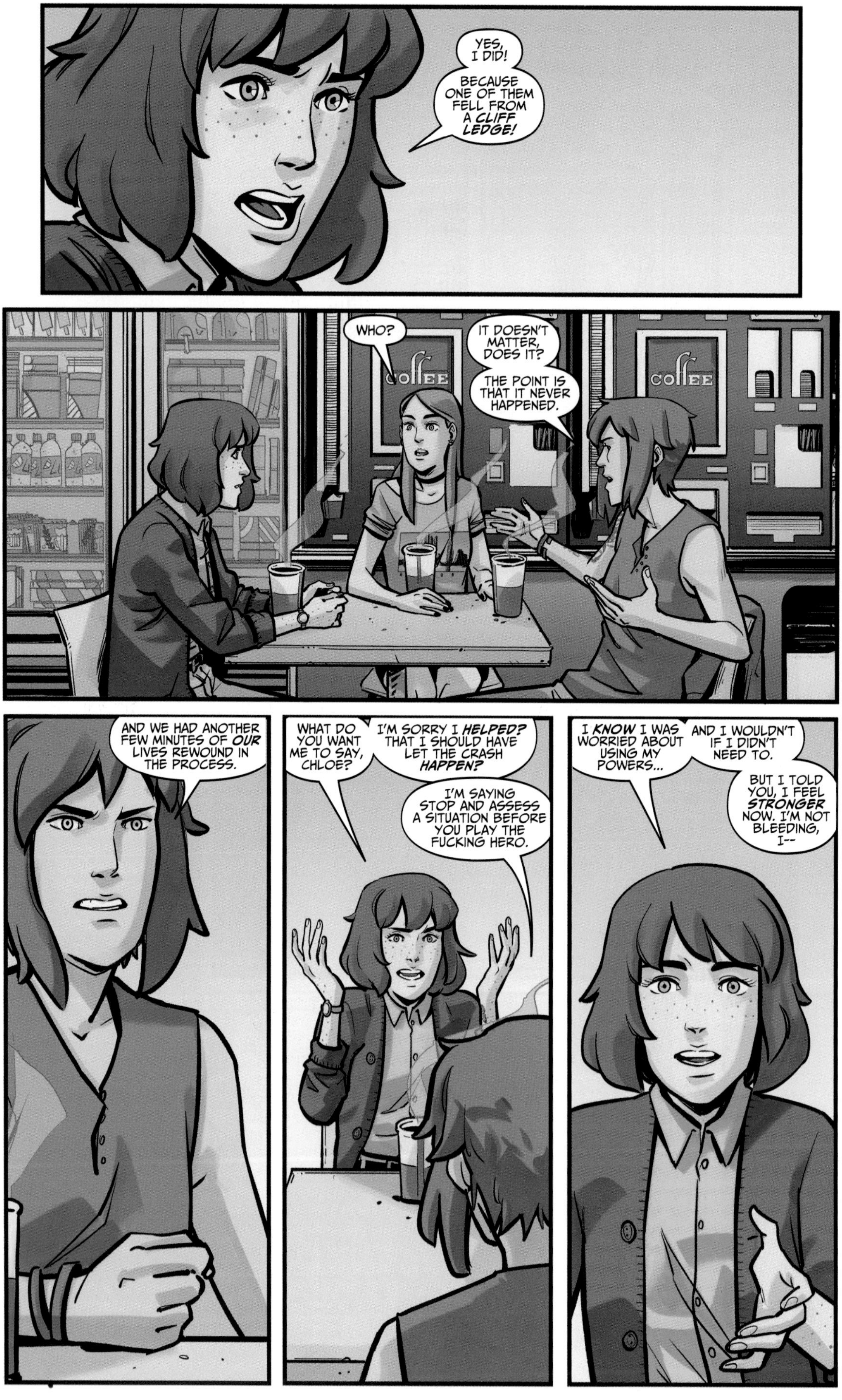
YES, I DID!
BECAUSE ONE OF THEM FELL FROM A CLIFF LEDGE!
WHO?
IT DOESN'T MATTER, DOES IT?
THE POINT IS THAT IT NEVER HAPPENED.
COFFEE
COFFEE
AND WE HAD ANOTHER FEW MINUTES OF OUR LIVES REWOUND IN THE PROCESS.
WHAT DO YOU WANT ME TO SAY, CHLOE?
I'M SORRY I HELPED? THAT I SHOULD HAVE LET THE CRASH HAPPEN?
I'M SAYING STOP AND ASSESS A SITUATION BEFORE YOU PLAY THE FUCKING HERO.
I KNOW I WAS WORRIED ABOUT USING MY POWERS...
AND I WOULDN'T IF I DIDN'T NEED TO.
BUT I TOLD YOU, I FEEL STRONGER NOW. I'M NOT BLEEDING, I--

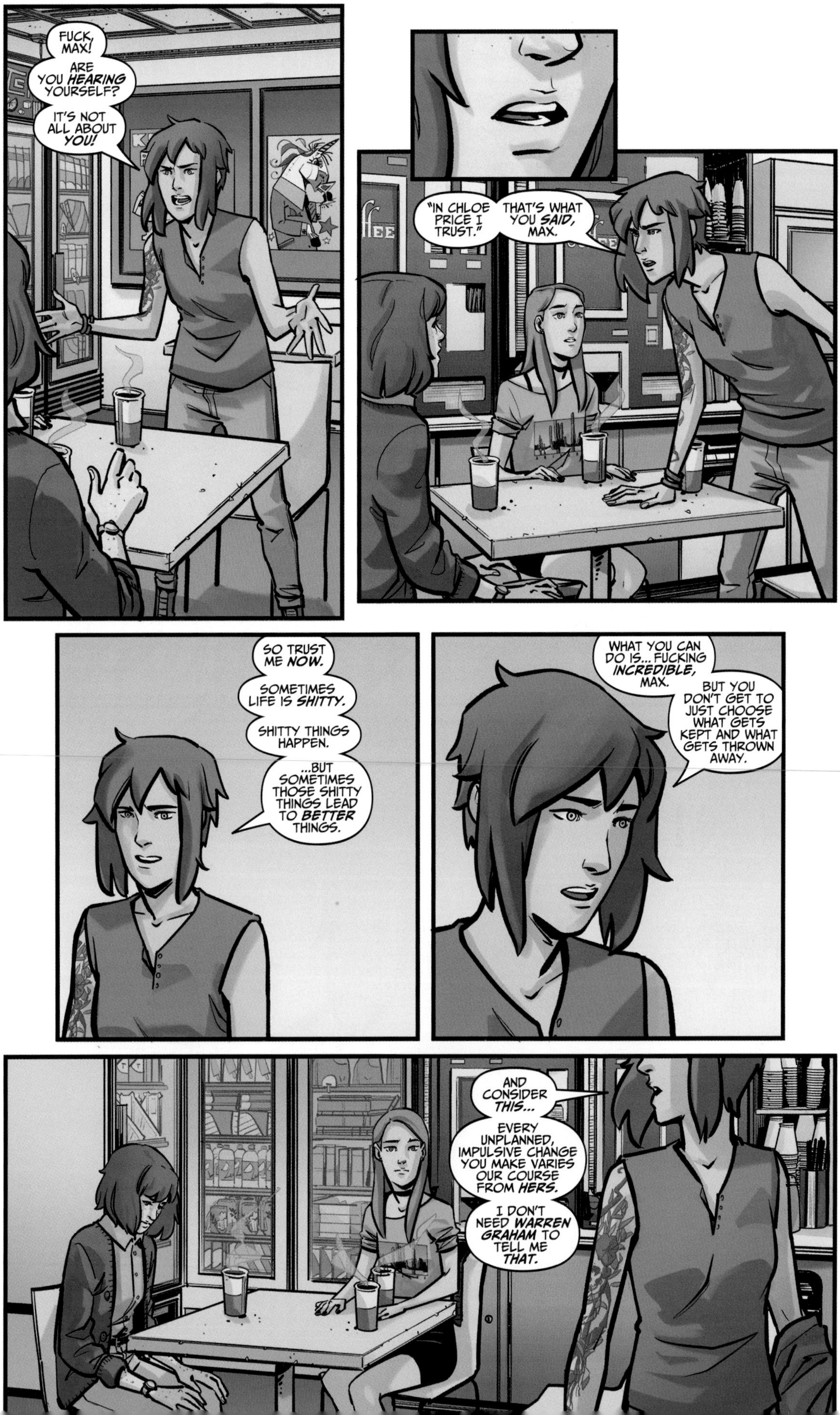
FUCK, MAX!
ARE YOU HEARING YOURSELF?
IT'S NOT ALL ABOUT YOU!
"IN CHLOE PRICE I TRUST."
THAT'S WHAT YOU SAID, MAX.
SO TRUST ME NOW.
SOMETIMES LIFE IS SHITTY.
SHITTY THINGS HAPPEN.
...BUT SOMETIMES THOSE SHITTY THINGS LEAD TO BETTER THINGS.
WHAT YOU CAN DO IS... FUCKING INCREDIBLE, MAX.
BUT YOU DON'T GET TO JUST CHOOSE WHAT GETS KEPT AND WHAT GETS THROWN AWAY.
AND CONSIDER THIS...
EVERY UNPLANNED, IMPULSIVE CHANGE YOU MAKE VARIES OUR COURSE FROM HERS.
I DON'T NEED WARREN GRAHAM TO TELL ME THAT.

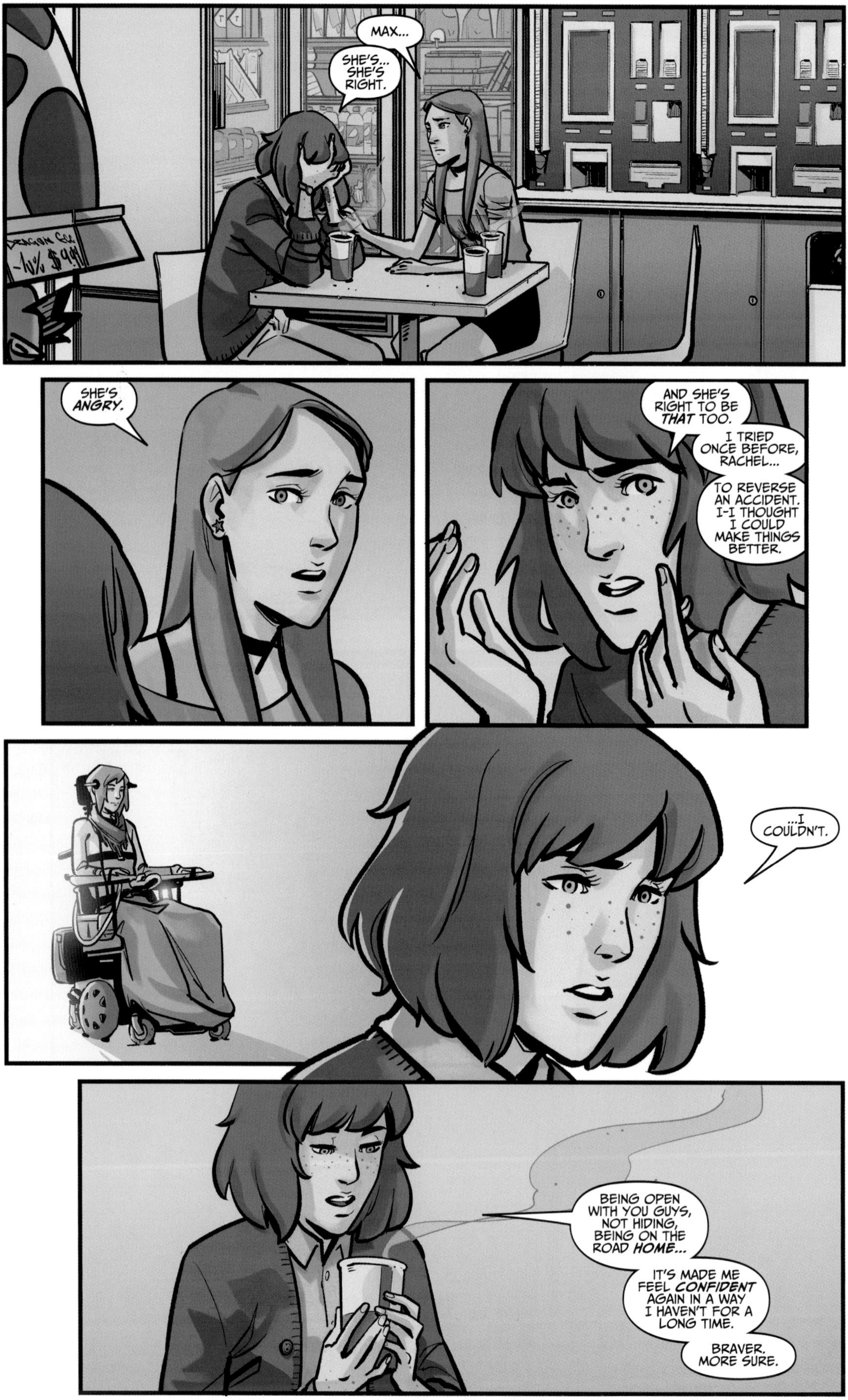
MAX...
SHE'S... SHE'S RIGHT.
SHE'S ANGRY.
AND SHE'S RIGHT TO BE THAT TOO.
I TRIED ONCE BEFORE, RACHEL...
TO REVERSE AN ACCIDENT. I-I THOUGHT I COULD MAKE THINGS BETTER.
...I COULDN'T.
BEING OPEN WITH YOU GUYS, NOT HIDING, BEING ON THE ROAD HOME...
IT'S MADE ME FEEL CONFIDENT AGAIN IN A WAY I HAVEN'T FOR A LONG TIME.
BRAVER. MORE SURE.

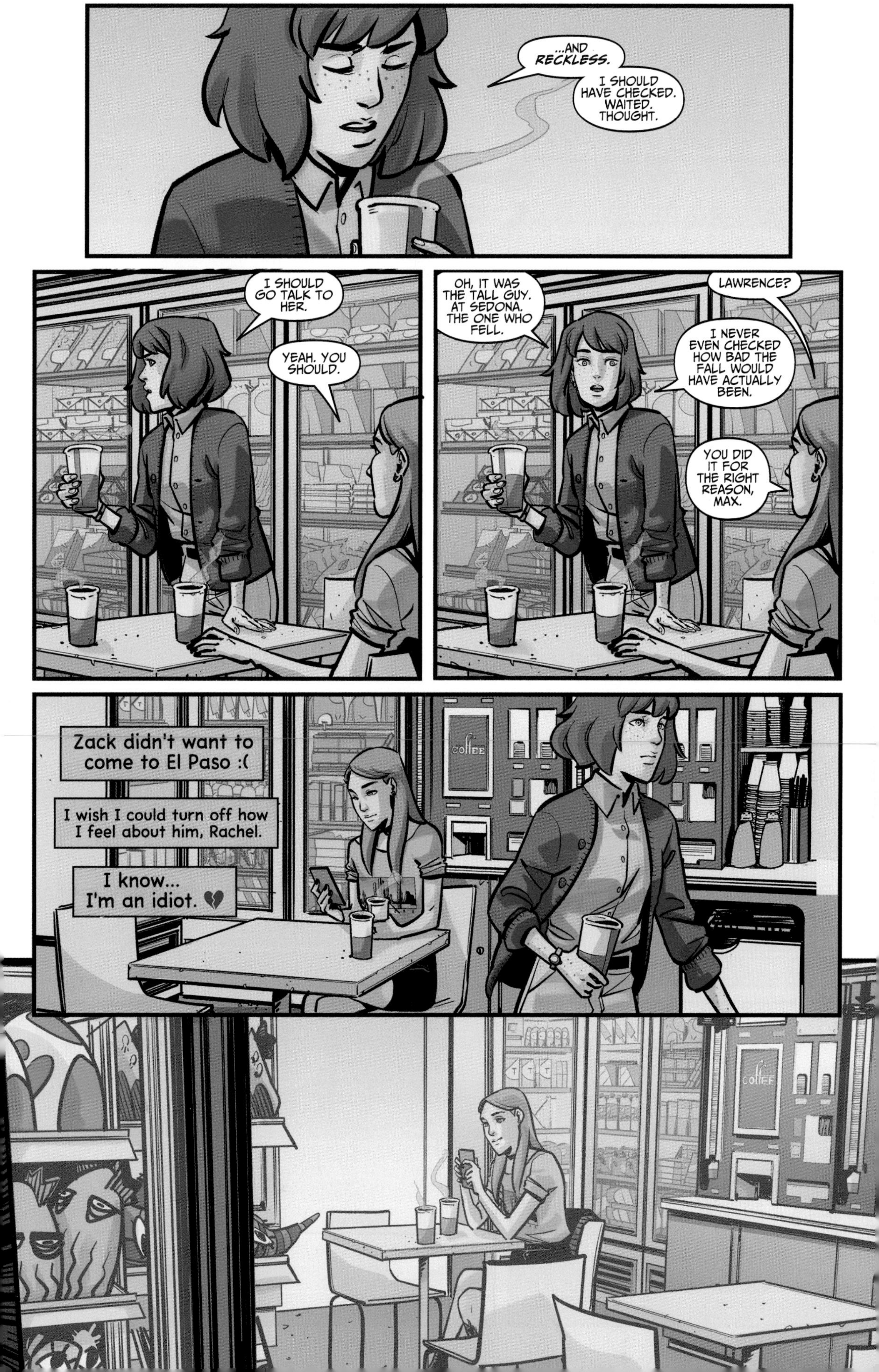
...AND RECKLESS.
I SHOULD HAVE CHECKED. WAITED. THOUGHT.
I SHOULD GO TALK TO HER.
YEAH. YOU SHOULD.
OH, IT WAS THE TALL GUY. AT SEDONA. THE ONE WHO FELL.
LAWRENCE?
I NEVER EVEN CHECKED HOW BAD THE FALL WOULD HAVE ACTUALLY BEEN.
YOU DID IT FOR THE RIGHT REASON, MAX.
Zack didn't want to come to El Paso :(
I wish I could turn off how I feel about him, Rachel.
I know... I'm an idiot. 💔
COFFEE
COFFEE

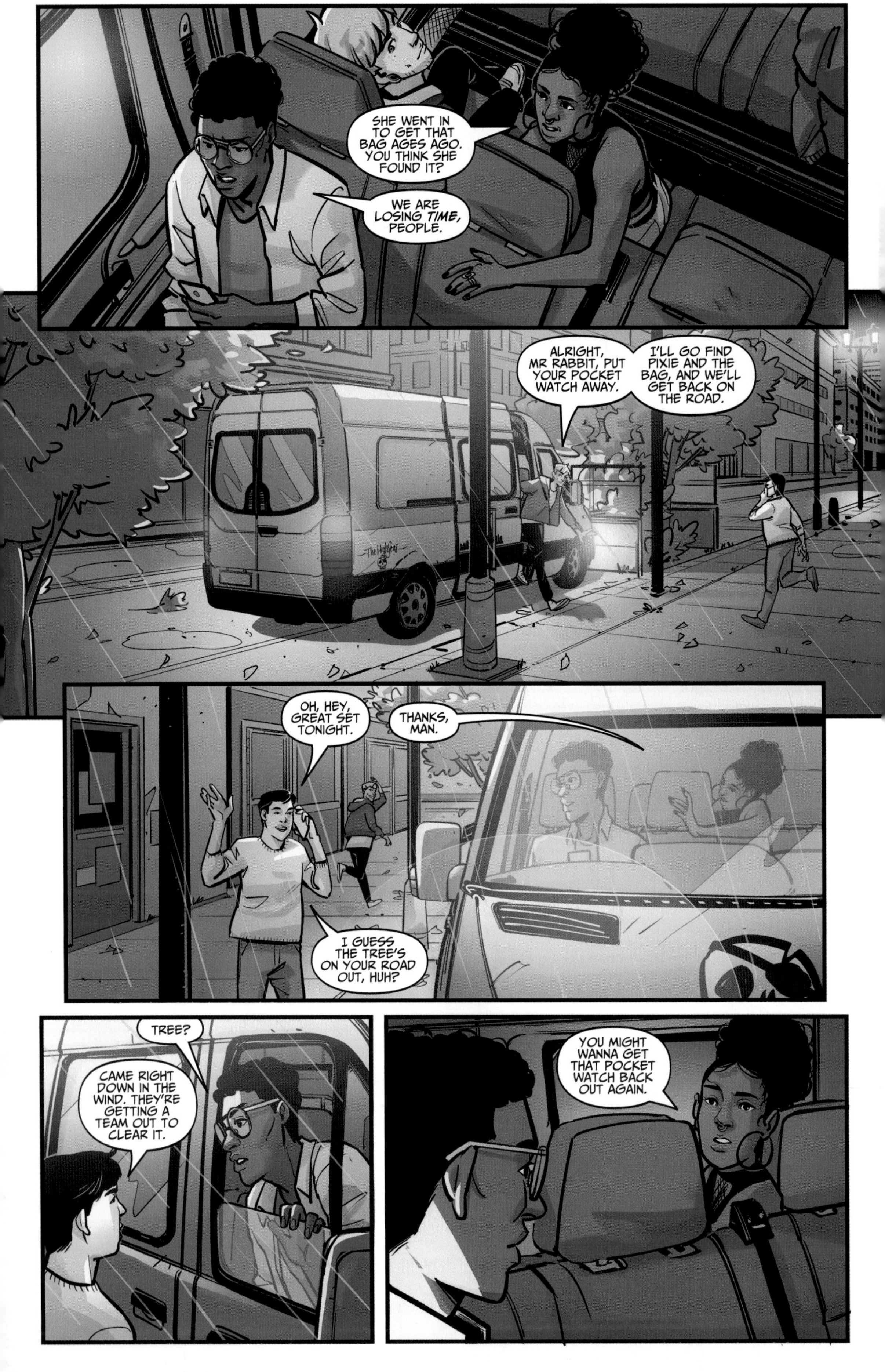
SHE WENT IN TO GET THAT BAG AGES AGO. YOU THINK SHE FOUND IT?
WE ARE LOSING *TIME*, PEOPLE.
ALRIGHT, MR RABBIT, PUT YOUR POCKET WATCH AWAY.
I'LL GO FIND PIXIE AND THE BAG, AND WE'LL GET BACK ON THE ROAD.
OH, HEY, GREAT SET TONIGHT.
THANKS, MAN.
I GUESS THE TREE'S ON YOUR ROAD OUT, HUH?
TREE?
CAME RIGHT DOWN IN THE WIND. THEY'RE GETTING A TEAM OUT TO CLEAR IT.
YOU MIGHT WANNA GET THAT POCKET WATCH BACK OUT AGAIN.

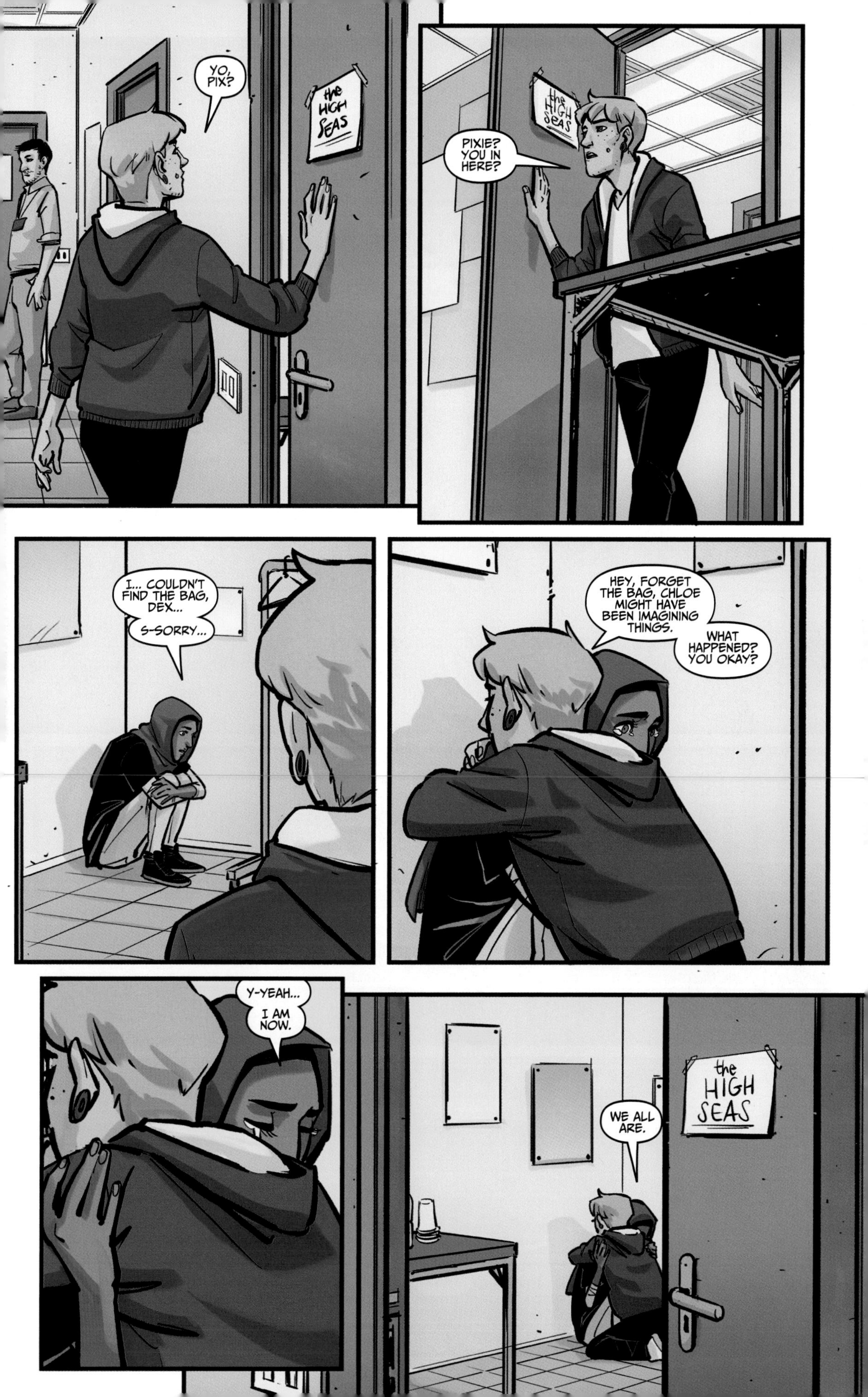
YO, PIX?
the HIGH SEAS
PIXIE? YOU IN HERE?
the HIGH SEAS
I... COULDN'T FIND THE BAG, DEX...
S-SORRY...
HEY, FORGET THE BAG, CHLOE MIGHT HAVE BEEN IMAGINING THINGS.
WHAT HAPPENED? YOU OKAY?
Y-YEAH...
I AM NOW.
the HIGH SEAS
WE ALL ARE.

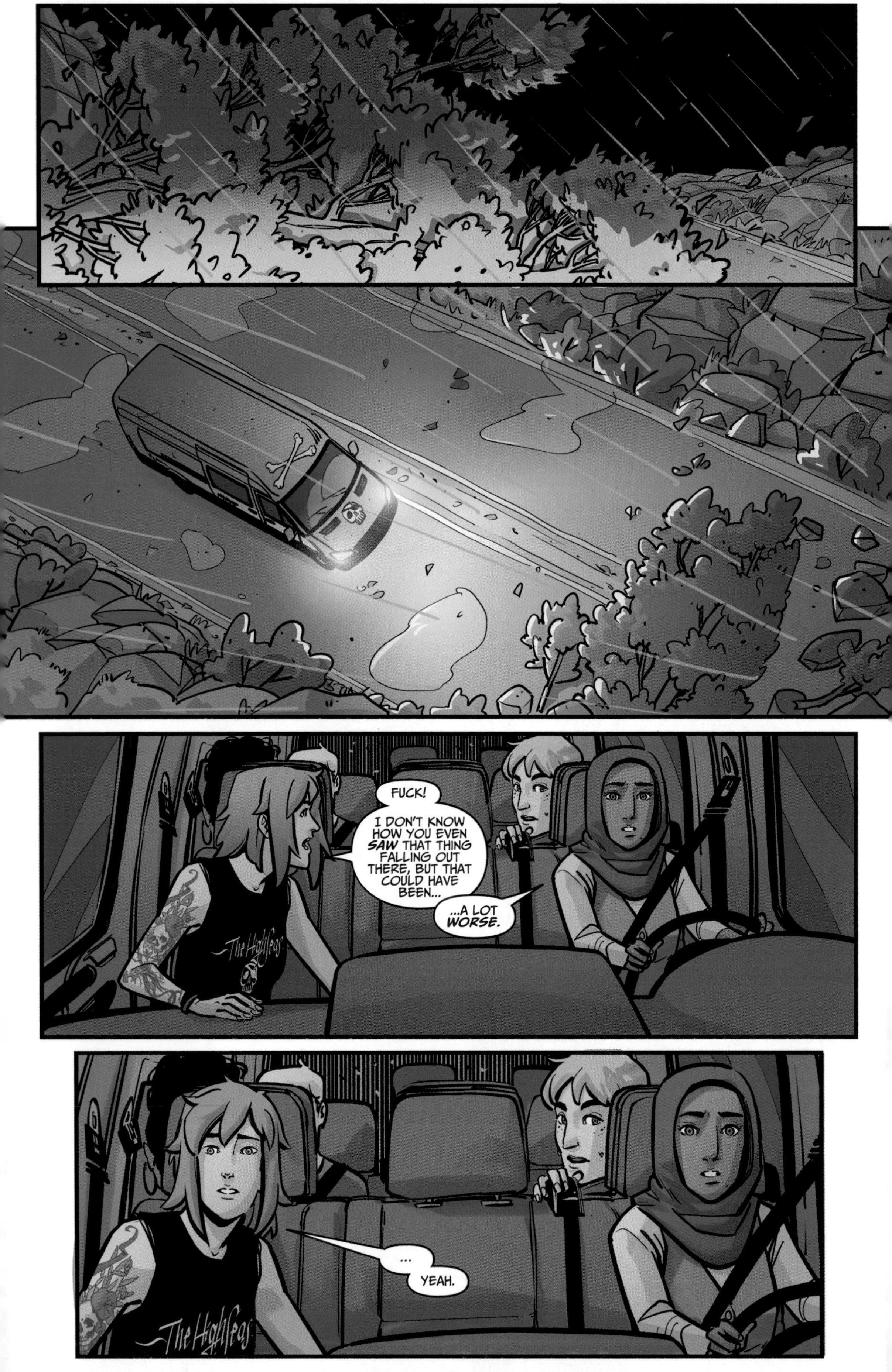
FUCK!
I DON'T KNOW HOW YOU EVEN SAW THAT THING FALLING OUT THERE, BUT THAT COULD HAVE BEEN...
...A LOT WORSE.
...
YEAH.

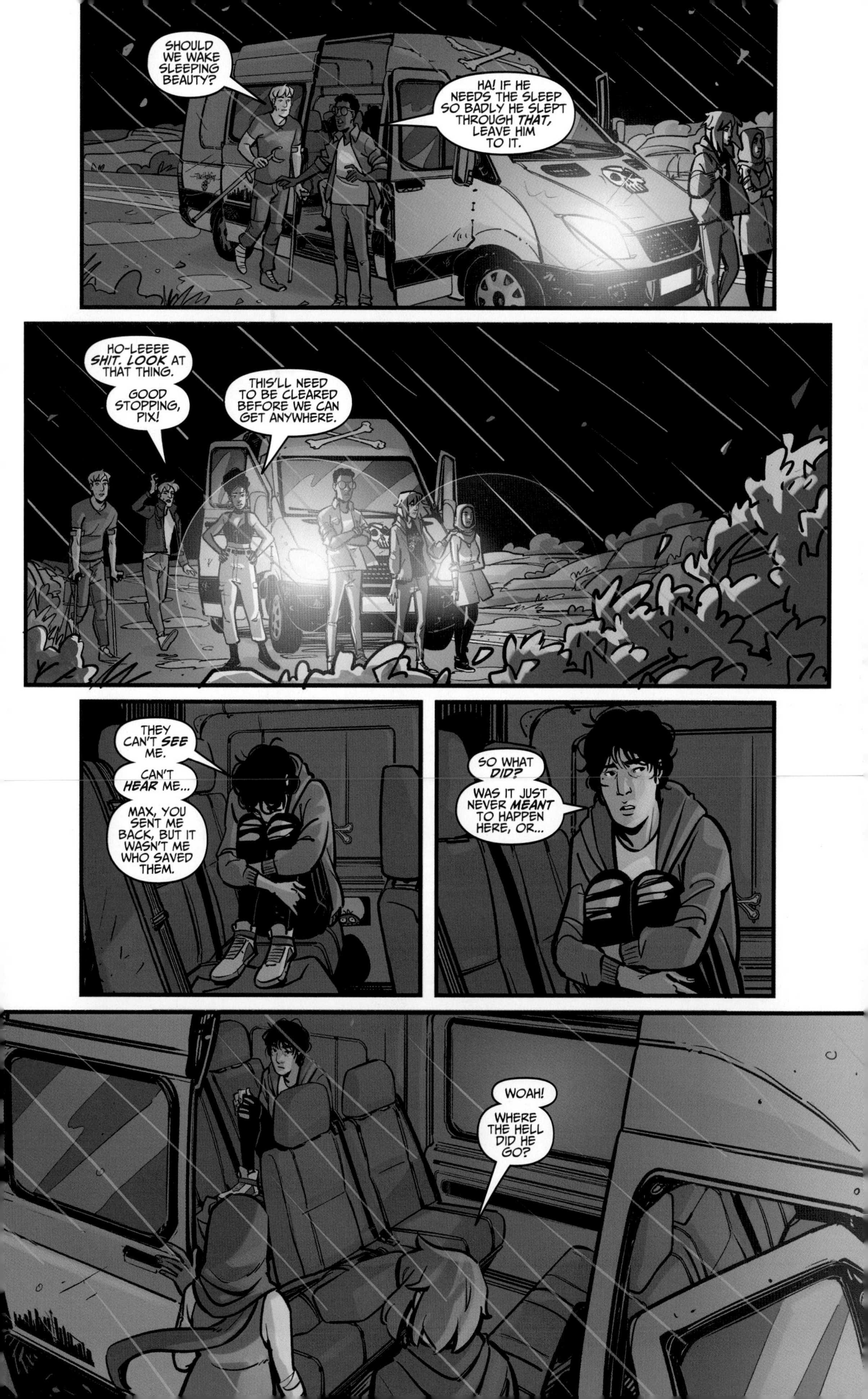

SHOULD WE WAKE SLEEPING BEAUTY?
HA! IF HE NEEDS THE SLEEP SO BADLY HE SLEPT THROUGH THAT, LEAVE HIM TO IT.
HO-LEEEE SHIT. LOOK AT THAT THING.
GOOD STOPPING, PIX!
THIS'LL NEED TO BE CLEARED BEFORE WE CAN GET ANYWHERE.
THEY CAN'T SEE ME.
CAN'T HEAR ME...
MAX, YOU SENT ME BACK, BUT IT WASN'T ME WHO SAVED THEM.
SO WHAT DID?
WAS IT JUST NEVER MEANT TO HAPPEN HERE, OR...
WOAH!
WHERE THE HELL DID HE GO?

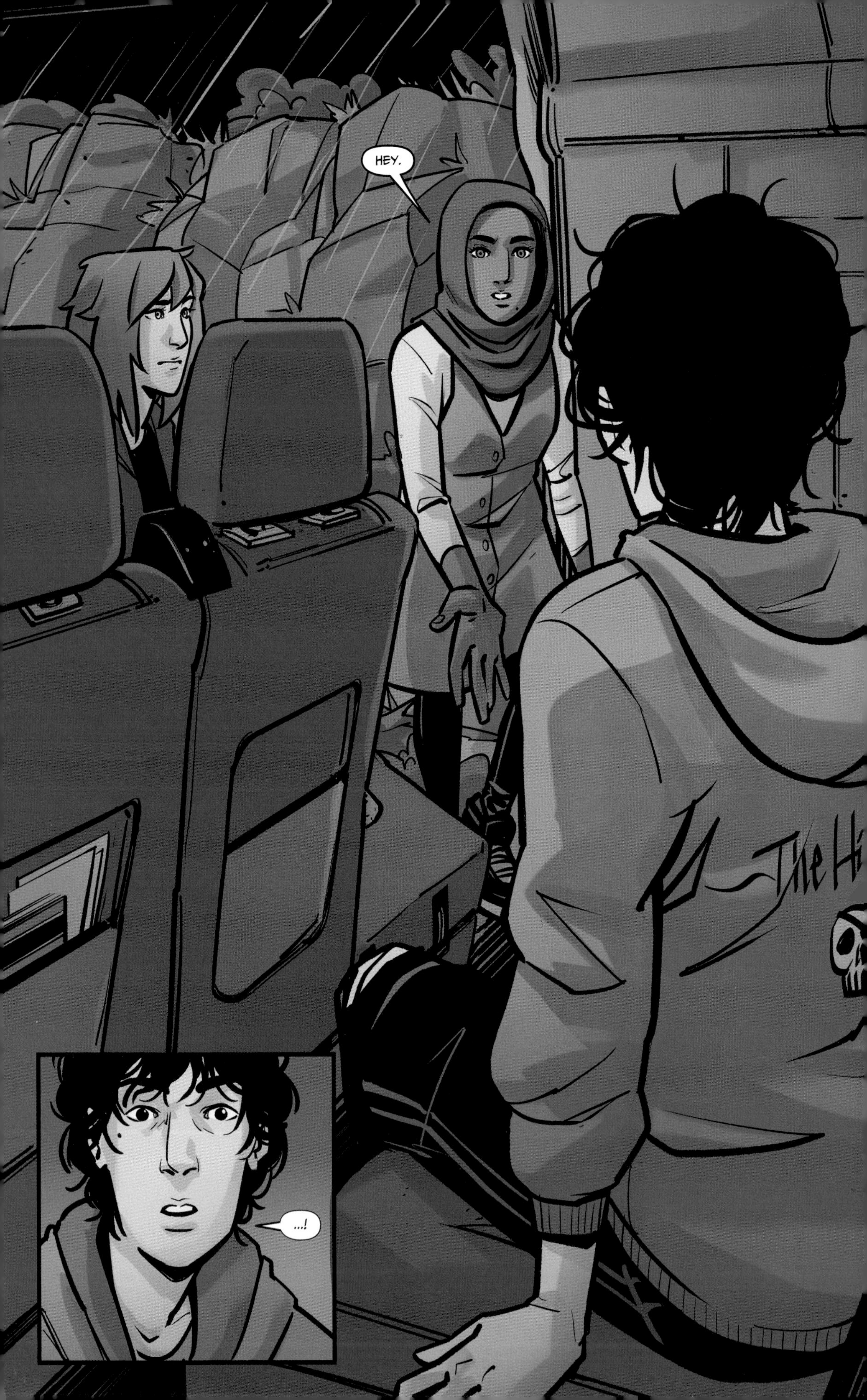
HEY.
...!

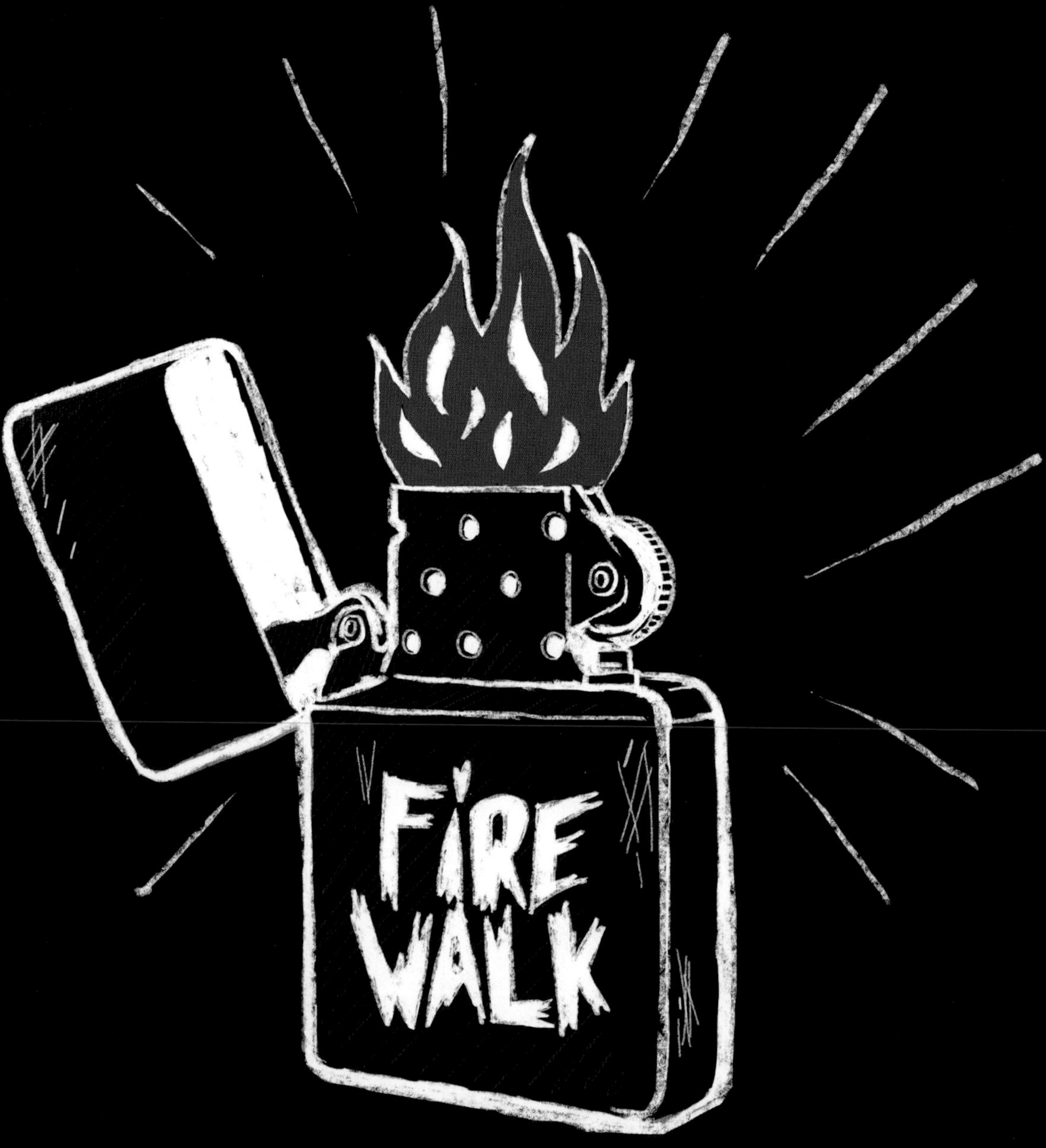
FIRE
WALK

COVER GALLERY

BY SARAH GRALEY

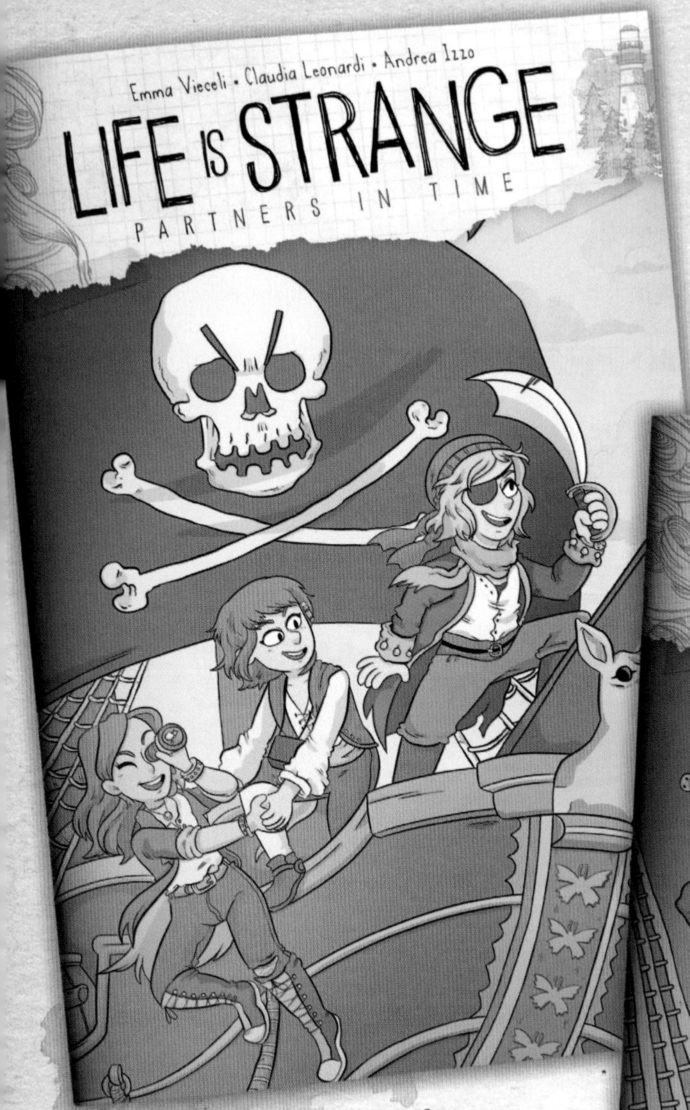
Emma Vieceli • Claudia Leonardi • Andrea Izzo
LIFE IS STRANGE
PARTNERS IN TIME

ISSUE #2.1

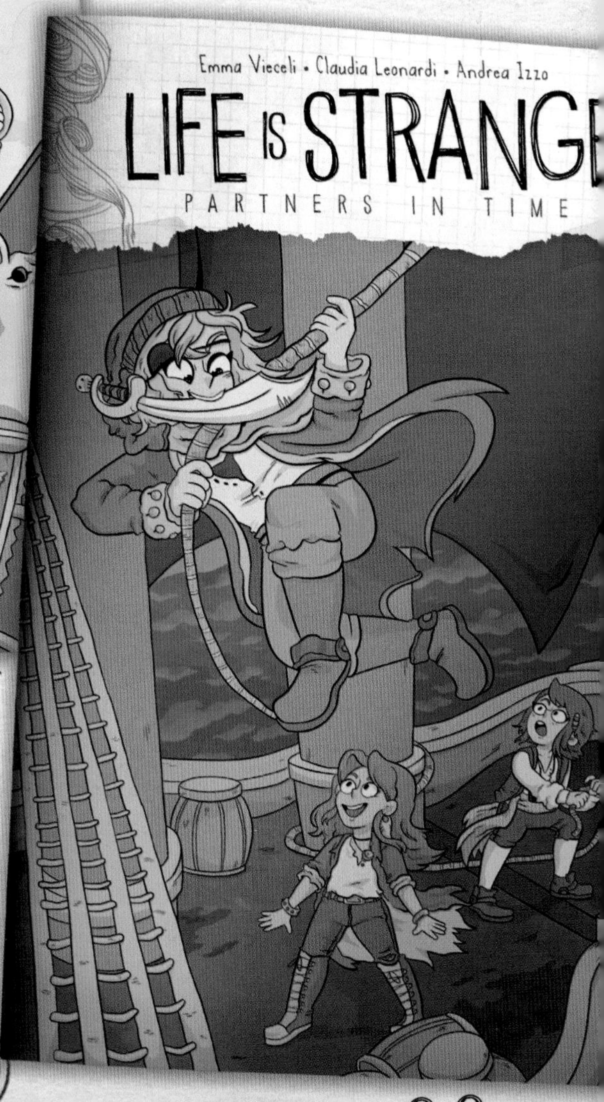
Emma Vieceli • Claudia Leonardi • Andrea Izzo
LIFE IS STRANGE
PARTNERS IN TIME

ISSUE #2.2

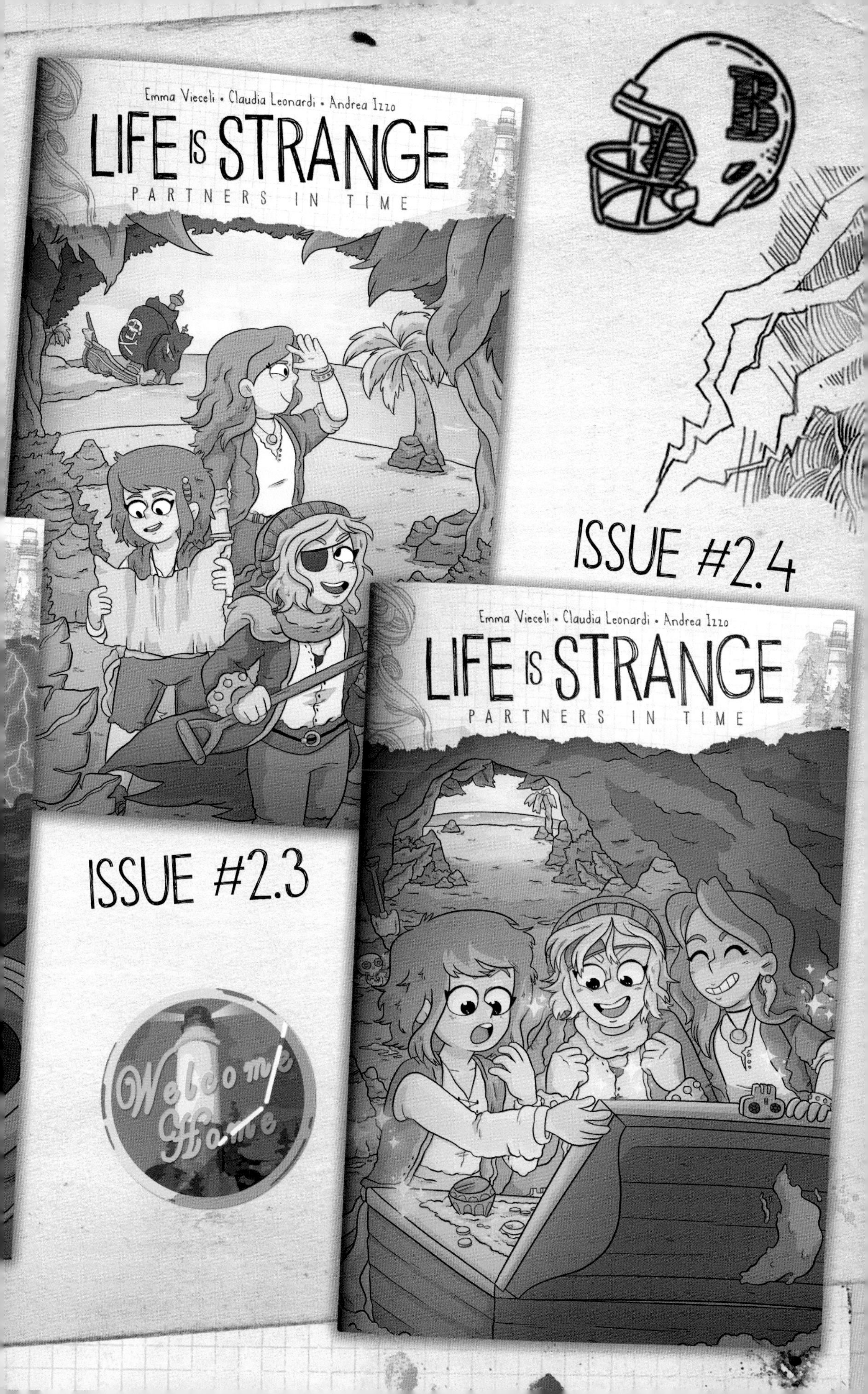

Emma Vieceli • Claudia Leonardi • Andrea Izzo
LIFE IS STRANGE
PARTNERS IN TIME
ISSUE #2.4
ISSUE #2.3
Welcome Home
Emma Vieceli • Claudia Leonardi • Andrea Izzo
LIFE IS STRANGE
PARTNERS IN TIME

COVER DEVELOPMENT

Follow Sarah Graley's cover series from concept to completion!

STEP 1

When designing and planning covers for the brand-new arc of Life is Strange, it was decided that some of the covers would tell a story across the four issues. One of Max's most treasured memories is from her childhood, pretending to be Long Max Silver to Chloe's Captain Bluebeard. From here, Sarah Graley sketched up a series of covers which would reinvent the pirate tales for the girls as grownups and give Rachel the chance to join in the fun!

LIFE IS STRANGE

Emma Vieceli • Claudia Leonardi • Andrea Izzo
LIFE IS STRANGE

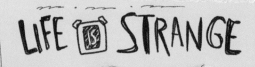

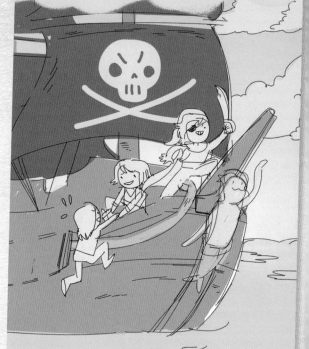

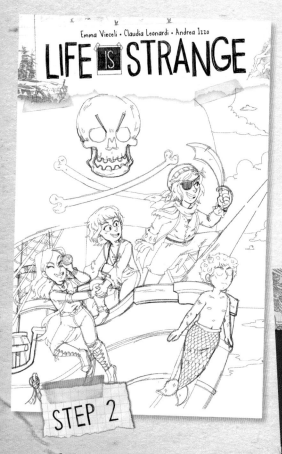

STEP 2

Initially, Sarah drew in Tristan as a dashing merman in the place of the ship's figurehead. Each sketch was done with the logo in mind, so that no details were lost in the final image.

Emma Vieceli • Claudia Leonardi • Andrea Izzo
LIFE IS STRANGE
PARTNERS IN TIME

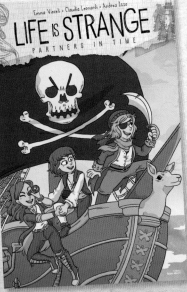

STEP 3

Tristan was replaced by a doe's head in the final cover, which brought the focus back to the girls as they set off on their four-part pirate adventure!

CHARACTER SKETCHES

BY CLAUDIA LEONARDI

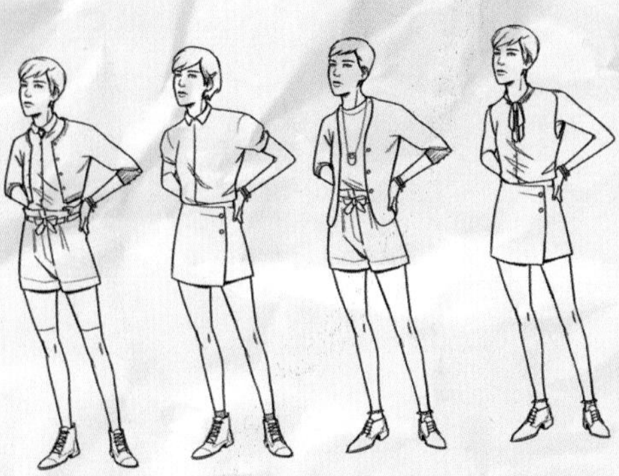

VICTORIA

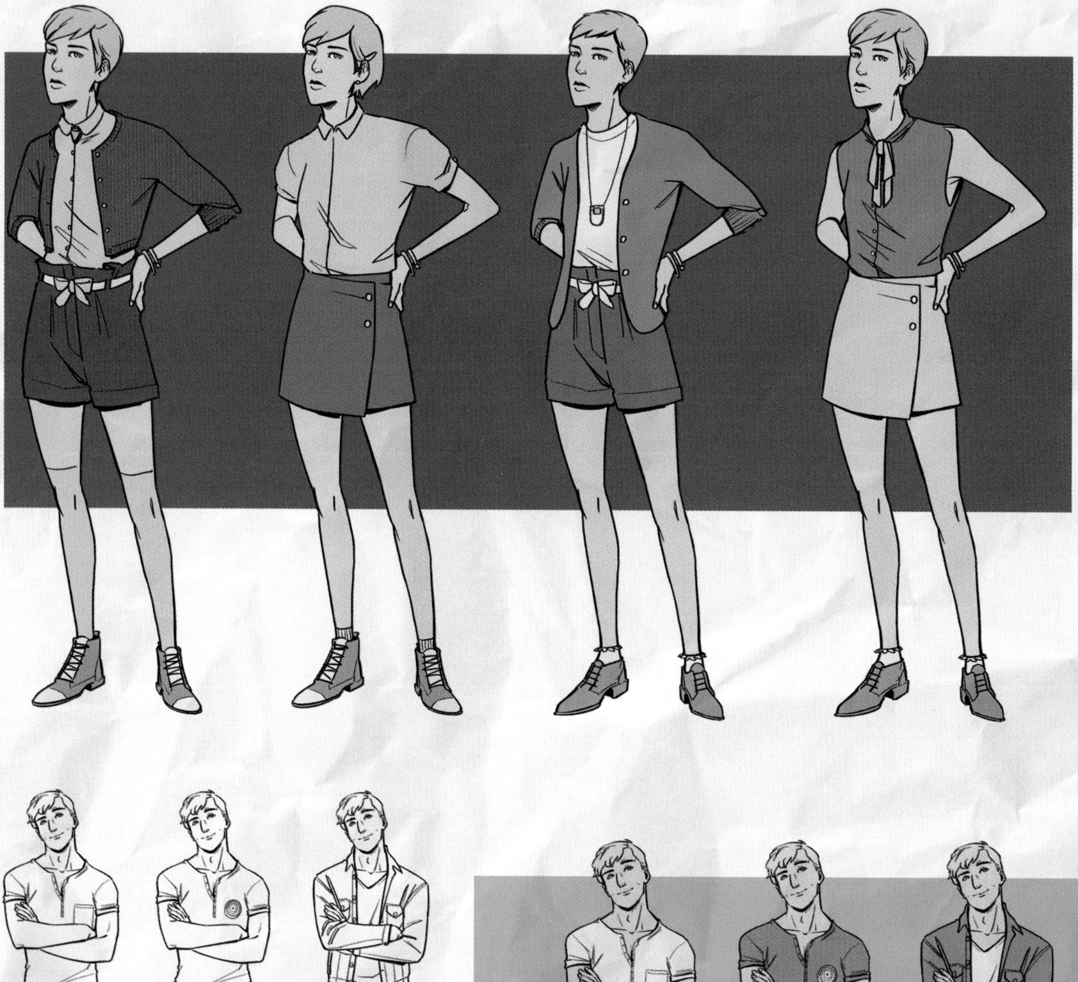

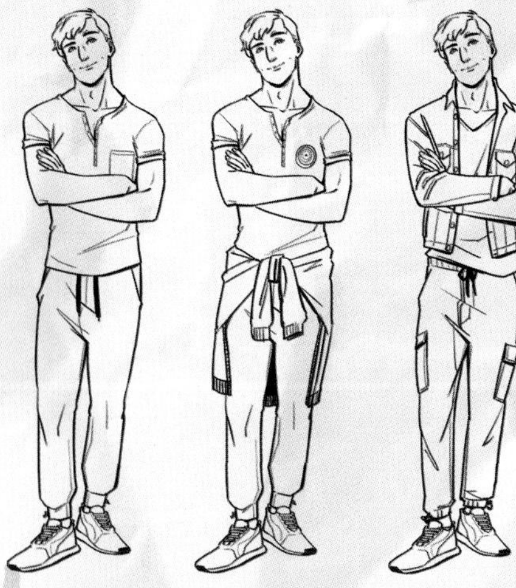

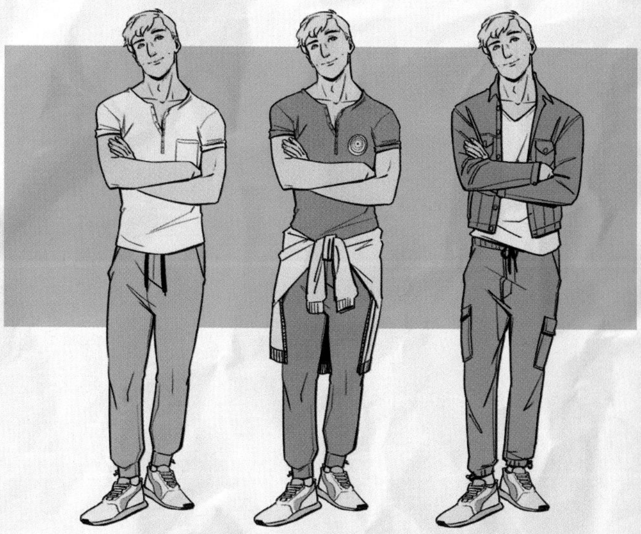

LAWRENCE

ZACK

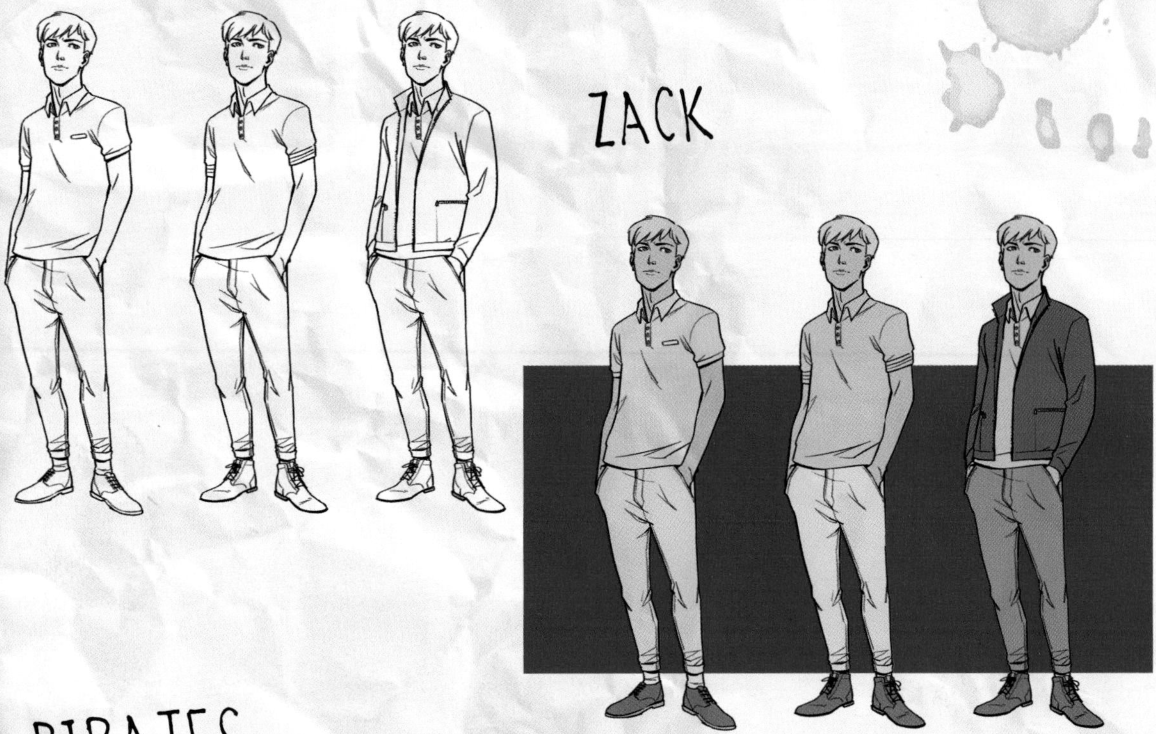

PIRATES

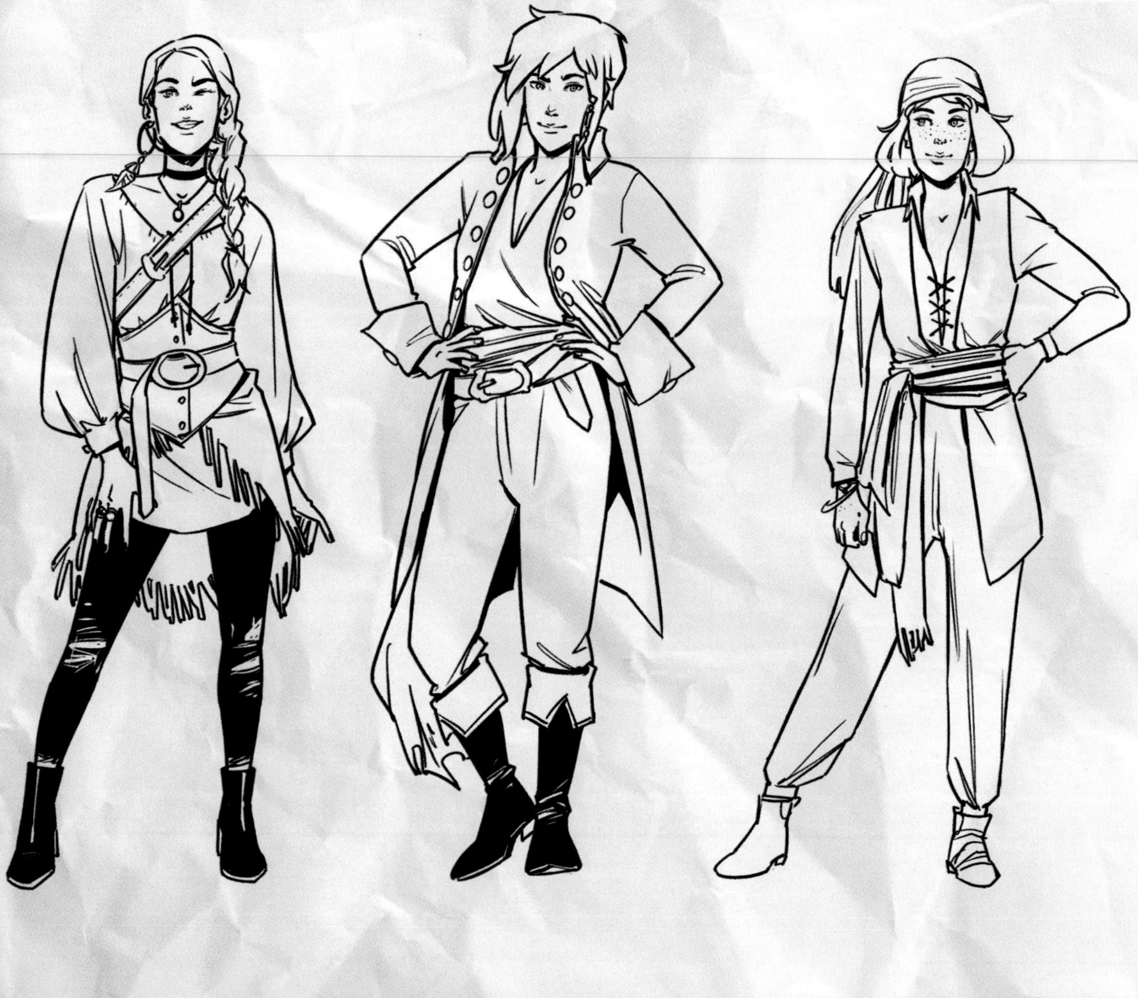

THE ROADTRIP CONTINUES!

Emma Vieceli • Claudia Leonardi • Andrea Izzo

LIFE IS STRANGE
PARTNERS IN TIME

— ECHOES —

"This comic will leave you desperate for more."
Bleeding Cool